Corporate finance

Going public and issuing new equity and
takeovers, mergers and disposals

Corporate finance

Going public and issuing new equity and takeovers, mergers and disposals

Martin Sabine, BA, MBA
Chairman of Somerley Limited, Hong Kong

London
Butterworths
1987

United Kingdom	Butterworth & Co (Publishers) Ltd, 88 Kingsway, LONDON WC2B 6AB and 4 Hill Street, EDINBURGH EH2 3JZ
Australia	Butterworths Pty Ltd, SYDNEY, MELBOURNE, BRISBANE, ADELAIDE, PERTH, CANBERRA and HOBART
Canada	Butterworths, A division of Reed Inc., TORONTO and VANCOUVER
New Zealand	Butterworths of New Zealand Ltd, WELLINGTON and AUCKLAND
Singapore	Butterworth & Co (Asia) Pte Ltd, SINGAPORE
USA	Butterworths Legal Publishers, ST PAUL, Minnesota, SEATTLE, Washington, BOSTON, Massachusetts, AUSTIN, Texas and D & S Publishers, CLEARWATER, Florida

© Martin Sabine 1987

Reprinted 1988, 1989

British Library Cataloguing in Publication Data

Sabine, Martin
   Corporate finance.
   1. Corporations—Finance   2. Industrial
   management
   I. Title
   658.1'5   HG4026

ISBN 0 406 25956 9

Typeset by Cotswold Typesetting Ltd, Gloucester
Printed by Bookcraft (Bath) Ltd Avon

To Maureen, for her love, support and guidance

Preface

This book describes the theory, principles and practice of corporate finance, that is to say the major activities carried on by the corporate finance department of a large merchant bank or similar institution. The book is divided into three parts: the first is a brief introduction to the characteristics of corporate securities which are important for corporate finance transactions; the second part covers going public and making further issues of equity capital, the traditional 'issuing house' function; and the third part deals with takeovers, mergers and disposals, perhaps the most glamorous aspect.

Merchant banks have tended to encourage a mystique about their business. This is particularly true of the corporate finance area, ranging as it does from the complexities of prospectus documentation to the drama of public takeover battles. Reluctance to let 'daylight in on magic' creates difficulties for those who need to know (or are simply interested in knowing) about corporate finance in general or a particular aspect of it. As a practitioner, I believe this book describes the field in sufficient detail to serve as an introduction for executives starting work in merchant banking organisations. I hope it will prove a useful supplement to checking proofs, reviewing calculations, making the coffee and generally being thrown 'in the deep end', which passes for basic training in many corporate finance departments. On the other side of the table, it should provide some guidance to company executives in using the services of corporate finance specialists and knowing what to expect. The book is also designed to assist other professionals—accountants, lawyers, stockbrokers, fund managers, registrars, valuers and financial journalists—who are intensively involved in certain aspects of corporate finance transactions but do not always have the chance to see the overall picture. The use of technical terms has been kept to a minimum so that the book can also be readily understood by investors, students or anyone else who may wish to take an interest in the subject of corporate finance.

This book is based on 14 years' practical experience of corporate finance in the Asia-Pacific region, the UK and a number of other international financial markets. It has been written as a practical handbook and not from an academic or theoretical point of view. No formal survey of the available literature has been attempted, although of course a number of the topics covered in this book are dealt with in various works of reference which have proved useful sources. Colleagues and friends may recognise parts of cherished arguments and discussions held with them over the years.

Local regulations, for example as regards taxation and the issue of securities, vary widely from country to country and affect the structure and methods adopted for a particular transaction. This book is not intended to replace the need for specialist advice on individual cases. However, it has been my experience that many corporate finance projects can be reduced to common denominators.

Similar factors recur in slightly different guises. Motivation remains remarkably constant although means vary. The material set out in this book should provide the reader with a framework which can be applied to the analysis and understanding of corporate finance transactions in whatever market they take place.

M.S.
January 1987

Contents

Part 1

Corporate securities: Characteristics, valuation and pricing

Introduction

(i) What is meant by corporate finance as covered in this book

The term 'corporate finance' in this book is used to refer to two major areas of activity. The first is going public and raising capital by further issues of listed shares and other types of equity. The second is takeovers, mergers and disposals. These areas form the core of specialist corporate finance work in a merchant or investment bank. The other types of financing options available to corporations such as bonds, syndicated lending, commercial paper and swaps are distinct subjects in themselves. Neither do topics in financial analysis and capital budgeting fall under this definition of corporate finance.

The whole process of going public is reviewed in Part 2, beginning with the advantages and disadvantages and the reasons people embark on this sometimes frustrating venture. A checklist is provided so that management can assess for itself without incurring substantial professional fees whether a company can go public. A guide to the structural changes which may be required is given. If a decision is made to proceed, it is necessary to form a team to co-ordinate all aspects of the flotation. The budget will be substantial but meeting the expenses is less painful if money is successfully raised by the operation. Correct timing and pricing are critical elements and difficult to get entirely right, even with a fair slice of luck. They are among the more glamorous and exciting problems of a flotation. Meanwhile, the laborious process of putting together the nuts and bolts of a prospectus and a timetable for monitoring progress must also proceed. After the preparations are complete, come the launch, allocation of shares and the start of trading.

There are other ways of gaining a listing apart from a full scale prospectus, such as acquiring a shell company or spinning off a subsidiary. Once a listing has been obtained, it is a much simpler process to raise further capital by way of rights issues to existing shareholders. Placings to new shareholders can also be carried out. Use may be made of equity-linked securities in addition to ordinary shares.

Part 3 of the book deals with takeovers, mergers and disposals. The wide range of motives for takeovers is discussed. They vary from carefully calculated financial gains to personal empire building. The first step is to identify acquisition candidates and subject them to a preliminary screening to avoid too much wasted effort. Despite this, a high proportion of unsuccessful projects is inevitable in the mergers and acquisitions field. When a likely candidate has been identified, a more intensive effort in collecting and evaluating information must be mounted.

The objective of gaining control can be tackled from various different angles. There are also many options open regarding the structure of an offer and the terms of payment. After this review, there comes a moment when analysis and pre-planning must stop and action start. A skilful approach and sensitive

3

negotiating style are important but sometimes the blunt instrument of a high cash bid is required. Winning a recommendation by any method possible is the single most critical factor determining the outcome.

For every aggressive move there are counter measures. Some need considerable planning to put into place, others can be used tactically in the midst of battle. Engaging in a contested takeover bid is possibly the most publicised event that a company and its management will experience. Willpower and personalities can become as important as fundamentals. The formal procedures and techniques of how to carry an offer through still apply and meticulous attention is required. Offer documentation is relatively complex. A number of specialist professionals have their own role to play in dealing with the technical aspects which arise.

It would be logical for management to spend as much time and energy on disposals as on acquisitions. This is rarely the case. The considerations relevant to disposals are the mirror image of the acquisition process but a deliberate policy is required on management's part if this important responsibility is not to be neglected.

(ii) How the subject is approached

The book contains sufficient detail to be of assistance to executives beginning their careers in investment or merchant banks. The material is drawn from practical experience of working on corporate finance transactions, alongside corporate finance specialists of various backgrounds, in different countries. Some of the detailed techniques are most closely derived from the UK or markets modelled on the UK. However, the majority of the principles discussed can be validly applied to corporate finance transactions worldwide.

The approach to the material should also prove suitable for professional advisers and company executives who are from time to time involved in corporate finance projects but whose main area of work and responsibility lies outside this area.

Institutional shareholders often hold the key to the success of a corporate finance transaction either by being prepared to act as major sub-underwriters in an issue or by controlling critical blocks of shares during a takeover battle. They are increasingly being called upon to exercise responsibility commensurate with this power and it is hoped that the material presented will provide some relevant background. It may also prove of use to financial journalists and consultants in financial public relations along with shareholders and investors generally and those who simply have a passing interest in the stock market.

It has been the intention to approach the subject of corporate finance from as practical a viewpoint as possible. The book is not intended to be an academic survey of the outstanding literature on the subject but rather a summary of factors which have been found to be important from actual experience and a study of techniques which are in regular day-to-day use. Some of the theory of corporate finance is discussed but not beyond the extent to which it is relevant to these techniques. A complex exposition of a statistical method of evaluating risk which the average shareholder neither understands or trusts has rarely advanced a corporate finance transaction.

(iii) Who is involved

At the level of the company itself, it is usual for senior management to be closely involved in corporate finance projects. The decisions being taken may affect the future direction of the group, particularly as regards flotations and major takeovers. Further issues of securities may be handled by the finance director or the treasurer. In almost all corporate finance transactions, accounting staff will be involved in preparing and assessing up-to-date financial statements about the company. The documentation will require participation by legal and company secretarial staff. A team of analysts, researchers and co-ordinators may also be required, depending on the size of the transaction.

The staff of a corporate finance department in a merchant bank is usually young. Executives in their mid- to late-twenties will take considerable responsibility for transactions. They are stronger in educational qualifications than on business experience. On many occasions, merchant banks have found themselves out-manoeuvred by businessmen with shrewd instincts but little formal training. Some companies are adept at allowing merchant banks to feel they are running the show while keeping their own objectives firmly in view. The background of corporate finance staff is likely to be accountancy or business schools specialising in finance, the law, stockbroking or, on occasion, even 'real' banking.

Accountants prepare studies on working capital and profit forecasts and investigate and confirm key aspects of corporate finance transactions. Lawyers will be widely engaged not only in drafting, verification and documentation but often in negotiating with principals, devising bid tactics and dealing with regulatory and anti-monopoly bodies. Stockbrokers will mastermind market operations and provide critical input on pricing and underwriting decisions. They will also liaise with stock exchange authorities. Property valuers, share registrars, receiving banks and specialist printers all have important roles to play.

(iv) What a corporate finance department does

A company only goes public once and therefore most managements will be novices in this particular field. They will look for overall guidance on rules, procedures, documentation and timing. Even inexperienced managements will have strong views on pricing, especially if some of their own shares are being sold. As the merchant bank is ultimately standing behind the underwriting it has considerable leverage in the pricing negotiations.

A company which has gone public will look to its sponsor for guidelines as to what is expected from the management of a public company. It may also wish an experienced party to monitor the market in its shares. The merchant bank which arranges the initial flotation should have a strong advantage when it comes to suggesting further transactions. If a close association develops, the bank may also act as advisers to some of the directors of the company in their personal capacity.

Takeovers tend by their nature to be one-off projects. The most valuable service is generating ideas and providing information about available companies. The merchant bank which is able to bring deals is likely to be given responsibility for that particular piece of business. Analysis of the market and the price to be paid will be required. The merchant bank may be involved in approaching the target company and opening negotiations. Most companies have little direct experience of negotiating with stock exchange authorities and bodies regulating takeovers. This will normally be left in the hands of the merchant bank or stockbroker.

As companies become more experienced in making takeovers, they may look to the merchant bank less for handling procedures and more for arranging a package. This will include offering or arranging suitable loan finance, handling purchases of shares (sometimes with buy-back arrangements) and providing support through underwriting. Depending on the strengths of individual management, the merchant bank may also be involved in press and investor relations.

Payment for these services is largely on a 'no foal, no fee' basis. Fees are calculated on a percentage of the size of the transaction, perhaps 1/2–1% on a largish transaction and up to 5% on a small one. In issues, market practice varies as to whether fees are paid outright or are included in a 'spread' between the price at which an underwriting syndicate takes shares and the price at which they are sold to investors. Fees for new issues of small companies can be as high as 10% for some very risky propositions but are normally perhaps in the 2–5% range, varying widely in different markets. Depending on what services are included, a documentation fee may also be charged.

In merger and acquisition work, it sometimes happens that a simple introductory fee is charged by the person putting up the idea. The detailed work is carried out by another house on a separate basis. Many merchant banks charge out-of-pocket expenses in addition. It can be irritating for a company to find it is charged with telexes and taxi fares on top of a very substantial fee.

Other categories of professional fees will normally be based on time spent at a certain rate per hour with a loading for urgency, complexity and general inconvenience. Corporate finance transactions can involve anti-social hours.

(v) Organisation of the book

The remaining two chapters of Part 1 deal with the characteristics of corporate securities and principles of valuation and pricing. These subjects are fundamental both to the issue side of corporate finance activity and to takeovers and mergers. Part 2 deals with issues by public companies in the rough chronological order of the various steps involved and Part 3 follows the same basic format for the area of mergers, acquisitions and disposals. The processes should be more readily understandable if the chapters are read in order but a reader interested in only one aspect should find that the topics are more or less self-contained.

CHAPTER 1

Characteristics of corporate securities

This chapter deals with the characteristics of the different types of securities issued by companies. The characteristics described are those which are particularly relevant to corporate finance transactions. It is not intended to present an exhaustive account of all the rights attaching to each type of security.

The following section deals with shares, both ordinary shares (common stock) and shares with rights which differ in some way from those of the ordinary shares. 'II Loan stocks and warrants' below, deals with loan stocks, particularly convertibles and loan stocks with warrants which are equity-linked.

I SHARES

The shares which form the basic capitalisation of a company are called ordinary shares or common stock. Other shares are distinguished from them by having different rights in certain specified respects, notably as regards voting and preferred or deferred claims on income and return of capital.

(i) Ordinary shares

Ordinary shares are the most familiar type of security to the average investor. They are likely to be a greater number of shares and a greater spread of holders than for the other types of securities a company may have in issue. This makes them more marketable and generally more easy to value than other securities. A framework for analysing the worth of ordinary shares has become well established and widely understood, involving such measures as the price earnings ratio, dividend yield, asset backing and the variability of the expected return compared with the market as a whole.

(a) Cost of ordinary shares

Ordinary shares carry no fixed servicing obligations. Of course, shareholders are none too pleased if no dividends are paid but there is no legal sanction triggered against the company. Whether to pay or recommend dividends lies in the discretion of the directors.

This gives rise to different attitudes to the cost of ordinary shares. In theory, as ordinary shares (other than certain types of deferred shares covered below) carry the greatest risk of all the securities issued by the company, it would be expected that holders would demand the greatest return. Expressing this from the company's point of view, ordinary shares are in some sense the most expensive type of capital for a company to employ. However, in cash terms they are the cheapest, both in the sense that no dividends are actually required and because a normal dividend payment is likely to put a share on a lower yield than the interest rate on debt. From the point of view of cash servicing costs, it is cheaper and safer for a company to raise a given sum by issue of shares than it is by bank borrowings or issue of other securities.

Financial theory suggests that the difference between the cash returns on shares and the interest payable on loan stock or bank borrowing should be more than made up by the expected capital gain to holders of the shares. On the other hand, some managements may regard the share price of the company in the stock market as capricious, particularly in the short term, and largely beyond their control. Whether shareholders will actually reap a capital gain to compensate them for the lower cash income depends on many factors, including the timing of the investors' purchase and sale, the mood of the stock market and the economic cycle. What the directors of the company can control is the level of dividend payments. While theory tells them shares are the most expensive form of financing, they may be tempted to measure reality in terms of cash paid out.

(b) Timing and pricing of issues

Another paradox concerns the timing and pricing of issues of ordinary shares. Directors may feel that money raised by issues of ordinary shares is 'cheapest' when the share price is high. Issue activity tends to intensify at market peaks. To the shareholder, this may prove the most expensive time to increase his holdings. Shareholders may look back and rue an issue made near a market peak while the directors congratulate themselves on their foresight, having raised money for the company cheaply and at the right moment. This policy may expose shareholders to capital losses on their investment rather than the capital gains needed to supplement the dividend yield.

(c) Voting rights

A fundamental right of ordinary shares is that they normally carry the voting control of companies. In most takeover bids, the premium for acquiring control of a company attaches entirely to the ordinary shares. Preference shares or loan stock which may be more valuable on an income basis do not share in this bonanza unless they carry unusual rights to block or hinder a takeover.

A register of shareholders is usually maintained by the company, in which case the registered holder has the power to vote at meetings of the company or to appoint a proxy to vote on his behalf. Shares held in 'street names' and not yet registered by a purchaser cannot be voted by the new owner until transfer of ownership has been registered by the company. Some companies (mostly private) have issued securities in bearer form which allows the person in physical possession of the certificates to attend meetings and vote the shares he holds.

(d) Claims on income and assets

Holders of ordinary shares participate pro rata in the profits of the overall business attributable to them. The dividends they receive and capital gains they enjoy should be determined over a period of time by the performance of the company.

The articles of association of a company usually contain provisions preventing the dilution of shareholders' claims on the company's income and assets. In some jurisdictions, further issues of shares for cash are required to be made by 'rights', which ensure that the existing shareholders have the opportunity to maintain their percentage shareholding in the company. Bonus issues, sometimes called 'scrip' or 'capitalisation' issues, are made to existing shareholders out of the company's share premium account or by capitalising reserves.

When a bonus issue is made, no cash is paid by shareholders or received by the company. In theory, the issue should leave the value of a shareholder's holding unchanged. For example, if a shareholder holds 100 shares with a market price of $1 and a one-for-ten bonus issue is declared, the total shares he owns will increase to 110 but the price should decline to approximately $0.91 ($1 multiplied by a factor of 100/110). However, in some markets bonus issues are well received, perhaps as a sign of favourable progress by the company, and the total market value of a shareholder's investment in the company may be observed to increase instead of adjusting fully.

(ii) Shares with different voting rights

Standard voting rights are for each shareholder to have one vote if a resolution is to be considered on a show of hands, while if a poll is demanded the formula is usually one vote for each share. In some instances, usually for historical reasons relating to the founding shareholders' wish to retain control and raise new capital, shares will be created with differing voting rights. There may be 'A' shares with one vote per share and 'B' shares with say ten votes per share. The original shareholders can then raise capital by issuing more 'A' shares to the public while retaining voting control through their 'B' shares. The public may well value their shares in relation to the earnings, dividends and asset backing which would be identical to the 'B' shares, without much concern over the inferior voting rights.

The current attitude of stock exchanges to differing voting rights is unfavourable. They will not normally grant listings to new issues on these terms. Where shares with different voting rights have been in existence for many years, it is difficult to insist on a change. Pressure may be applied by the authorities or by institutional holders for the directors voluntarily to propose that all voting rights should be made identical. It is common practice to give holders of shares with superior voting rights a bonus issue (say on the basis one-for-ten) to compensate them for the loss of their voting advantage.

(iii) Preference or preferred shares

Shares which have generally superior rights to the ordinary shares are called 'preference' shares. Shares whose rights differ only in one area may be called 'preferred' shares.

(a) As regards income and capital

Shares may be issued with rights to income and return of capital which are superior to those of ordinary shares. The dividend on a preference share is normally expressed as a fixed percentage of the par value or the issue price, for example 8%. Preference shareholders may, on occasion, participate in some percentage of the dividend paid to ordinary shareholders, giving holders some possibility of increasing income. Preference shares can be issued with a dividend linked to other variable factors such as the rates obtainable in the money market, but this is unusual.

The dividend rights of preference shares are normally 'cumulative'. If a dividend is not paid for one period, it must be subsequently paid together with the current dividend before dividends may be paid on the ordinary shares.

As with ordinary shares, there is no legal sanction on the company for failure to pay a preference dividend. Missing a preference dividend, as well as involving restrictions of payment of dividend to ordinary shareholders, may trigger voting rights or other powers for the preference shareholders. Preference shareholders cannot usually vote at general meetings of the company except on matters which affect their rights.

(b) Issues in place of ordinary shares

Issues of preferred or preference shares can be useful when it is difficult to issue ordinary shares. If the price of the ordinary shares is low, perhaps close to or even lower than the par value (in jurisdictions where a par value applies), an issue will not be possible. In such jurisdictions, it is not legal to issue shares at below par value. However, a new class of shares may be issued, designed to be valued at par because of its superior rights. This may also prove useful in a takeover bid, where there may be some doubt about the value of the ordinary shares or the bidder wishes to argue he is being generous to the target company's shareholders.

In situations where it is not practical to pay a dividend on the whole of the share capital owing to poor performance, it may still be possible to pay a dividend on a lesser number of preference shares. Preference shares are widely used in reconstructions. A company's equity needs to be increased but new investors are not willing to put in fresh money unless their investment ranks ahead of that of the original shareholders. As preference shares are counted as equity, an issue of preference shares serves to reduce gearing and to increase borrowing limits while giving new investors greater protection. An issue of unsecured loan stock, which might have similar rights, would not achieve this purpose.

(c) Ability to redeem

Preference shares are usually redeemable. This is a useful right in jurisdictions which prevent repayment of capital without court sanction and may restrict a company in purchasing its own shares. In such jurisdictions, it is possible for a company to redeem its preference shares out of a further issue of preference shares or if it has sufficient distributable reserves in its balance sheet and adequate financial resources. The possibility of redemption of a part of the share capital adds a flexibility in adjusting the overall level of gearing of the company. This feature has been found useful in some investment trusts to cater for the objectives of different types of investors.

(iv) Shares with deferred rights

Shares may be issued with deferred rights, usually as regards income. For example, a company may acquire by an issue of shares assets (such as development sites) which may not yield income for some years. The company may not be able to maintain its dividend if the new shares rank for dividend before the assets acquired can contribute income.

In this case, the shares may be issued on terms that they do not rank for dividend for a certain period of time, estimated to be the period before the assets generate profits. At the end of this period, the deferred shares will automatically become ordinary shares and rank for dividends equally with them.

This device may also assist in maintaining reported earnings per share. Shares which do not rank for dividends are not normally included in the earnings and dividends per share calculation. However, 'fully diluted' earnings per share, that is assuming all shares rank for dividend, should also be shown in the accounts, either on the face of the profit and loss statement or as a note.

Deferred shares have also been used as a fundamental part of tax schemes to lessen the amount of transfer duty. If the shares transferred have such inferior rights that their value may be argued to be negligible, their transfer may be effected with little or no transfer tax. This method of avoidance has been tolerated in certain jurisdictions in the past but it seems likely that changes in legislation will render it obsolete.

(v) Treatment in takeovers

Shares which lack voting rights in normal conditions are largely ignored in takeovers and treated as part of a tidying-up exercise at the end of the day. However, as noted above, if a dividend is not current, preference shareholders are likely to have votes and, in some circumstances, may even have a majority of votes. In addition, provisions to protect their preferential right to assets may give them a veto over certain types of reorganisation planned as part of the takeover or merger. Preference shares with special rights may be used specifically to put in place a 'poison pill' defence, giving the holders rights which make a takeover of the company prohibitively expensive to a hostile predator.

(vi) Convertibility

Shares may be issued with rights that they can be converted into ordinary shares. The method and terms of conversion are normally the same as those applying to convertible loan stock which is described below. Convertible preference shares are very close to outright equity. They would typically be issued in circumstances where the company would prefer to issue ordinary shares except for the technical or tactical reasons mentioned above.

Deferred or preferred shares may become identical to ordinary shares on the triggering of some event to which their preferred or deferred status specifically relates. For example, preferred shares may be entitled to a higher dividend than ordinary shares initially. When the income on the ordinary shares increases so that it exceeds the preferred share dividend, the preferred shares automatically become ordinary shares. Deferred shares which, for example, do not rank for dividends for a certain period become ordinary shares when that period has elapsed.

II   LOAN STOCKS AND WARRANTS

Unlike shareholders, holders of loan stock do not participate pro rata in the earnings of the company. The return is fixed at the level of the coupon on the loan stock and does not vary if the profits increase. If profits decrease or indeed are eliminated altogether, there is still a legal obligation on the company to pay the interest or be subject to various legal sanctions which may be taken by or on behalf of the holders of the loan stock. The rights of the holders are set down in a trust deed or other document showing the terms on which the issue is made.

Two main types of loan stock are relevant for corporate finance transactions, unsecured loan stock with no conversion rights and convertible loan stock. On occasions, loan stock without conversion rights is issued in conjunction with warrants.

(i) Unsecured loan stock

Issues of straight unsecured loan stock tend to appeal mainly to institutional investors, particularly pension funds and insurance companies. These institutions have long-term obligations which they seek to match with assets providing steady long-term income. Unsecured loan stocks have final maturities ranging from say 5 to 15 years or longer. At least for a proportion of their portfolio, institutions prefer a conservative investment, ranking ahead of ordinary shares and protected by various covenants. The degree of added security compensates such holders for the lack of any potential increase in their income. A serious breach of the convenants of the loan stock will constitute a default by the company on its obligations and will trigger repayment of the loan stock and other sanctions.

(a) Restrictions on issuing group

The trust deed which constitutes the loan stock contains restrictions on how the issuing company is financed and managed. These restrictions may include an overall limit on the borrowings of the company and its subsidiaries and a lower or 'inner' limit on borrowings which rank ahead of the loan stockholders. Loan stock may be issued by a holding company or a special-purpose off-shore subsidiary guaranteed by the holding company. If this is so, all borrowings by subsidiary companies conducting the group's main business rank ahead of the loan stockholders in practice, assuming the major assets of the group are held by such subsidiaries. The inner limit therefore includes both secured borrowings and borrowings of subsidiaries.

There is usually a covenant not to dispose of any major assets (unless the proceeds are reinvested in similar assets or used to repay debt) without the consent of loan stockholders or to make a major change in the nature of the business. It is assumed that stockholders will have made their decision to invest on the basis of the assets and business of the group at that time and might not take the same attitude if substantial changes are made. Trustees for the stockholders will represent their interests as a class and act as a representative available for discussions with the issuing company on points the company may wish to take up relating to the terms of the loan stock.

(b) Interest

The coupon on the loan stock is normally fixed and payable semi-annually. The stock will be valued by discounting the stream of interest payments and the final repayment of principal at maturity by the rate considered appropriate by the market from time to time for a stock of that particular risk and maturity. If interest rates drop, the value of the stock will rise and vice versa.

It is possible to set the coupon by reference to some floating rate, for example the rate of interest payable in the inter-bank market. Obligations of this kind are called floating rate notes. The interest rate may vary by reference to other benchmarks, provided there is some objective way of determining what the interest payment should be. Some floating rate bonds have a maximum and minimum payment built into their terms. Others may become fixed when the interest rate drops or rises to a certain specified amount.

Some bonds have been issued without any coupon payable at all, called, appropriately enough, zero coupon bonds. Such bonds are issued at a substantial discount to their face value. The discount is calculated to compensate holders for the lack of income until maturity by reference to the rates of return available on bonds of a comparable maturity and risk. This type of bond is attractive to some holders, as the 'income' is automatically reinvested at the same rate of return. If interest is actually paid, the recipient must seek a similarly attractive investment. Zero coupon bonds may be considered a speculative investment by bond standards. Their market value will fluctuate more than any other kind of bond for a given rise or fall in interest rates.

Unsecured loan stocks with low or poor investment ratings but high coupons have become extensively used to finance leveraged buy-outs. They are known in the market as 'junk bonds' and some curbs on their use seem likely to be imposed. However, unsecured loan stocks have an important role in takeover offers, being used not only as a means of raising capital for the offeror but also to provide an increase in income to the target company's shareholders. The coupon on an unsecured loan stock will almost certainly be higher than the dividend yield of the target company's shares at the offer price.

(ii) Warrants

A warrant represents a right to subscribe a certain sum of money for a company's securities at a fixed price for a stated period. Most usually, the securities in point are ordinary shares but they may also be, for example, preference shares or loan stock. Warrants can be listed on a stock exchange and traded. They impose no obligation on the holder and may be considered as a type of traded call option.

(a) Rights

The rights of warrantholders are set out in the warrant certificate or other document. They are not as extensive as the rights of most other securities, concentrating on protecting the right to subscribe, the price at which subscription is made and the worth of the securities which can be subscribed for.

Warrants are exercised by sending in a subscription form to the company with a cheque for the number of shares being subscribed for at the subscription price. A warrant may confer the right to subscribe one share or the right to subscribe a fixed sum of money for shares at a price which may be adjusted for various events. The right to subscribe may be exercised up to some fixed date, which may be say five years from the date of issue of the warrants. If the holder does not exercise the warrants by that date, they expire and become worthless. The company cannot force the warrantholder to exercise his warrants, although in certain circumstances they may be cancelled if he does not.

(b) Value of warrants

Warrants tend to have vogues. In a rising market, an option to subscribe shares at a fixed price has obvious attractions. Even in a falling market, warrants will have some value. Warrants will have more speculative appeal in a volatile market and when issued by companies with a cyclical share price record. As warrants will probably never attract significant interest from conservative investors, the more speculative operators set the tone of the price movements and dealing activity.

Apart from the volatility of the particular market and of the price of the share to which they relate, the value of warrants is affected by three main factors. The first is their expiry date – the longer the warrant life, the more valuable it will be. The second is the exercise price. If the exercise price is below the current share price, the warrant has a real value equal to the difference and is said to be 'in the money'. Even when the exercise price is far above the market price of the share, the warrant will still have a 'hope' value.

The third factor is the level of gearing a warrant offers an investor. For a given sum, an investor can buy a certain number of shares. Alternatively, for the same sum he can buy warrants which give him the right to subscribe for a greater number of shares. The ratio between the two numbers of shares is the gearing.

Several models exist for valuing call options and warrants which may provide some theoretical basis for attributing value when warrants are issued. However, it seems that markets and professional advisers do not yet fully understand or trust this approach. It is rare to see a company or its bankers being prepared to estimate the value of warrants in a formal document prior to the start of trading.

Prices for warrants are often assessed in the market by reference to the 'premium'. The premium is the additional amount it costs an investor to purchase a share by buying a warrant and exercising it as compared to an outright purchase of the share. Whether a premium is expensive or not is judged chiefly by the three factors mentioned above. The premium is not a useful measure in all circumstances. If the exercise price is substantially higher than the current market price of the shares, the premium will inevitably be high but the actual cost to buy the warrant will be low.

(c) Uses of warrants

Warrants have been frequently issued with loan stock to reduce the coupon payable on the stock. Instead of assessing the coupon required for the stock to stand at par, the issuer can deduct the assumed value of the warrant. The exercise price of the warrant is normally set at the current market price of the shares, or at a small premium, say no more than 10%. Typically, the total amount of subscription rights attached to the warrants will equal the nominal amount of stock to be issued, although it can be less (say half) or, rarely, more than the loan stock issue. If the market premium for warrants is in the 15–20% range, the issuers can afford to price the loan stock element to stand at say 85%, and not 100%, producing a significant saving in interest costs.

The warrants are detachable and are traded separately. As they appeal to another category of investor from the loan stock, it is not uncommon to find that stock and warrants issued together become held by largely different investors after a short period of time.

Warrants are occasionally used as 'sweeteners' in takeover offers or issued to shareholders by way of bonus issue. It seems that on such occasions the issuing company derives little immediate benefit from the exercise, owing to the difficulty the market finds in knowing how to value the warrants.

The issuing company may not be greatly concerned. On the face of the accounts, there may be little sign that warrants even exist. If the warrants are exercised, the company receives cash. If they are not, they simply expire at no cost to the company. However, there must be an opportunity cost in giving a third party an option to subscribe. If the option is over a significant percentage of a company's share capital, the resulting 'overhang' may prevent the share price rising much above the exercise price of the warrants. Shareholders will also be exposed to dilution in the earnings and asset backing of their shares.

(iii) Convertible loan stock

(a) Rights and restrictions

The rights and restrictions contained in the document which constitutes a convertible loan stock tend to be along the same lines as those for a straight loan stock. If anything, covenants may be less strict, as the holders of the convertible are likely to be regarded partly as shareholders as well as holders of debt.

The right to convert will be carefully defined and protected. Conversion rights usually start shortly after the stock is issued and last until it is redeemed. The conversion price may be at the present market price of the shares or at a small premium, normally not more than 10%. The holder converts by completing a form on the back of the stock certificate. The number of shares he receives is calculated by dividing the nominal value of the loan stock he tenders by the conversion price. If he tenders a stock certificate with a nominal value of $1,000 and the conversion price is $2, he will receive 500 shares. The market value of the stock and the shares is not relevant for this purpose. It should be noted that the stockholder pays no cash but simply exchanges his stock for shares. Likewise, the company receives no cash. Its outstanding debt is reduced by the nominal amount of stock redeemed and its issued share capital (and share premium account, if appropriate) goes up by the same amount. A conversion therefore has a doubly beneficial effect on gearing, reducing debt at the same time as equity is increased. Many convertibles contain a clause which enables the company to force all holders to convert if over 75% of the holders have converted their loan stock. More controversially, conversion may also be forced if the share price exceeds the conversion price by a minimum amount (say 50%) for a minimum period. Such a provision puts a 'cap' on the value of the stock. The conversion procedures normally contain provisions which prevent an investor collecting interest and dividends in respect of the same period.

Most convertible loan stock is convertible into the ordinary shares of the company which issues the stock. However, there is nothing to prevent the stock being converted into the shares of another company if the issuing company has such shares under its control. In this case, a convertible issue could be a disguised method of placing out a significant holding in another company which might not be marketable as one block. The convertible loan stock could also be converted into, for example, straight loan stock or preference shares.

(b) Reasons for issue

A convertible loan stock may be issued by a company which wishes to issue further equity but not at a discount to market price (as is usually necessary), or when it is unable to issue equity because of market conditions or other constraints. On the other hand, a company may prefer to issue debt but is prevented because the straight debt market does not view its paper as of sufficient quality. In this case, the company may compensate for the additional risk by including an element of equity in the package.

On the other hand, the coupon payable on convertible loan stock will be lower than that on a standard unsecured loan stock reflecting the value of the conversion right. Straight debt has no possibility of price appreciation in line with expected rises in the price of the shares.

In takeovers, a convertible loan stock is often used to increase the value of an offer while avoiding dilution in earnings per share. A detailed example of this is given in ch 4 of Part 3 below.

(c) Valuation

The valuation of convertible loan stock can be approached in two ways. If it is considered as 'deferred equity', it will be valued on the basis of the market price of the number of shares into which a holding can be converted, added to which is the income advantage in receiving for a period a higher level of interest than dividend. Alternatively it can be considered to have a base value as straight debt; the convertible feature can be regarded as a kind of option and valued as such. This may be illustrated as follows:

EXAMPLE

Method 1

Coupon on convertible loan stock is 8%. Stock is issued in $100 amounts.

Dividend yield on ordinary shares at the conversion price is 4% and dividends are expected to grow at 15% per annum.

Tax on interest and dividends is ignored for this example.

Year	Interest	Dividend income	Differential	Present value of differential at 10%
1	8%	4.0%	4.0	3.64
2	8%	4.6%	3.4	2.81
3	8%	5.3%	2.7	2.03
4	8%	6.1%	1.9	1.30
5	8%	7.0%	1.0	0.62
6	8%	8.0%	—	—
				10.40

Conversion price is set at 21, a 5% premium to market price of 20.

Value on conversion is $\frac{100}{21} \times 20 =$ 95.2

Present value of income differential   10.4

Estimated value of convertible   105.6

Method 2

Straight unsecured loan stocks with an 8% coupon and similar maturities and perceived risks are standing at approximately 88%.

Warrants of similar life and gearing issued by comparable companies are selling at a 15% premium.

Value as straight bond   88

Value of conversion option, say   15

    103

The results of the two methods will not be identical (except by coincidence) but should not be far apart.

(d) Timing of conversion

Experience shows that convertible loan stocks are generally converted. An investor will tend to convert when dividends rise on the ordinary shares to such an extent that the dividend income receivable after conversion (adjusting for the tax position of the investor) is greater than the interest receivable from the loan stock, provided that the investor believes the dividend level can be maintained. The other reason for conversion before maturity is to increase marketability. The convertible loan stock of a company may be less marketable than the ordinary shares because of fewer holders, a lower amount in issue and a tendency for such issues to be 'salted away' in portfolios.

It should be noted that conversion will not necessarily occur simply because the market price of the ordinary shares is greater than the conversion price. Subject to marketability, the market price of the convertible will in this case rise above par and the investor can take his profit by selling the loan stock. He has no need to convert. The income differential should still be the main determining factor until the end of the conversion period approaches.

CHAPTER 2

Principles of valuation and pricing

An important part of most corporate finance transactions is valuing a company and putting a price on its shares or other securities. The two are obviously closely related as the valuation forms part of the basis of the price of an issue or, in the case of a bid, the price at which the transaction is carried out.

There is, however, an important distinction between valuation and pricing. Valuation tends to be at least in part a theoretical exercise. It is normal to consider a range of valuations. To claim that any one figure can be the precise valuation of a company is unrealistic. There are too many variables to be taken into account for absolute precision to be attainable. The weighting given to each factor in the valuation is largely a question of judgment, not mathematics. The range of valuation will therefore be partly subjective owing to the way it is calculated.

Valuation will be affected by the attitudes of the people preparing it. A big project or a complex company would perhaps be approached cautiously by most purchasers but others might see additional opportunities rather than risks. Experience of a particular industry may have given some buyers encouragement, others burnt fingers. Value, like beauty, is at least partially in the eye of the beholder.

Pricing on the other hand is a much earthier process. It is disastrous to stray from the practical disciplines of the market-place. Whereas valuation can be a somewhat leisurely, almost academic pursuit, prices are fixed rapidly and tested immediately in the market. Timing is vital. Sentiment can change abruptly.

If an issue price is set too high in the opinion of the market on the day of subscription, the issue will flop; too low and there will be embarrassing over-subscriptions. In either case, substantial amounts of money will be lost and months of careful planning will be largely wasted.

In the case of a bid, the acid test is success or failure. Price is always a (if not the) determining factor. If the price is too low, the entire campaign may fail; if it is too high, funds which may later be badly needed are lost to the company. Whether the pricing of a corporate finance deal has been correct tends to be all too obvious.

I VALUATION

In a corporate finance transaction, valuation cannot usually be taken to very sophisticated lengths. There are two main reasons for this. First, there tends to be a severe constraint on time and manpower; second, the information available may be incomplete, out of date and not in the most relevant form. This is seen in its most extreme form in a contested takeover but holds true to a greater or lesser extent in most corporate finance transactions.

When investors refer to the 'worth of a company', they usually mean the worth of all the ordinary shares or common stock of that company. This is almost always the case with a public listed company, although care may be needed if other classes of securities are also listed. A private company often has a small share capital. The bulk of its funding will be provided by shareholder loans, which is a more flexible and perhaps more tax efficient method of providing the necessary base of stockholders' investment. In such a case, the definition of worth can be usefully extended to include any shareholder loans.

(i) Earnings multiple/price earnings ratio

'Earnings multiple' or 'price earnings ratio' has become over the last 25 years a measure of valuation with which even infrequent stockmarket investors or observers are comfortable and familiar. However, some refinements in the way earnings are calculated and how the multiple is applied are necessary to ensure the earnings multiple concept is as appropriate as possible in a particular case. The main considerations include:

(a) How should 'earnings' be defined?

Earnings for this purpose can most usefully be regarded as the profits of the company and its subsidiaries and associates after deduction of the charges which rank ahead of the shareholders entitled to those earnings. Consequently, all interest charges owing to bankers or others should be deducted as these claims on the company's income and assets rank ahead of shareholders. Tax should also be deducted for this reason. If any proportion of income is attributable to outside shareholders of a subsidiary (for example if a subsidiary is not wholly owned by the company), this proportion, called 'minority interests' is also deducted. The above represents standard accounting treatment of 'earnings' as they would appear in an audited profit and loss statement in most countries, that is consolidated profit after interest, tax and minority interests.

(b) 'Attributable' earnings

The principle is to match what is being valued with the earnings attributable to it or generated by it. If there are preference shares outstanding which are entitled to receive a certain dividend, this should be deducted from the earnings before the ordinary shares can be valued. If there are convertible securities outstanding which are likely to be converted, the interest should be added back to earnings (with appropriate adjustments for tax) and the earnings related to the enlarged number of shares in issue after conversion.

(c) 'Recurrent' earnings

If a multiple is applied to a particular year's earnings to calculate a valuation, the implication is that the elements included in the earnings will be present in each year's earnings for the foreseeable future. Profits or losses which are made from activities which are not part of the company's regular business, such as the sale of a fixed asset used in the business, are separately listed in the profit and loss account under the heading 'extraordinary items'. Such items should not be included in 'earnings' to which the multiple is applied for valuation purposes.

'Recurrent' earnings imply that the business is a going concern. For this reason, depreciation should not be added back to earnings, as it is in a cash flow calculation. It is assumed that regular reinvestment at the level of the depreciation charge will be required to ensure that the earnings are indeed recurrent.

(d) Timing

Earnings are expressed over a single financial period, often a calendar year. Trading conditions may not fall conveniently into annual patterns. If a company has made a loss of 5 in the first half of the year and a profit of 10 in the second half, the accounts will show earnings of 5 for the whole year (10 for the second half minus 5 for the first). In this case, other things being equal, the year-end profitability is running at the annual rate of 20. To use the published figure of 5 for the basis of valuation is likely to be misleading.

(e) Forecast vs historic earnings

In assessing earnings, analysts will attempt to form as up-to-date a picture as possible. Past earnings are only of interest as a guide to the future. Reliable estimates and forecasts are much sought after. However, the degree of uncertainty in the estimates is likely to increase sharply beyond a few months in the future and the analysis will become more speculative.

(f) Other adjustments

The above are the first steps in identifying the most appropriate figure from a company's accounts to take as the starting point. No change is attempted to the numbers as presented by the company itself. At this point, the analyst must begin to think for himself what actual adjustments might be needed to ensure his valuation is soundly based. It must also be constructed so as to be comparable with valuations of other similar companies, a highly relevant consideration in most corporate finance transactions. The types of adjustments to look for include the following:

Accounting policies. Have accounting policies been recently changed and with what effect? Most changes are linked to developments in accounting and auditing practice but the introduction of a change in accounting policy often seems to increase profits rather than the reverse. Popular areas are the valuation of closing inventory, the treatment of research and development expenditure and the circumstances when interest can be capitalised.

Components of income/profits. In using a multiple of earnings to value a company, it is critical to ensure that all the elements included in the profits being multiplied are in fact appropriately treated in this fashion. This is particularly important where a very high or very low multiple is being used. Items which are not best treated in this manner include:

INTEREST ON SURPLUS CASH DEPOSITS OR INVESTMENT INCOME ON FUNDS UNDER MANAGEMENT.   Cash can hardly be worth more than its face value. If interest is earned at 10% on surplus cash of 100 and interest income included in earnings to which a 15 times multiple is applied, cash of 100 will in effect be valued at 150.

RENTS.   If a property is owned by a company but not for the moment used in its business, rent may be earned. In this case, it is preferable to value the surplus property separately and not include rentals in profits to which a multiple is applied. The multiple may bear no relationship to the capitalisation rate appropriate to the property.

FOREIGN EXCHANGE INCOME.   In times of unstable foreign exchange rates, a company with an international range of business may make substantial gains or losses from the timing of payment for its purchases and conversion of its foreign exchange sales income. The company might argue that this is part and parcel of its regular activities. An analyst might well feel uncomfortable at putting a multiple on substantial foreign exchange gains (or losses) and risking distortion of the valuation. A better treatment is to exclude such items on the grounds that in the longer term gains and losses of this type will probably balance out.

INCOME FROM SALES OF ASSETS.   Some asset-based companies regularly buy and sell major assets as well as utilise them in their business. Examples of industries where this is common practice are transportation (particularly shipping and airlines) and property development. The companies may argue that it is their regular involvement in a particular line of business that enables them to make sales of assets which outsiders could not achieve. Nevertheless, asset-based industries are often highly cyclical so that the reliability of such profits is hard to gauge. Differing accounting treatments by companies in the same industry complicate the picture, some including such profits (or losses) in earnings and others showing them as extraordinary items.

ASSOCIATES.   If a company is accounted for as an associate, the attributable percentage of its earnings (rather than just dividends received) will be taken into the profits of the company holding the stake. Associated companies are defined as companies in which the holding company has a substantial interest (say a minimum of 20% of the equity) and some influence over management, evidenced for example by being able to appoint at least one board member. However, board membership may confer little control. The holding company has no access to the associate's cash flow which may be a weakness. There appears to be some merit in the verdict of a well-known City of London financier that 'associated company accounting is for the birds'.

SALES AND EXPENSES NEAR YEAR END.   By accelerating or delaying shipment of goods or completion of projects, management can adjust profits to some extent from one year to the next. Many types of indirect or non-variable costs can be deferred by management on a short-term basis, for example an advertising campaign, a branch-opening programme or the hiring of additional administrative staff. It may well be legitimate to smooth profits to reflect underlying business trends but the analyst should beware of the effect on a single year's figures.

If a business is highly geared, increases or decreases in interest costs will have a marked effect on profits before taxation. Consideration should be given in such cases to applying the multiple to earnings plus interest paid and then deducting the amount of the debt to reach the valuation.

The underlying principle behind the above adjustments is that the multiple of earnings method is most satisfactory where the earnings are recurrent earnings generated from continuing business activities. If the earnings figure is substantially influenced by net financial income such as interest and foreign exchange gains, rents and sales of non-current assets, distortions are inevitable.

(g) Setting the multiple

When an adjusted figure for earnings has been established, it remains to set an appropriate multiple. Multiples vary by market, sector and individual company.

It is possible to try to calculate a suitable multiple on a theoretical basis. The major determining factors are the expected rate of growth, the perceived risk and the marketability of the shares. However, a more usual starting point is to identify comparable companies and use their multiples as a basis. Adjustments can then be made to reflect factors such as growth, risk and marketability. The higher the rate of growth which is anticipated, the higher the multiple. A company which is expected to exceed the average rate of growth for its sector should be accorded a premium. The estimate of risk should encompass if possible both commercial aspects, such as areas of business activity engaged in, and financial aspects, such as level of gearing. Most listed shares should be adequately marketable. A private company would be allocated a lower multiple than a public listed company.

The multiple appropriate for historic earnings figures will be higher than for forecast earnings. The historic multiple will reflect expectations of growth which are already being included in the forecast earnings. In addition, the forecast will contain some element of risk whereas the historic figures are definite.

A comparison of multiples may be distorted by different treatments of tax, when the apparent amount of tax due on the basis of pre-tax profits differs from the actual amount of tax paid. In financial statements, standard tax charges are normally applied but care must be taken if this is not so. Even if the deduction for tax is comparable, a company which is able to reduce or delay its tax payments by skilful tax planning may be able to achieve faster growth by use of the additional resources. This factor may also make it difficult to compare an average market multiple in one country with another. Tax rates may differ sharply, but not necessarily tax payments.

(ii) Net assets

The most obvious way to value a company is perhaps to value its assets and then subtract its liabilities as shown in the balance sheet.

An example of a typical consolidated balance sheet laid out in vertical form is given below:

	$m	$m
Fixed assets		
land		25
buildings		10
machinery and equipment		15
		50
Associated company		8
Investments		7
Current assets:		
stocks and work-in-progress	28	
accounts receivable and pre-payments	13	
bank balance and deposits	20	
	61	
Current liabilities:		
accounts payable and accrued charges	15	
bank loans and overdrafts	20	
taxation	5	
proposed dividend	5	
	45	
Net current assets		16
Goodwill on consolidation		5
Intangible assets		5
		91
Less: deferred liabilities		
long term loans	25	
deferred taxation	5	
		30
minority interests		13
Consolidated net assets		48
Consolidated net tangible assets		38
Net assets per share		
(75 million shares in issue)		$0.64
Net tangible assets per share		$0.51

In carrying out a valuation on a net asset basis, each item must be examined critically. Most time will probably be spent on the fixed assets, typically the largest items in the balance sheet. If they have been owned by the group for a number of years, substantial differences may have arisen between book value and current market value.

A number of important considerations must be borne in mind when a company instructs a professional valuer or attempts to make its own estimate. In the case of a flotation or issue of securities, it must be assumed that the business in which property is used will continue as a going concern, otherwise the entire exercise would be in doubt. In this case, only an existing use basis can be used for valuation. Property which is of a specialised type may be difficult to value except as an integral part of the business.

Property which is surplus or which could be sold independently of the business can be regarded in a different light. The valuer should be asked to give his opinion of the best alternate use, that is the use which would produce the highest valuation of the property. The value of vacant land depends on what planning permissions have been obtained. A completed building may be valued on the basis of the income it generates from rental or on the assumption that it will be sold on the open market, either as a whole or perhaps floor by floor. Major income generating assets such as hotels, quarries and mines may be valued by discounting the net cash flow attributable to their operations.

Associates are held at cost plus share of profits or losses since acquisition. It will be hard to check the validity of this figure without access to the associate's accounts. If advances have been made to the associate, they will also be included in the figure for associates. If the associate is a private company with a small share capital and large loans, the recoverability of the loans may be in doubt. Long-term holdings in companies which are not associates may be held under 'investments'.

Stocks and accounts receivable are the most vulnerable part of a manufacturing concern's balance sheet. A fresh look at the real value of these items sometimes produces some startling differences of opinion. If the business is not continued, stock may become largely worthless and receivables difficult to collect.

Goodwill on consolidation represents a premium paid for control of a company over the fair value of its net assets. Most service companies can only be purchased at a premium to net asset value. Goodwill is regarded as an intangible asset although it might well be backed up by excellent earnings prospects. Other intangible assets might be expenditure on such items as trademarks, licences, patents and costs incurred in flotation or reorganisation. Some of these items will have more continuing worth than others.

A provision for deferred tax may be made when capital allowances for taxation purposes are significantly higher than the depreciation charges applied by the company in its accounts. A provision is made on the assumption that a lower tax charge now means more tax must be paid later. Some managements feel that they can manage their tax affairs so that the low tax charge will continue indefinitely and argue that deferred taxation reserves should be counted as equity.

Minority interests will arise when a group owns less than 100% of the share capital of a subsidiary.

In addition to liabilities shown on the face of the balance sheet, there may be guarantees outstanding or other contingent liabilities. Liabilities can also arise through litigation, contractual arrangements, capital investment commitments, lease obligations, severance payments and unfunded pension plans.

Net assets are of most relevance in acquisitions where the acquiror will obtain 100% control, conferring direct access to the target company's assets. The net asset value may be the single most significant figure for takeover exponents whose chief objective is to acquire assets at a discount to improve their own balance sheet or to sell off at a profit.

A holder of a minority interest has no direct access to the assets underlying his shares. The net asset backing in a flotation may therefore be less relevant, although the preference in some markets is to have an issue price which is fully backed by net assets. It is felt that if the earnings collapse at least the net asset backing will provide some support for the share price.

The net asset statement will be scrutinised closely for the level of gearing which is shown. Net assets may be compared to total liabilities or just loans. Any cash resources will normally be taken into account. Issuers should also consider the question of potential dilution of net asset backing when issuing shares other than to existing shareholders.

(iii) Composite basis

If sufficient information is available, a composite approach to valuation is more satisfactory than taking an earnings multiple or net asset backing by itself. Where a group consists of a number of essentially different assets or businesses, it is preferable to look at each on an individual basis. This requires constructing a valuation on an unconsolidated rather than consolidated basis. In a large company, this may have to be taken further involving a valuation of each major category of asset.

The main reason for building up a composite valuation on an unconsolidated basis is the different nature of businesses or assets which may be included in a group. Some businesses are able to make a considerable profit from a very low capital investment. They may require a high level of recurrent expenditure on, for example, advertising which is expensed year by year without an asset base being built up. A well-known brand name with immense commercial value does not appear on a balance sheet. Other assets may have a high book value but a relatively small income. For example, the more prime the location of a property, the lower its yield.

If a group consists of these two types of assets, a consolidated valuation will result in an under-estimate of the worth of the group. On a consolidated basis, the group may appear to be worth approximately the same, as if an earnings multiple and net asset backing is used. However, examined separately it will be readily apparent that the value is greater.

An example of this principle would be as follows:

	$m	$m
Land and buildings		50
Plant and machinery		5
Investments		10
Current assets: stock	30	
accounts receivable	15	
cash	25	
	70	
Current liabilities: creditors	15	
overdraft	15	
	30	40
		105
Less: long-term debt		10
Net assets		95

For the latest financial year the company reported earnings of $10 m and the current year's budget is for a small increase. A typical price earnings multiple for this industry is 8.

On the face of it it would appear that a fair value for the above company is about $80–90 m representing an industry average multiple and a small discount on net assets. On further enquiry the following facts emerge:

(i)   Land and buildings are factories only half occupied by the company itself. The remainder are vacant or rented to third parties.
(ii) Investment of $10 m consists half of an investment in a research and development company engaged in design work for the business and half of listed shares unrelated to the business.
(iii) Cash balances of $25 m are not utilised in the business but are managed separately by an investment adviser. There is no foreseeable requirement for additional working capital in the business.

A composite valuation of the business would be as follows:

(i)	Earnings	10
	Less: Income from rentals and surplus cash	(2)
		8
	Business valued on 8 times multiple	64
(ii)	Surplus land and buildings at valuation	25
(iii)	Surplus investment at market value	5
(iv)	Surplus cash after allowing for a $5 m contingency	20
	Total valuation	114
As compared with initial valuation		80–90

The composite method is likely to place the highest valuation on the group. It is most relevant where there is at least a possibility that the group might be broken up and sold to realise full value for each independent unit. When a hostile bid reaches this level, the directors of the target company have to consider whether it is in the shareholders' interests to continue to resist.

(iv) Other methods

As mentioned above, valuations can also be carried out by reference to various other methods. The main ones are discussed in (a) and (b) below:

(a) Dividends

The dividend paid on an ordinary share divided by the share price and expressed as a percentage is called the 'dividend yield'. It is normally expressed gross, without taking any account of the recipient's tax position. Income-conscious investors may place a high weight on annual income received although they would acknowledge that capital gain is also part of the total return equation. Companies which pay out almost all earnings as dividend may be valued on this basis alone. Of course, as dividends and earnings are virtually identical in this case, valuation on the basis of dividends is also an earnings valuation.

In some markets, the stock exchange authorities will pay particular attention to the amount of dividend paid. They regard this as a more concrete return than the more speculative nature of capital gains. The fact that the company is able to pay out a substantial cash dividend is taken as a reliable test of strength.

(b) Cash flow

Using cash flow as a basis for valuation is essentially similar to using earnings or dividends. However, as the format of analysis based on cash flows involves setting out figures for a significant number of years ahead, the analyst is forced to spell out assumptions on such matters as capital investment and working capital requirements, inflation and timing of tax payments. In addition, risk can be incorporated more systematically by using expected values for the various components of cash flow rather than single point estimates. A computer model can be constructed by assigning probability distributions to each variable. A large number of possible outcomes are then calculated to produce a probability distribution of valuation estimates.

The snag of carrying out such a valuation in the context of corporate finance transactions is that there is rarely sufficient reliable data about a company and its many variable features to make the numerous assumptions required for the analysis. If general assumptions are made concerning estimated flows, little is gained by using the cash flow method. The net cash flow for an average year begins to look like an adjusted figure for estimated earnings. If it is assumed that cash flows continue indefinitely, the discount rate begins to look like a reflection of the multiple.

Relatively simple businesses owning a single major capital asset such as a hotel, quarry or mine may be usefully assessed by the cash flow method. The nature of the investment in such a company is quite close to a capital investment in its major asset. The discounted cash flow method has for a considerable period of time been widely used in industry to make decisions about capital investments.

II   PRICE

Pricing is essentially a practical skill whereas valuation is at least partially academic.

(i) Flotations

In flotations, pricing is chiefly based on comparison. An investor has a choice between buying a large number of existing shares or the new one which is being floated. Although novelty can have some appeal, investor inertia and a sentiment of 'better the devil you know' may prevail unless there is a tangible incentive. The pricing of a flotation is therefore normally pitched at a discount to the ratings of the most comparable companies. The ratings of comparable companies themselves of course are influenced by fundamental factors such as price earnings ratio, net asset backing and dividend yield. However, setting the price is effectively at one stage removed from these fundamentals. It must also be remembered in a flotation or any other market exercise that the average investor is buying only a small number of shares and no premium for control or access to underlying assets is appropriate.

(ii) Rights issues

As rights issues are made by definition to a company's existing shareholders, the question of pricing is not so sensitive. Most markets will have a standard approach to pricing which again is based on the principle of a discount. In this case, the discount is not so much related to comparable companies as to the price of the company's own shares. Some incentive must be given to shareholders to take up the rights issue rather than simply buying more shares in the market which is a quicker and more convenient process. It is unlikely that fundamentals will be very relevant to the pricing discount itself, although of course they may have a significant bearing on whether to proceed with the rights issue in the first place.

(iii) Placings

As in the case of a rights issue, markets normally have their own standard discounts which apply to a placing of shares to investors other than existing shareholders. In this instance, the position of the existing shareholders is highly relevant. They will wish to see the shares placed as close to market price as possible so that share price does not come under pressure. They will also be concerned if their attributable earnings or assets per share are likely to be significantly diluted.

(iv) Takeovers

In launching a takeover particularly if it is contested, some premium over market price is required if the bid is not to fall flat on its face. It is also helpful if it can be demonstrated that shareholders of the target company will receive an increase in their income. If it is possible to offer them an increase in asset and earnings backing, this will also be of some effect particularly as it deprives the defence of a major argument.

At this stage, however, valuation becomes relevant. If the price for success is too high and exceeds the valuation on a theoretical basis, the board of the bidding company must consider whether they should withdraw from the fray. In this connection it is useful to set limits in advance, even if they are somewhat flexible. On the other side of the table, the board of the defending company must consider whether they should accept an offer at this level. Even if it could be successfully resisted, is it really in the shareholders' interests to continue the struggle?

The relationship between pricing and valuation is clearly a very close one with pricing in many cases being the direct descendant of valuation. However, it may be that the price needed for a successful issue is, for example, too low to be in the company's interests. In these circumstances, it needs a strong will and determination to resist being carried along by the momentum and impetus a transaction can generate. In takeovers, one of the most difficult decisions is to recognise that the price necessary for success cannot be justified in terms of valuation. It is also a bitter pill for a board which believes it can resist an unwelcome bid successfully to acknowledge that they have lured an offeror too far and must lose in order to win.

Part 2

Going public and making further issues of equity capital

Introduction

SOME BASIC TERMS AND CONCEPTS

Part 2 of this book deals with going public and making further issues of equity capital. As with many specialised types of financing, a certain amount of jargon is used in describing the procedures, the participants and their role. This review is intended to introduce some basic terms and concepts and to present an overview of the more detailed aspects covered in the individual chapters.

(i) Terminology

The terms 'going public' or 'flotation' are applied to the situation where a company first seeks to obtain a listing for one or more classes of its securities on a recognised stock exchange. This process is referred to in the US as an 'initial public offering'. Going public usually involves the raising of funds either by the company or its shareholders or both. Occasionally, all that is sought is a listing on an exchange without any further marketing of shares. This procedure is called an 'introduction' and can only be used when a sufficient spread of shareholders to ensure adequate marketability is already considered to exist.

The term 'prospectus' refers to the formal documents which have to be filed with the relevant authorities when a company offers its securities to the public. The amount of information to be included in the prospectus is the greatest on the occasion when a company first goes public.

Prospectuses may well have to be filed when subsequent issues of shares or other securities are made. Much of the information required in the first instance does not need to be repeated. Subsequent issues therefore tend to involve less documentation and expense. In the US, it is now possible to have a prospectus on file with the authorities in approved form which can be used at short notice as the basis of further issues by a public company, normally of debt.

The procedures for an issue are likely to be simplified and considerable time saved if a prospectus does not have to be filed. The legal advisers to a company making an issue will devote considerable time and research to devising a structure for the issue which if possible does not involve filing a prospectus.

The term 'promoters' has a legal definition in some countries. In this book, it is used in a more general sense to describe people closely connected with the company going public and who are the prime movers of the issue. Such people are likely to be existing shareholders or directors of the company.

'Underwriting' is a term derived from the insurance industry. It can be explained as a kind of insurance for the company and its shareholders if the issue does not prove popular with the market in general. The basic function of an underwriter is in return for a fee to take on the risk that an issue will not be fully subscribed by the investors at which it is directed. Flotations are open for subscription by the public at large. Rights issues are offered to existing shareholders. Placings are aimed at a select group of major investors. The risk that the underwriters run of having to take up shares varies in these different circumstances. An underwriter will normally expect to have some investment demand for issues that it underwrites.

The financial institution which takes the lead in managing and underwriting an issue is variously referred to as an investment bank, merchant bank or issuing house. Sometimes this institution may not be a bank at all but rather a stockbroker or other financial services company. For convenience the term 'merchant bank' is used throughout.

Merchant banks are a considerable influence in the occurrence of flotations. Flotations represent attractive business for merchant banks, as they give prominence to the bank's name and enlarge the number of their public company clients. The relationship which develops between the lead manager of an issue and the top management of the company being floated can be close and long-lasting. This stems from the essential co-operation between them during the preparation of a prospectus and the detailed knowledge of the company which the merchant bank acquires during this period. If the issue goes well, the success is a shared one and the merchant bank in question has obtained a loyal customer. One of the problems with mergers and acquisitions from the merchant banking standpoint is that, at least on the vendor's side, the merchant bank tends to lose a customer at the end of the day however well it performs.

As well as the basic management and underwriting fees, there may well be benefits to merchant banks in terms of other financial services which can be offered to the new public company including insurance, management of pension funds, deposits and foreign exchange.

(ii) 'New issue' and 'offer for sale'

Going public normally involves the widening of the shareholder base by attracting a range of new shareholders. The mechanism by which this is achieved may be either:

  (i)   an issue of new shares by a company to investors who subscribe for them in cash, referred to in this book as a 'new issue'; or

 (ii)   a sale of already issued shares by existing shareholders, referred to as an 'offer for sale'; or

(iii)   a combination of the two.

In some jurisdictions, new shares are issued in renounceable form, enabling shareholders to renounce them in favour of a third party during a certain period of time without the payment of transfer duty. In such cases, a company going public via a 'new issue' will issue the shares first to the merchant bank which is leading the issue. The merchant bank will 'offer for sale' all the shares comprised in the issue, whether they are new shares just issued by the company or existing shares. The term 'new issue' is not used to distinguish between the two.

In jurisdictions where shareholders cannot renounce their holdings without the payment of transfer duty, there is no advantage in using the renounceable format. In such cases, interposing the merchant bank in a 'new issue' increases costs. The company going public will therefore offer new shares to the public directly, under the guidance of the merchant bank.

There are important differences between the position following a new issue and the position following an offer for sale. In a new issue, the company going public raises new capital whereas in an offer for sale, the existing shareholders selling their shares receive the proceeds. The company itself receives no cash. It is important therefore to establish from the outset whether the company requires or would benefit from new capital and how this is to be reconciled with the objectives of the shareholders.

The second difference concerns the size of the issue. In most countries, the stock exchange sets rules regarding the minimum percentage of the company's capital which must be in public hands before a listing is granted. This percentage is considered the most convenient measure of whether there will be sufficient shares available in the market to form a satisfactory basis for trading. Frequently the size of the issue will be determined by the need to satisfy this minimum which is typically around 25% of the amount of the security for which a listing is sought. If it is necessary to ensure that a minimum percentage be in public hands, the money amount involved in a new issue will be greater than for an offer for sale. This is illustrated below.

EXAMPLE

A company wishes to go public and is forecasting after-tax profits of $20 m. The terms agreed with the merchant bank are that the price earnings ratio will be 15 times the forecast earnings. The valuation of the company for the purpose of the flotation is:

$$15 \times \$20 \text{ m} = \$300 \text{ m}$$

The stock exchange requires a minimum of 25% of the share capital to be in public hands.

If an offer for sale is employed, existing shareholders will arrange to sell one-quarter of their shares and the size of the issue will be:

$$\$300 \text{ m} \times 0.25 = \$75 \text{ m}$$

If a new issue is employed, the position is different. It is assumed (for the purpose of the analysis) that with the addition of the amount to be raised by the new issue the worth of the company, previously assessed at $300 m, will be increased by exactly the size of the new issue. The size of the new issue (x) required so that 25% of the issued share capital will be in public hands is therefore found by:

$$x = 0.25 \ \$(300 + x) \text{ m}$$
$$x = \$75 \text{ m} + 0.25x$$
$$0.75x = \$75 \text{ m}$$
$$x = \$100 \text{ m}$$

Consequently, the size of the new issue, at $100 m, is one-third larger than the size of the offer for sale, at $75 m. The company itself is worth $400 m in market terms, rather than $300 m, and has an additional $100 m in cash.

The above equation can be re-arranged to solve for the percentage of a company's share capital which would have to be issued to raise a given amount of money, which is sometimes the question which concerns the promoters more. For example, if $125 m were needed, the percentage of the company's enlarged share capital (x) which would have to be sold to the public would be:

$$125 = x(300 + 125)$$
$$125 = 425x$$
$$x = 29.4\%$$

To raise $125 m for the company rather than $100 m, existing shareholders suffer a 29.4% decrease in their shareholding rather than a 25% decrease. This type of decrease in a shareholder's percentage shareholding in a company is often referred to as 'dilution'. Dilution is also used to describe any decrease in shareholders' attributable earnings and assets caused by issues of new shares.

It is sometimes considered that investors are likely to be more receptive to a new issue than an offer for sale. The money raised by a new issue goes into the company to strengthen its balance sheet or provide funding for future growth. An offer for sale on the other hand puts money into the pocket of existing owners. If the owners (who may be presumed to know more about the company and its prospects than a new investor) are selling, investors may ask themselves whether they are well advised to buy. To counter this reaction, the company going public may issue some new shares even when the main purpose of the flotation is to allow existing shareholders to sell. In any event, the existing shareholders are decreasing their percentage holding in the company and so may be considered to be disposing of an interest.

(iii) Overview of topics covered

(a) Reasons for going public – advantages and disadvantages

The factors involved in deciding whether to go public mostly have two aspects. Along with the attractions come responsibilities, constraints and costs. The pluses and minuses may appear to offset each other. The decision may well hang on the weighting that the promoters give to a particular factor. Some may consider their privacy is paramount and draw back. Others may emphasise the increased growth possibilities and press on. Where the balance of advantage lies will depend on the particular circumstances of the company and the personalities and ambitions of its directors and shareholders.

Chapter 3 is based on the assumption that the company's shareholders and management are considering going public from scratch, via a new issue or offer for sale. In ch 9 below, alternative methods of gaining a listing are considered which may be suitable if the promoters' objective is to obtain a listing and they are not primarily concerned with increasing the spread of shareholders or raising money at the initial stage. Other things being equal, the management of a company which is capable of going public in its own right will probably wish to do this rather than utilise the methods described in ch 9. Most of the advantages and disadvantages discussed in ch 3 are also relevant to the decision as to whether to obtain a listing by other methods.

(b) Going public – is it a realistic prospect? – what structural changes are needed? (see ch 4 below)

After weighing up the factors involved, the promoters may conclude that the balance of advantage lies in the company going public. However, this does not necessarily mean a flotation is a practical possibility. Before committing their own time and starting to incur substantial professional expenses, the promoters need to take a hard-headed look at their chances. A list of the criteria which might be used to make this assessment is set out in ch 4 below.

It is assumed for the purpose of this chapter that the promoters wish the company to gain a listing on a major stock exchange. There are an increasing number of alternatives to full listings. A company which may not qualify for a 'big board' listing may nevertheless be suitable for trading on an 'unlisted' securities market or 'over-the-counter'. In these markets, the rules concerning degree of disclosure about the company, track record and the percentage to be held in public hands are likely to be less stringent.

Chapter 4 also deals with the structural reorganisation which may be needed in preparation for going public. Private interests are rarely formed up ready-made in an orderly group. The gearing, voting rights and number of shares in issue may also require some tailoring to suit market preferences. Some merchant banking and legal advice will begin to be needed at this stage.

(c) Forming a team and estimating expenses (see ch 5 below)

Once the review outlined in ch 4 below has been completed, the company and its promoters have come as far as they can on their own. If the decision is taken to proceed, a team of advisers must be formed, starting most probably with the appointment of a merchant bank.

The calls on the company's own resources of manpower are frequently underestimated. The involvement of senior executives cannot be avoided. It is important that their team of advisers be experienced in the specialist business of flotations and capable of working harmoniously together over a protracted period. Work on a flotation requires close co-operation and liaison in sometimes trying circumstances. The individual roles of the advisers are described in ch 5 below.

Expenses begin to mount rapidly and are considerable. With the appointment of advisers, the major categories of expenses (and who is responsible for meeting them) can be identified and the approximate amounts estimated. Expenses can be reduced by careful planning. Interest on over-subscriptions may provide a contribution. The availability of funds from the flotation at least means a ready source of cash for paying the expenses is at hand.

(d) Timing and pricing (see ch 6 below)

The skill in timing lies in identifying when favourable periods in market and sector cycles coincide with a good performance from the company itself. Ideally, a 'window' of some months should be established as the cumbersome nature of new issue procedures makes fine tuning difficult.

Pricing owes something to fundamental techniques of valuation, which also play a part in determining more informal views on price. Comparison with the ratings of similar companies already traded in the market is probably the single most important aspect of pricing. A shrewd feeling for what the market will stand, based on discreet soundings among potential investors, is a valuable cross-check. The most market-orientated method of pricing is by tender. This may inhibit large subscriptions by 'stags'. The realities of the market-place are ignored by issuers and underwriters at their peril.

(e) Components of a prospectus and timetable (see ch 7 below)

The main components of a prospectus and the expected timetable are set out in ch 7 below. A prospectus has a dual function. It provides information about the company and its management as required by law or the stock exchange regulations, so that investors will have sufficient information to make an informed judgment. Strict penalties apply if false or misleading information is given. At the same time, it serves as a selling document to persuade investors to take the plunge. These two functions sit rather uneasily with each other at times.

While much of the work can be left to the professional advisers, ultimately the contents of the prospectus, even the technical sections, are the responsibility of the directors of the company. The directors can delegate the preparation and supervision of the prospectus but they cannot delegate responsibility for it. The best strategy is to avoid giving any hostages to fortune in the statements made.

The timetable suggested by the advisers (a minimum of 4 months) may seem leisurely to the company's executives when the work is starting. Delays are the rule rather than the exception and the timetable should have some slack in it to allow for contingencies. No matter how methodical the preparations, the final stages seem always to be completed in something approaching a panic. In the last days before publication, it is difficult to make significant changes and the participants become locked into meeting a particular date, the alternative being a significant postponement.

(f) Launch, allocation and the start of trading (see ch 8 below)

Preparations for the launch must be set in hand well before the actual publication of the prospectus. Tell-tale signs of a company being groomed for flotation may appear some months in advance. Underwriting the issue guarantees receipt of the funds by the company and/or its shareholders and ensures a reasonable spread of investors even if the issue does not prove attractive to the market in general. As the company is an unknown quantity to the market, the underwriters do run a considerable risk.

Application procedures should be kept as simple as possible. Deciding on the basis of allotment is one of the more pleasant problems in a flotation, since the greater the difficulty, the bigger the success of the issue.

The first day of trading takes place in an atmosphere of some excitement with hectic activity in turnover as positions taken before the start of official trading are unwound. Turnover will subsequently subside to more normal levels. If the shares go to a discount on the issue price, a feeling of anticlimax will set in. It is interesting to compare the initial subscription list with the register of members of the company at some time later. The latter may be significantly smaller.

(g) Alternative methods of gaining a listing (see ch 9 below)

There are alternative methods of gaining a listing if it is decided not to go through the full flotation process. Control of a small but listed company (called a 'shell' company) may be obtained and the assets or business for which a listing is desired injected into it. A premium over net assets will be required to secure control of the shell and concluding satisfactory terms may prove difficult. However, this method does allow a full listing to be gained for businesses which might not otherwise be able to achieve this status.

Variations on this theme are possible. For example, the shares of a subsidiary company may be 'spun-off' to shareholders of an existing listed company.

The independent company will normally be granted a listing via an introduction on the strength of the spread of its shareholders. A variety of expedients may be adopted by companies to achieve a wide enough spread of shareholders to qualify for a listing by means of an introduction.

These methods are suitable principally for those whose major requirement is to obtain a listed vehicle. The marketing and fund raising aspects must be handled separately.

(h) Rights issues (see ch 10 below)

Once a listing has been obtained, capital can be raised more simply by subsequent issues. Issues which are first offered to existing shareholders are said to be made by way of 'rights'. Issues of further ordinary shares of a listed company for cash are often required by law, the company's articles or stock exchange regulations to be made by rights. Other types of security, including shares of other companies, may be offered by way of rights on occasions.

Rights issues have proved a reliable means of raising further equity. They are pitched at a discount to the market price 'ex rights' and aimed at 'the converted', i e investors who have already bought shares in the company. In these circumstances, management could, but rarely does, decide to dispense with underwriting and instead increase the discount at which the issue is priced.

Documentation and expenses are considerably less for a rights issue than for the initial flotation. The timetable has to allow for a period of trading in the rights 'nil paid'.

(i) Placings and other issues of shares and equity-linked securities
(see ch 11 below)

Shares and other equity-linked securities may be issued on various occasions other than rights issues. Issues or sales for cash are called placings and are subject to certain restrictions. They may be carried out before a company goes public, as part of the flotation or subsequently. The placing procedures are also suitable for the sale of large blocks of existing shares and for debt securities.

Bonus issues are further issues of shares to existing shareholders where no consideration is involved. Dividends may be paid in the form of shares instead of cash.

Shares may be issued as a result of the exercise of options (perhaps related to an employee incentive scheme), the conversion of convertible securities and the exercise of warrants. Debt instruments with conversion rights or warrants attached find favour with the market from time to time.

Shares and equity-linked securities are an important form of payment in making acquisitions, both of other companies and of assets. On such occasions, an important principle is whether the interests of existing shareholders are diluted or not. Some immediate dilution may be tolerable in return for the prospects of improved future growth.

If the parties receiving the shares as consideration do not wish to retain them, a 'vendor placing' may be organised.

(iv) Approach adopted

In approaching the subject of going public and raising equity capital, emphasis has been placed on concepts and techniques which are valid in financial markets generally. To follow too closely the detailed practices of a single market at a particular time is not very helpful in an era of rapid change in regulations and investor preferences. Company law and taxation are in any event specialist subjects in their own right.

The basic questions facing a company and its promoters when it goes public or issues further equity and the appropriate responses have substantial common elements. In the following chapters, a practical approach has been adopted and the comments are based on actual experience. Sufficient detail is given to assist those actively involved in equity issues but the treatment is not tied to a unique set of market circumstances. Changes in local rules and practices and variations from market to market will not invalidate the principles discussed.

CHAPTER 3

Reasons for going public – advantages and disadvantages

Owning and running a public company has become one of the major milestones in a successful career in business and finance. The attractions of public companies appear undimmed despite extensive tightening in many countries of regulations governing disclosure, share dealings and management.

The most appropriate god to watch over companies going public might be Janus, reflecting the different aspects of the factors involved. The intending promoters must look back to the comforts of a private company and forward to the potential of a public company and see where the balance of advantage lies. Going public represents a coming of age, a time of significant change for the company and its associates. The motivation to attempt this transition is likely to reflect not only the needs of the business but the character and requirements of the individuals who own and manage it.

The main factors and the advantages and disadvantages associated with each are summarised in the table below and discussed in more detail in the remainder of the chapter.

I OUTSIDE INVESTORS PARTICIPATE SUBSTANTIALLY FOR THE FIRST TIME

(i) Advantages

(a) From the company's point of view – increasing equity capital

If the flotation involves an issue of new shares, the funds raised are received by the company. It may be desirable for the company to increase its equity base to underpin business expansion plans, to introduce new products or to reduce borrowings. Forecast requirements for capital may exceed amounts that the original shareholders can contribute, placing limits on the company's development if further sources of capital are not tapped.

The initial flotation paves the way for fund raising exercises in future. This applies not only to the equity markets but to other capital markets. The company's public status in itself is likely to be an advantage. The increased level of information available makes credit analysis and assessment easier and more reliable.

(b) For the original shareholders – realising profits, securing tax advantages, diversifying and raising money

Existing shareholders may have been financing the company for a prolonged period of time, often without a commercial rate of return on their funds. They

Factors	Advantages	Disadvantages
I Outside investors participate substantially for the first time.	(a) From the company's point of view, increasing equity capital. (b) For the original shareholders, realising profits, securing tax advantages, diversifying and raising money.	(a) Time and expense required. (b) Duties of directors become more onerous and the interests of public shareholders have to be considered. (c) Constraints on management's actions increase.
II Marketability.	(a) Shareholders may buy and sell more readily. (b) Value of the shares is enhanced. (c) Shares are more acceptable as security for loans. (d) Shares are more acceptable for use in acquisitions.	(a) Company and its directors must abide by listing rules of the exchange. (b) Care needed over dealings by 'insiders'. (c) Spread or gradual loss of control.
III Company becomes more visible.	(a) Extensive publicity accompanies the flotation. (b) Standing of the company increases and attitudes to it change.	(a) Level of disclosure increased. (b) Share price is taken as a barometer of the company's fortunes.
IV Changes of philosophy.	Catalyst for company to develop from family-run to professionally-managed business.	Ruffled feathers and higher overheads.

may have been working without an arm's length salary to compensate them for their time. Going public provides a convenient opportunity for the original shareholders to take their profits.

It may be more tax efficient for the original shareholders to realise a capital gain on their investment rather than to receive large dividends or salaries. Public company status may also offer tax advantages in countries where tax legislation includes a concept of a 'closely held' company.

Shareholders may wish to avoid having 'all their eggs in one basket' and sell shares in order to diversify their investments. There may be a need to raise funds to assist in provision for death duties or other personal matters.

Going public provides controlling shareholders with the opportunity to have their cake and eat it, i e to sell part of their interests while still retaining control of the company.

(ii) Disadvantages

(a) Time and expense required

The amount of time required to be devoted by top management to a flotation is very extensive and consistently under-estimated. Management finds itself distracted from the day-to-day running of the company at the very time when they would like it to be performing at its best.

The main expenses incurred in going public are discussed in ch 5 below. They can be divided into underwriting and professional fees and other charges such as capital and transfer duties. Some professional fees are likely to be incurred before it is certain that a flotation can proceed.

(b) Duties of directors become more onerous and the interests of public shareholders have to be considered

Once a company ceases to be private and becomes public, the responsibilities of controlling and managing it broaden and become more onerous. Instead of being answerable only to a small group, usually relatives or close associates, the directors must recognise a duty of trust to a body of public shareholders who will not necessarily be aware of or sympathise with the aspirations of the original shareholders. The precise duties of directors vary from country to country but two problems which can cause particular difficulty are:

(i)   The directors may well have been accustomed to deal with the company's liquid resources as if they were available for their personal requirements. The discipline of segregating the public company's funds may be irksome. The system to safeguard this money may be operated by relatively junior employees previously accustomed to carrying out the controlling share-holders' wishes without question.

(ii) In many private groups, there is a considerable amount of intermingling of funds and assets between companies. If money is required for a particular project, the assets of other companies may be pledged to raise it, as is most convenient and efficient. A considerable amount of inter-company and inter-group borrowing and lending may go on without security or formal arrangements about charging interest and repaying principal.

(c) Constraints on management's actions increase

Once a company has become public, certain corporate actions may require a meeting of shareholders rather than simply a meeting of directors. Transactions which are likely to be subject to a vote of shareholders include the issue of more than a certain number of new shares and the sales or purchases of assets which are significant in relation to the size of the business as a whole.

In a private company, even if a shareholders' meeting is required, the proceedings are likely to be similar to a directors' meeting. A general meeting of a public company on the other hand can be a very lively affair. If the matters under consideration are controversial, an intensive question and answer session and considerable press coverage can be expected. Even strong executives have been known to quail at the prospect of a stormy public meeting.

If a public body of shareholders needs to be consulted, relevant information will have to be provided to them well in advance, usually by means of a printed circular. The preparation of such a circular needs senior management time. If incomplete or biased information is presented, the results of the meeting may not be valid and the directors will be vulnerable to a charge of misleading their shareholders.

In some jurisdictions, any transaction or contract of material size with directors or substantial shareholders must be approved at a general meeting by a vote of the independent shareholders. This sometimes gives directors and major shareholders of a former private company their first taste of having to submit their actions to the veto of an outside body of opinion. The controlling shareholders and directors may be unable to force the proposals through, since, if they are interested parties in the transaction, they will be unable to vote their shares.

II MARKETABILITY

(i) Advantages

(a) Shareholders may buy and sell more readily

Over the course of time a controlling group of shareholders (often a family) is likely to develop different interests and attitudes towards a company. Some will remain actively involved in the company and its management whereas others, perhaps through marriage or migration, may become remote from its affairs. Not only are the shares of a private company not traded in an organised way but the articles of association usually contain restrictions on the transfer and registration of shares. They will also include a 'pre-emption' provision, to the effect that shareholders wishing to sell must first offer their shares to the other shareholders. This procedure is cumbersome and may involve the price being set by a neutral party (perhaps the auditors) based on a formula which reflects the limited marketability of the shares. Once a company goes public, the articles of association will be amended to eliminate such provisions. The ability to sell shares freely provides a more satisfactory route for shareholders who wish to go their separate way.

(b) The value of the shares is enhanced

Marketability in itself will tend to increase the value of an investment. Some institutional investors are severely restricted as to their holdings of unlisted shares and may not be able to buy the shares at all before they are listed. All investors will look on the increased liquidity of their holding favourably. In a valuation exercise, the multiple applied to the earnings of a public company would be higher than to those of a similar private company, resulting in a higher valuation.

(c) Listed shares are more acceptable to banks as security for loans

Once a share is listed, it becomes more acceptable to banks as security for loans, either on its own or as part of a portfolio. This provides an alternative for shareholders who do not necessarily wish to sell but need to raise money from time to time. Provided the shares are reasonably well traded, banks who engage in this line of business will normally be prepared to advance a percentage (say 50%) of the market price of shares pledged to them.

(d) Listed shares are more acceptable for use in acquisitions

Sellers of assets or shares in companies are normally not willing to accept unlisted securities as a form of payment. Once a company is listed, it may use its shares as consideration in acquisitions, widening its financing options and allowing it to consider bigger targets.

The information publicly available about the company will be sufficient to sustain a listing for, say, new loan stock or preference shares offered to the target company's shareholders, provided adequate details are given of the rights of the security to be issued. The security would need to have a minimum number of holders to ensure marketability, but this will be achieved if a reasonable proportion of the target company's shareholders accept it or satisfactory underwriting arrangements are made. Acceptance of paper rather than cash may have attractions from the vendors' point of view, both from tax considerations and by allowing them to feel they still retain an interest in the asset or business they are selling.

In the early days of a public company's life, it may be necessary to make arrangements for vendors who receive securities in this way to place them on to third parties. As the securities become more widely held and actively traded, these 'back-up' arrangements become less critical.

Controlling shareholders and management must bear in mind that issuing shares in the context of acquisitions will tend to dilute their own control and bring cohesive groups of shareholders, sometimes of significant size, into the company. The new shareholders may have interests and attitudes which could lead to a clash of wills at some future occasion.

(ii) Disadvantages

(a) The company and its directors must abide by the listing rules`of the relevant stock exchange(s)

By definition, the process of gaining a listing on a stock exchange involves compliance with stock exchange rules. A recognised stock exchange is likely to require signature of an extensive formal undertaking to comply with the regulations of that stock exchange for companies whose shares are listed on it. The rules will include requirements that the company follows certain administrative procedures and provides relevant information promptly, particularly regarding results, dividends and other significant corporate developments.

(b) Care will be needed over dealings by insiders

Directors and other senior executives must accept that they will normally know more about the company than the general body of shareholders. This will restrict the occasions on which they can buy and sell shares. Restrictions are necessary to prevent them being exposed to criticism and possible legal action for dealing in the shares on the basis of privileged or 'inside' information.

Directors of a company often feel that the market does not understand or appreciate properly the particular merits of their company. They may also feel strongly that purchases of the shares are an expression of confidence in the company itself. However, if purchases are made, for whatever reason, shortly before the release of price-sensitive information (for example unexpectedly good results), the actions of the directors may be questioned. Less frequently, directors may consider the market is unreasonably optimistic about the company's prospects, while they themselves have misgivings. They may feel an obligation to sell shares to protect the interests, for example, of wives and children for whom they are trustees. The same dangers apply to the sales of shares as to purchases.

(c) Spread or gradual loss of control

An anxiety commonly felt by shareholders and directors of a private company is the possible loss of control once the company becomes public. Although this is not usually an immediate threat, a potential danger may have been created.

Small shareholders in the context of a private company have little practical recourse if they are unhappy with the way the company is run. Once their shares become marketable, they may be tempted to sell so that for example an apparently solid family block may fall apart. Sometimes even the possibility of a group of outside shareholders appointing a director who is not familiar to the major shareholders seems threatening.

To counter the disintegration of a controlling block, at least 51% of the shares of the public company may be put into a separate private company and the control of that company vested in certain individuals. If family members want to sell they must then sell shares outside the controlling block in such a way that absolute control is not threatened. While for some purposes a 75% voting majority is required, even the most anxious of controlling shareholders normally accept that their control is secure if they can command over 51% of the votes at a general meeting of the company.

As the company grows and the spread of shareholders becomes wider, for practical purposes control of as little as 10 or 20% of the company may be sufficient to constitute control of the whole company. This is particularly true if there are a large number of relatively passive shareholders.

III   COMPANY BECOMES MORE VISIBLE

(i) Advantages

(a) Extensive publicity accompanies the flotation

A flotation is a process which requires the publication of a high degree of information about the company. For a company identified with well-known branded consumer items or luxury products, the publicity may become an end in itself, an effective form of image advertising.

In the months leading up to the launch, the promoters will prepare the ground by a series of strategically placed press articles and announcements to arouse media interest. Coverage of the flotation when it actually occurs brings the company, its management and its products before investors' and the public's minds. Although some shareholders and managers dread this part of the transaction, other more flamboyant characters revel in it. Previously unknown businessmen may become national figures for a while at the time of flotation of 'their' company.

The attention drawn to the company and its business may increase awareness of its attractions as a business or joint venture partner. Sometimes a recently floated company immediately attracts a bidder. As the company will normally still be under the majority control of its original shareholders, any such bid could only be on a friendly basis.

(b) Standing of the company increases and attitudes towards it change

A public company is generally regarded by its customers, suppliers and creditors as having a higher standing than a private company. Employees may take a pride in working for a public company rather than an individual or family-owned business. A share incentive scheme may be offered to foster a sense of participation. Shareholders, whether employees or not, can become useful advocates if the company is threatened by actions of government such as unfavourable changes to legislation affecting the company.

Although it is difficult to pin down, there is perhaps a feeling that a company of a certain size and reputation ought to be a public company. Some general appreciation exists of the rigours and difficulties of going through a flotation. The fact that a company and its management have passed this test is taken as a seal of approval.

There may be a strong streak of 'me too' as competitors see their rivals going public and fear that they may obtain some market or financial edge. A similar attitude can be observed among institutions. Once the ice has been broken by a successful flotation, a series of companies in that sector are often brought to market. Individual investors and institutions begin to feel comfortable with a particular type of company and sector of the market and the band-wagon effect is under way. After considerable research and investigation to learn about an unfamiliar industry, there is a natural tendency to try to capitalise on the base of knowledge gathered.

(ii) Disadvantages

(a) The level of disclosure is increased

Directors of public companies have to come to terms with a substantially increased level of disclosure of information. In a private company, only limited disclosure to 'outsiders' is necessary. In the context of a public company, the information to be published will cover important financial data including announcements of results and dividends, events which affect the management of the company, such as changes in the directors, and alterations in capital structure and shares in issue, which are relevant to investors trading in the shares. There may also be a sweeping provision to disclose any information which is likely to have a material impact on the price or the level of trading of the shares in the market.

Insistence on disclosure may sometimes be interpreted by management as a questioning of their good faith. They may consider holdings of shares and dealings by themselves and their families as nobody's business but their own. Disclosure of terms of employment such as salary and benefits may be a potential source of embarrassment compared with the anonymity of a private company.

(b) Share price is taken as a barometer of the company's fortunes

Once a company is listed, details of the share price movements and trading volume are released daily by the stock exchange. Arrangements may be made for the share price to appear in major newspapers. Share price movements reflect rumour and market whim as well as fundamentals. Management may experience pressure to promote good performance while feeling that the daily ups and downs of the market are largely irrational. Bitter comments may be muttered about the 'tyranny of the share price'.

If a company is seen as part of a market sector, its performance will be compared by analysts to others in that sector. This may lead to decisions being taken on a short-term basis. For example, if the sector as a whole has shown strong profit increases, actions a particular company might wish to take for long-term development of its business, but which might prove a short-term drag on profits, may be deferred.

If the company is performing well but the sector as a whole is out of fashion, it may be difficult for the market to accept a rating for the company much above the sector average. With the same results but located in a more glamorous sector, the company might be accorded a significantly higher rating.

IV   CHANGES OF PHILOSOPHY

(i) Advantage: catalyst for company to develop from family-run to professionally-managed business

At some stage in a company's development, a change in management style tends to occur. The paternal attitudes often found in a small company give way to a more systematic and objective approach required to control and manage a larger group. Preparation for becoming a public company affords an opportunity and a catalyst for achieving this transition without the appearance of a direct attack on entrenched interests.

An important part of this process involves directors and top management. Prior to a flotation, a company is likely to appoint outside directors, typically one or two non-executives of standing in the political, business or financial community. These individuals bring a new perspective to the way problems are tackled and decisions taken. Perhaps for the first time, executive directors will have to explain and justify their actions to independent individuals of comparable age, standing and abilities.

A review of the depth and areas of expertise of management conducted as part of the flotation preparations may identify a need for additional qualified executives such as a specialist finance director. A professional middle management structure may be missing or inadequate in a private business. To assist in recruiting and retaining suitable executives, a share option scheme may be introduced. Extended service contracts may be negotiated for senior executives, giving them a greater degree of security and independence.

The more obviously distinct identity of a public company and the existence of outside directors and shareholders create the framework for strengthening professional management. This need may have been previously recognised. However, without the external stimulus of the flotation it can prove difficult to overcome internal inertia and vested interests.

(ii) Disadvantages: ruffled feathers and higher overheads

There may be resistance to change from those who have seen the company grow from its beginnings and recognise no need to alter a winning formula. One of the chief skills required in a flotation may be the art of diplomacy.

Many of the changes in personnel and systems which may be instituted in the context of the flotation cause higher overheads without bringing any immediate improvement in performance or increase in profits. In the short term, there may be a period of confusion while new executives find their role in the company and new procedures become established. Developments along these lines may be vulnerable to attack and fall victim to internal politics unless they carry very senior support and are given time to show their worth.

CONCLUSIONS

The factors involved in the decision to go public and the pluses and minuses associated with each have been discussed under four general headings. Those taking the decision must weigh up where the balance of advantage lies and decide whether the compromises involved are worthwhile.

It seems a consistent experience that the time taken and the work involved in going public is greater than anticipated and that frustration, change and delay are the rule rather than the exception. At points of crisis, the determination of the principals that they are pursuing the right course will be severely tested. They must be convinced at the outset that the reasons for going public are sound and the underlying advantages strong enough.

Substantial amounts of management time and considerable expense are necessary if a flotation is to be carried through to a successful conclusion. Before large-scale commitments are made, it is useful as a first step to review briefly and from a strictly practical standpoint whether a flotation is a realistic prospect. Some criteria for doing this and for considering the need for reorganisation of the interests to be floated are given in the next chapter.

CHAPTER 4

Going public – is it a realistic prospect?
– what structural changes are needed?

After weighing up the advantages and disadvantages of going public, the promoters may have decided they wish to proceed. They next need a checklist of key points against which to consider how realistic the prospects are. They should also assess what structural changes may be necessary and whether they are feasible.

A list of criteria to judge whether a flotation is a practical proposition or not is set out in 'I Criteria' below. Changes which may be needed in the organisation of the group and in its gearing, voting arrangements and issued share capital are discussed in 'II Structure' below.

In some countries, a hierarchy of markets has emerged. There may for example be a major stock market, an unlisted securities market and an over-the-counter market. This chapter deals mainly with the requirements for going public on a major stock market where a company would be bound by a full listing agreement. The points discussed apply also to a company considering alternative markets, the main difference being the degree of compliance.

I CRITERIA

A convenient starting point is to review recently issued flotation documents. This exercise serves to identify the main categories of information which need to be given and to see how the group compares. Companies in a similar sector should be chosen if possible. While some elements in a prospectus are common to all flotations, critical factors and the emphasis which is placed on them vary from sector to sector. What is required for a flotation of a retailing chain will not necessarily ensure success for a computer company.

A useful checklist would include the following points:

(i) Size and period of existence

Most stock exchanges impose a minimum size for the aggregate value of securities they are prepared to consider for listing. Size will be measured by the market value at the flotation price of the securities to be listed and is based on the whole class of such securities, not just the percentage in public hands. The purpose of the minimum size criterion is to ensure reasonable marketability in the security. Marketability is largely a subjective concept, so that the minimum size in force may be somewhat arbitrary. It depends in part on the type of security and varies widely from market to market. Within individual markets, the size criterion is updated periodically by the stock exchange authorities and is most easily found by aspiring promoters by enquiry through a stockbroker or merchant bank.

Many markets require a company to have existed or to have recorded profits for a minimum period of time, say three to five years, but this is not always the case. A recently incorporated top company used to reorganise a group prior to flotation is considered to inherit the track record of its subsidiaries.

(ii) Profit trend and prospects

If the company is likely to be primarily assessed on an earnings basis, the audited profits for, say, the last five years will be critical, together with a forecast for the current year. A smooth progression of profits is desirable. If there are departures from the trend, can they be readily explained? Are they due to cycles in the general economy or sector, or are they attributable to some special circumstances in the company? If a loss has been incurred, can the problem be clearly identified and factors responsible shown to have been isolated and remedied?

(iii) Sector/industry

What sector or industry would the company expect to be classified under? Is this sector in favour with investors? Are the prospects for the sector regarded as encouraging?

If a particular market sector is depressed, it may be virtually impossible for even a sound company in that sector to go public on acceptable terms. On the other hand, when for example the high technology sector is in vogue, flotation of a company with little more than a few promising projects on the drawing board is quite possible. Indeed, it seems that promise – allowing investors full range to their imaginations – is frequently preferred to performance.

(iv) Balance sheet

Does an analysis of the balance sheet reveal any areas of weakness? The levels of gearing and the requirements for working capital should be examined to see if they are out of line with other companies in similar businesses. Are there any contingent liabilities, guarantees or litigation outstanding which could increase the company's financial obligations? Is lack of capital likely to be a constraint on growth?

(v) Image and management

Does the company have some feature which will serve to identify it in the minds of investors? If not, is there some way that the company's attractions can be described so that it will be differentiated from existing investment opportunities? How can the promoters counteract the inertia which prompts investors to stick to more familiar shares?

Is the management known at all to the general public? Does it have a reputation for competence and integrity among its peers and in financial circles? Are there any non-executive directors of standing? Are there any obvious gaps in management competence, particularly as regards the finance and control functions?

(vi) Uncertainties

Major areas of uncertainty are likely to act as a significant barrier to investment. The market likes the extent of the risk of a new investment to be clearly established. If there is uncertainty for example in the outcome of litigation, the most likely reaction of financial institutions is to suggest a delay until the problem is resolved or at least until the maximum exposure can be quantified.

(vii) Timing

A prospectus requires the inclusion of audited accounts. In many markets, these should be not more than six months' old. Even if the audit can be completed promptly, the available 'window' is quite narrow. A profit forecast is also likely to be needed. For prudence, management may wish to see some months' actual results and a reasonable level of business and orders on hand before committing itself for the whole year. Management may be torn between the need to be certain of their forecast and the flotation deadline. Other factors affecting timing are more general, such as the state of the market and any queue of pending issues, with a danger of 'crowding out'.

(viii) Relationships with existing shareholders/directors

Are there any dealings between existing shareholders, directors and other related parties and the group which might be inappropriate in a public company but would be difficult to unwind? For example, any material amounts owing by such parties to the company should be cleared prior to the flotation. The need for the public group and private interests to deal with each other on an arms-length basis may involve unacceptable levels of complexity and expense.

If a reasonably clean bill of health can be given under headings (i)–(viii) above, it will be worth proceeding to the next stage, reviewing the structure of the group to see what changes may be required for flotation.

II   STRUCTURE

Formal changes must be considered in the corporate organisation of the group. Market preferences on gearing, voting arrangements and share price must also be taken into account.

(i) Corporate organisation of the group

A business built up by an individual or family may grow in size and complexity in a rather haphazard manner. A series of companies may be established as is most convenient at the time. These companies may well be owned by the same or very similar sets of shareholders. The result is a number of private companies with common ownership and related lines of business which have not been formed legally into a group. There is no one holding company having beneath it a number of subsidiaries or associates in an orderly family tree.

If the decision is taken to go public, a single company will have to be selected to have its shares listed on the exchange. A choice must therefore be made as to what company should be used. The largest or most well-known company may acquire all or some of the other companies or businesses and serve as the company which goes public. Alternatively, a new top holding company may be established which acquires the companies chosen to form the public group. This company will derive its track record from its new subsidiaries.

Care must be taken over transfer of ownership of a company holding a valuable licence or agency agreement. The change of control may well require time-consuming consents to be obtained. In some circumstances, it could jeopardise continuance of the arrangements or lead to renegotiation of their terms.

The method used for forming the group will normally be an exchange of shares. The companies acquired will become subsidiaries of the new top holding company by their shareholders exchanging their shares for new shares in the holding company. Depending on the gearing of the new holding company and the preferences of the vendor shareholders, some subsidiaries may be acquired for cash. Cash may be provided from the company's own resources, by identifying cash subscribers for new holding company shares or by bank borrowings.

In general, it is preferable not to leave minorities outstanding so that the holding company may have complete control over its new subsidiaries and full access to their assets and cash flow. In some cases, the managing director of an operating company may have a shareholding in that company as a performance incentive which it may be better to leave in place. The incentive will be weakened if he exchanges shares in the company he runs for shares in a holding company with interests in companies he is unable to influence.

A reorganisation of this type is likely to involve heavy expenses for capital duty on the share capital of the new holding company and transfer duty on acquisitions of subsidiaries or assets. The capital duty element is largely unavoidable when new shares are created and issued. In certain jurisdictions, it may be possible to reduce or largely eliminate the transfer duty. A change of control may be effected by subscription of new shares. Existing shares will only be transferred after drastic changes in their rights bring about a corresponding reduction in their value. Schemes of this type may be vulnerable to attack from tax authorities.

(ii) Gearing

The financial structure of the new holding company on an unconsolidated and consolidated basis should be reviewed. High gearing is a major reason for going public via a new issue to raise capital to retire corporate debt rather than offering existing shares for sale, with the proceeds going to the original shareholders. A group which is unusually highly geared may not be suitable for flotation at all until the level of borrowing can be reduced.

The appropriate level of gearing depends on a number of factors. An asset-based group, such as a shipping or property concern, or one which has highly predictable cash flows such as a utility, will be able to support a higher level of gearing than a business with unpredictable cash flows and little asset backing. The level of gearing in the group to be floated may be measured against existing listed companies in the same industry sector.

Market attitude to gearing can vary widely. At times when sentiment is positive, fairly high borrowing can be interpreted as an encouraging sign that an aggressive management is using the capital structure to increase shareholders' returns. At other times, particularly during or soon after a financial crisis, even modest amounts of borrowing are seen to be risky and a company with an ungeared balance sheet is given a premium rating.

(iii) Voting structure

Private companies will sometimes include in their capital structure founders' shares or some other special class of ordinary shares designed to ensure that control remains with the original shareholders. The articles of association may restrict the interest of any individual shareholder to a certain percentage (sometimes as low as 2%).

It is not normally acceptable to investors and the stock exchange for a company going public to have ordinary shares with unequal voting rights. Prior to flotation, new articles of association will be adopted so that all ordinary shares carry the same voting rights and any restrictions on holdings or transfer are eliminated.

This approach is justified because control is a valuable commodity. This is most obviously seen in the premium offered for control of a company compared with the prevailing market price for a share transaction of ordinary size. All shareholders who run the ultimate risk of financing a business should participate in the benefits of control. They should also be able to exercise their voting rights as a check on management.

An exception with which stock exchanges would sympathise would be a nationalised concern which the government of the day wishes to privatise. It may not be 'in the national interest' for the company to be controlled by any particular group, at least for a minimum period of years. In such a case, the government may be issued with a 'golden' share conferring certain preferential rights regarding control, for example as regards votes cast at a general meeting or over the composition of the board of directors.

Older established companies may have gained listings at periods when voting rights were not such a sensitive matter to stock exchange authorities and major investors. Although it is unlikely that existing listings would be cancelled because of refusal to change the voting structure, there are a number of examples where institutional investors have brought pressure to bear on the directors to propose that voting rights should be made equal. As compensation, a small bonus issue of shares (say on the basis of one-for-ten) may be given to the class of shareholders foregoing the preferential rights.

Companies with existing listings may seek to introduce a new class of ordinary shares with superior voting rights as a defence against hostile takeover bids. This action is likely to be highly controversial and brings a risk of de-listing of the shares.

(iv) Share price

For reason of historical accident or to save capital duty, private companies may have relatively few shares in issue. This would translate into a very high price per share if no changes were made prior to flotation. Many markets have a favoured price range at which popular shares tend to trade. Within markets, an appropriate price may vary depending on investor sentiment at the time and on industry sectors. A group intending to go public is often advised to aim at a share price in line with other similar public companies.

The expected market price of the share is found by dividing the valuation placed on the company by the number of shares in issue. The valuation will be negotiated between the promoters and the merchant bank and so for this purpose is a constant. The share price at flotation can only be reduced by increasing the shares in issue.

In order to achieve this, a number of measures may be taken. If the shareholders or other related parties have advanced money to a company under a loan account this loan account may be capitalised, i e cancelled in exchange for the issue of new shares. If the shares have a par value and this is relatively high, the shares may be subdivided so that, for example, one share of $10 may be converted into ten shares of $1 each. In addition, if there is a share premium account or reserves which can be paid up as a bonus issue, this may also be used to achieve the desired reduction in price. It may even be possible to use a share premium account created on the sale of new shares to pay up a bonus issue for which only the shareholders of record prior to the flotation are eligible.

EXAMPLE

For the purpose of flotation, a company going public via a new issue has been valued in its existing state by the promoters and the merchant bank at approximately $550 m. There are at present in issue 10,000 shares of $500 each which would result in a share price of $55,000 per share. Similar shares in that particular market trade at between $1 and $2 per share.

The following steps are taken:

1   Each of the 10,000 shares of $500 each are subdivided into 1,000 shares of $0.50 each, resulting in 10 m shares in issue.

2   Reserves of $70 m exist, sufficient to make a bonus issue of 140 m shares, resulting in 150 m shares in issue.

3   The new issue consists of 75 m shares at $2 per share to raise $150 m. A share premium account of $1.50 per share is created (equivalent to

$112,500,000) from which $75 m is used to pay up a further bonus issue of 150 m shares to the original shareholders. These final two steps result in an issued share capital of 375 m shares. The price at issue is:

	$m
Value of the company in its existing state	550
Money raised by new issue (net of expenses)	140
Total value	690
Shares in issue	375,000,000
Price ($690 m valuation divided by 375 m shares in issue)	$1.84
Desired range	$1–$2

CONCLUSIONS

A review of the basic requirements which must be satisfied before a flotation can be embarked upon with a reasonable prospect of success is essential if time, money and energy is not to be wasted. Designing the correct structure in terms of corporate organisation and the company's gearing, voting rights and expected share price is also a critical element in success. If the review is positive and a satisfactory structure can be put in place, the next stage is to begin selecting the team needed to get the project underway. The costs involved can then be estimated with a reasonable degree of accuracy.

CHAPTER 5

Forming a team and estimating expenses

A flotation is a team effort and the composition of that team will be a major factor in the outcome. Firms of advisers which individuals or the company have used in the past may not be best suited to the task because of the specialist expertise required. It is a question of 'horses for courses' and a flotation is more like a steeplechase than a sprint.

The cost of the exercise is highly relevant to the decision as to whether to proceed or not. The second section of the chapter sets out the main headings under which costs are incurred. The costs are borne by whichever party receives the funds from the flotation which perhaps makes them less painful. Some commitments for expense may have to be made before it is certain that the flotation can proceed.

I FORMING A TEAM

(i) The company

The company team typically consists of about four people. The decision to go public is usually a highly personal one. Very often the founder, major shareholder, chairman or chief executive will be directly involved. In a private company, the same person may well fill all these roles. As it is easy to be discouraged by the length and difficulty of the process of going public, his determination and enthusiasm will be of the utmost importance.

As well as the vital involvement of a very senior company executive, there are many more routine tasks for the company to undertake. The accounting department will be heavily engaged in producing past and projected financial information in conjunction with the reporting accountants and it is usual for the finance director or chief accountant to take a leading role. The company secretary is likely to be responsible for reviewing the legal aspects of the flotation, including producing details of the corporate history and liaising with the outside lawyers.

In addition, it is useful for one or two junior executives to be assigned as progress-chasers and co-ordinators. As soon as confidentiality permits, they should be involved full-time as the more senior members of the company team will inevitably have urgent and unpredictable calls on their time during the period the prospectus is being prepared.

(ii) Merchant bank

The first party to be involved outside the company is likely to be the merchant bank selected to manage the flotation and act as the underwriter. This choice is usually the first one as the merchant bank takes a central role in putting together the prospectus for the issue. It can also give, in the preparatory stage, a view on whether the flotation is feasible and at least an indication or moral commitment on underwriting.

The merchant banks alone of parties involved in flotations are actively involved in marketing the idea to flotation candidates. Consequently it is quite possible that a company which is beginning to be known in its industry will be itself approached by merchant banks to discuss the possibility of going public. This is increasingly so as the competition between merchant banks becomes more intense.

There are three major criteria for choosing a merchant bank to manage and underwrite an issue:

(a) Experience

It is essential that the merchant bank should have been actively and recently involved in the market. The number of flotations in a normal year is not very large and it may be surprising to find that even quite well-known names have handled rather few recent issues. Some claim an expertise which may barely exist in an active form and they will be, in effect, using the flotation to brush up their technique.

As well as the number of issues, it will be relevant to look at the results. It must be recognised that the outcome of a flotation depends quite heavily on short-term market forces which may be outside the power of the participants to control. However, a series of under-subscriptions would be of concern as would large premiums on the first day of dealing, indicating that the promoters could have obtained a better price. It is also instructive to look at the price say six months after the start of trading, adjusting for movements in the level of the market in general over the same period.

(b) Size and reputation

A major role of the investment bank, no doubt the single most important feature from the point of view of the company going public, is that it should be able to get the issue underwritten at a satisfactory price. This means it should either have the financial muscle and resolution to stand behind the entire issue if necessary or have reliable institutional connections and other placing power sufficient to find a safe home for the issue. Most commonly, a combination of the two is involved. Once an issue is underwritten and receipt of funds guaranteed, the company going public can take the attitude of an interested spectator in the actual level of subscriptions.

(c) Chemistry

A flotation requires long hours to be spent by the senior management of the company with the merchant banking executives involved. There will normally be a team of say three or four bank executives and it is important to meet at least the leader of the team. Without a personal meeting, it is impossible to know whether a good working relationship can be established.

Many problems will have to be tackled during the course of the flotation. Some of these will be sensitive matters for people who have not previously had to disclose substantial amounts of information about their operations to the public. A sympathetic approach is required to avoid turning drafting meetings into confrontations.

The rest of the team of professionals to work on the prospectus may well be drawn from the traditional connections of the company and its management. The merchant bank involved will be able to offer suitable introductions if required. A number of promoters, however, are uneasy at the idea of one professional adviser in effect appointing others and prefer to choose 'their own man'.

(iii) Reporting accountants

The obvious candidates are the group's traditional auditors who may be close business advisers to the private group. They start with the advantage of a good base of knowledge of the group and the way it has developed so that everything does not have to be explained from scratch. However, they may not be great large enough to devote a team of experienced staff to complete rapidly the great amount of accounting work which will be required. If the firm is not already well-known, its name may not be wholly acceptable to the merchant bank or give sufficient confidence to investors. It may therefore be necessary to appoint a larger accounting firm, either to replace the existing auditors, or to report on a joint basis. A joint appointment increases costs somewhat but allows the company to have the best of both worlds in terms of accumulated knowledge and reputation in the market. Usually little problem is experienced in establishing a smooth working relationship between the two firms of accountants.

A company which has an eye on eventual flotation may appoint an internationally known firm some years in advance or cultivate relationships with such a firm while not at that stage of appointing them auditors. In the absence of such contacts, the company will have to rely on the advice of the merchant bank in the choice of reporting accountants.

The reporting accountants will be instructed to report to the directors of both the company being floated and to the merchant bank. In addition to their report for inclusion in the prospectus they may also (depending on market practice) prepare a more detailed 'long form' report. This covers not only the financial position of the company but describes its business, management and systems. Some recommendations for change may be made.

The reporting accountants may be able to give valuable advice on any reorganisation of the group to be accomplished prior to flotation. If companies are purchased at above net asset values, goodwill may arise. Retained profits of companies acquired may be 'frozen', unavailable for distribution to the public company's shareholders. There are different possible accounting treatments of goodwill on consolidation and pre-acquisition profits and steps may be taken with the advice of the accountants to minimise these two problems, which can prove troublesome.

The accountant's report is the element of the prospectus which typically takes longest to produce and provides the raw material for much of the remainder of the prospectus. It therefore needs to be commissioned in good time. If the results show up some weaknesses, they should be highlighted as soon as possible so that the problems can be tackled or the flotation reconsidered.

As well as producing the accountant's report, the accountants have other major responsibilities. If there is a forecast of profits they will be heavily involved in checking and substantiating it. They may also be asked to check the statement of borrowings, contingent liabilities and commitments and to provide comfort to the directors on their statement concerning the adequacy of working capital. Their advice may be taken on taxation problems or planning for the company. If there is a trust deed or any loan agreement which contains limits on borrowings or other financial covenants, the accountants will check that these have not been breached. They will also have a major role in the verification of the prospectus in general and particularly as regards all figures and calculations.

As a separate matter, the accountants will produce a statement of adjustments setting out the adjustments they consider necessary from the audited accounts as produced by the company prior to its flotation. If the reporting accountant has been the auditor to the group over the period it is unlikely that there will be any material adjustments, except if accounting policies have changed. The statement of adjustments is normally filed with the stock exchange or other regulatory authorities.

(iv) Lawyers

It is likely that the promoters will have their own contacts with solicitors. The legal work involved in a prospectus is specialised and not all firms of lawyers will have suitable specialists available to work on a full-time basis. Again the merchant bank may be involved in introducing an experienced firm.

There are two separate aspects to the legal work in a prospectus, one for the company and its directors and the other for the merchant bank. While it is possible for different partners at one firm to carry out the two roles, it is more usual to appoint separate firms to ensure that no conflict arises. While for most purposes the company and merchant bank have similar interests, as regards pricing and the underwriting agreement they are on the opposite sides of the table. The merchant bank is likely to have a close relationship with a number of firms of lawyers specialising in corporate issue work.

The legal work in the prospectus starts very early with preparing a group structure. Formal sale and purchase and other agreements will be needed to document any acquisitions of companies or assets. The lawyers may be able to contribute helpful suggestions for simplifying the methods used for the reorganisation and in minimising tax and other costs.

As the work proceeds, the lawyers will be generally responsible for ensuring that all disclosures required by statute are included in the prospectus. Information which is not covered in other parts of the prospectus may be gathered for convenience in an appendix often headed 'Statutory and General Information'. This may include, for example, a summary of the new articles of association which will be appropriate for a public company, details of material contracts the group has been a party to and disclosure of directors' interests. Lawyers will also draw up the company's board minutes for the various corporate decisions and approvals required and will draft notes of evidence that all material points in the prospectus have been verified. Lawyers may also draft the share certificates and handle liaison with the legal authorities with whom the prospectus needs to be cleared or filed.

(v) Stockbrokers

In most markets it is required or highly desirable to have a sponsoring stockbroker for the issue. The broker will make the formal application for listing and handle relationships with the people in the stock exchange responsible for scrutinising new listings whom they will probably know on a personal basis. This relationship can be very valuable in ironing out problems on timing, procedures or documentation before they become major obstacles. The brokers will, if necessary, discuss with the stock exchange the mechanics of share registration, delivery of share certificates, dealing and settlement.

The brokers should be closely involved in sounding out large potential shareholders to evaluate their interest in the issue and be in a position to advise on pricing. The people they contact may also form the backbone of the sub-underwriting syndicate which, depending on market practice, the broker may take the lead in putting together. Very often a general market view will emerge on a reasonable level of price for the issue which it is dangerous to ignore even if it is out of line with the price fundamental analysis might suggest.

The brokers may be able to set the scene for the issue by publishing a helpful background circular on the sector or industry of the company going public. At the time of the flotation, they may circularise clients recommending the issue. Subsequently they serve as an effective channel of information on the company's progress to clients and shareholders.

(vi) Valuers

It may be required by regulation or desirable from a marketing and information point of view to show recent valuations of major assets.

In the case of a property company, the report of the valuer is likely to be the portion of the document which sets the tone for the whole issue.

The reputation and standing of the valuer is vital. The valuer should be recognised as a leader in his profession. There should be no question of his independence from the company. When the properties concerned are located in different countries, it is advantageous to use an international firm or one with strong international affiliations to ensure a consistent approach to valuation is adopted.

Other assets which are regularly revalued include ships, mines and quarries. Plant and equipment are not normally revalued. In choosing valuers for other fixed assets, the same general criteria will apply as for property revaluations. It must be recognised, however, that there may be some disagreement on the basis of valuation and its validity where a revaluation is carried out on a category of asset which is not regularly bought and sold in the open market.

(vii) Other professionals involved

Other professionals include:

(a) Public relations

It may be useful to engage a press and publicity agent. Their role can stretch from sowing the original seeds of interest in the months before the prospectus to an intensive media operation at the time of going public. A press conference to announce the issue can be very effective in obtaining coverage which the availability of a certain amount of food and drink does nothing to hinder. At a more nuts and bolts level, the prospectus will usually be reproduced in one or more newspapers and advice may be needed on the effectiveness of various alternative advertising strategies.

(b) Receiving bankers

The application forms with the cheques attached will normally be delivered to a bank specialising in receiving and checking such documents.

The bank chosen may be the clearing bank of the group or may be recommended by the merchant bank. Banks who specialise in this role have pools of experienced staff who can be drafted in to help at short notice in the event of a high level of applications.

The bank will charge a flat fee per application form processed. It may also act as a temporary registrar for an initial period.

(c) Registrars

After applications have been received (and the cheques detached), they will be passed to a registration company. It is their responsibility to tally the applications and carry out the procedure decided on for allocation. They will then draw up the first register of members.

It is unlikely that a private group will have any existing contact with a registration company. Such companies are often affiliated with firms of accountants or with banks. The company will normally act on the recommendation of one of its other advisers in choice of registrar.

(d) Printers

Although the role of the printer may not seem glamorous, their help with eleventh-hour changes to the documents is often vital. Their efficiency in updating and circulating the many proofs required is also a considerable factor in the smooth running of the operation.

II EXPENSES

There are three main types of expenses which are incurred in going public – the time of the company's own executives, the charges of the professional firms and taxes and fees paid to the authorities.

(i) The company's own costs

This element is often ignored because it is rarely separately calculated. Companies which do go through the exercise of costing in retrospect the time expended by their own executives may well be appalled at the result. The amount is likely to be higher than any of the professional charges, excluding underwriting.

As well as direct costs there are opportunity costs. The preparation of a prospectus requires heavy involvement on the part of senior management who are likely to be the major generators of new business. Even day-to-day management may suffer under the voracious capacity of the prospectus to absorb time.

(ii) Professionals

The major amounts payable to the various professional firms are as follows:

(a) Merchant banks

Underwriting fees vary widely from market to market, being perhaps most expensive in the US where fees for underwriting a small initial public offering can go as high as 10%. In the UK and markets influenced by the UK, underwriting fees tend to be about $2\frac{1}{2}\%$ of the amount raised. The total fee will be split into two. A management fee will be retained by the lead merchant bank(s) as their reward for bringing the company to market, putting their name to the prospectus and underwriting and managing the issue. The bulk of the fee, however, will be passed on to the underwriting or selling syndicate, for their risk in taking sub-underwriting or their efforts in selling.

On the whole, there seems to be little competition among institutions on pricing. Underwriting fees suggested by merchant banks for similar types of issues are not likely to vary sharply in a particular market. The major participants in the market probably know each other well enough to avoid a price war.

From the company's point of view, though the expense of underwriting is important, it is greatly outweighed by whether the issue can be underwritten at all. Bargaining takes place at the outset when the promoters may be ill-informed about the flotation process. Promoters pre-occupied about the overall success of the issue in the later stages are in a poor position to argue hard about the precise underwriting expense.

Underwriting and selling fees may be paid directly as such, or may be built into a spread between the price at which securities are acquired from the company or the vendor shareholders and the price at which they are sold to the market, depending on the type of issue being made.

In addition to underwriting fees, the merchant bank will sometimes charge a financial advisory or documentation fee to cover the work involved on the structure of the issue and in drafting the prospectus. As the merchant bank's major reward will come from underwriting fees, any additional fee is likely to be negotiable. Merchant banks would far rather reduce or even eliminate this element than disturb a relatively fixed underwriting fee structure.

(b) Accountants and lawyers

The fees of the merchant bankers will not vary significantly with the amount of work done. The accountants and lawyers on the other hand will charge primarily on a time spent basis. Most accountants and lawyers will also have a system of weighting a particular job by urgency, complexity and other factors. However, the final bill will principally depend on the number of man hours absorbed in the work required.

(c) Stockbrokers

The stockbrokers will be paid a fee (perhaps $\frac{1}{4}$% of the amount of the issue) directly by the company or by the merchant bank out of their overall underwriting fee for their involvement in putting together the sub-underwriting syndicate. They will also charge a flat fee for their processing work as regards the stock exchange.

The principal reward for a broker in being associated with a flotation may come later, from commissions when market dealings begin. The broker sponsoring the launch of a company is likely to be seen as a leader in the market for the securities of that company and would hope to gain a lion's share of the trading.

(d) Valuers

Valuers may be members of an association which publishes fixed fees for its members. In the context of a flotation, it may prove possible to negotiate a fee separately from the standard rate.

(e) Receiving bankers, registrars and printers

The costs incurred will depend on variable factors such as the number of applications received, shares allotted and prospectuses printed.

(iii) Taxes and listing fees

Two principal taxes are likely to be incurred:

(a) Capital duty

Capital duty may arise when the authorised share capital of a company is increased or when new shares are issued. The tax is usually based on a percentage (perhaps 1%) of the amount involved. If authorised share capital is used as the basis, it will be calculated on the face amount of the increase. If the tax is based on the issued share capital, it is likely to include any premium at which the shares are issued over par value.

If no acquisitions are made for shares and existing shares are sold via an offer for sale, no capital duty will be payable.

Capital duty will be hard to avoid if a new company is set up to act as the holding company for the group to be floated and acquires its subsidiaries by an exchange of shares. Capital duty will be payable in effect not only on any new shares issued at the time of the flotation but on the entire value of the group as reorganised for going public. There is a substantial cost saving if an existing company controlling as many of the interests to be floated as possible is suitable for use as the new listed company. Any reorganisation of the group should be designed with an eye to minimising the capital duty impact.

(b) Transfer duty

Transfer duty can arise in two ways. In the first instance it can arise upon the reorganisation of the group when assets or businesses are transferred to the new holding company. Transfer tax may be incurred whatever form of payment the holding company uses. Different rates may apply, however, on assets and shares so that it may be advantageous for example to transfer the share capital of a company which holds an asset rather than transfer the asset itself. Various tax avoidance schemes are available (depending on the jurisdiction involved) to limit the extent to which transfer duty may be incurred. Such schemes tend to be subject to periodic attack by tax authorities and changes of legislation.

The second area where transfer duty is involved is if existing shares are sold. In this case both the vendors and the purchasers will be obliged to pay transfer duty at the relevant rate, based on the issue price.

The payment of some tax is almost inevitable. A new issue does not involve transfer duty but will probably incur capital duty, an offer for sale of existing shares vice versa. The use of renounceable certificates may help in some jurisdictions. A corporate reorganisation prior to flotation may also trigger transfer duty and capital duty if a share exchange is used.

(c) Listing fees

The stock exchange will charge an initial listing fee, normally on a scale varying with the market value (at the issue price) of the entire class of capital for which a listing is granted. Thereafter, a lower annual fee is payable by all listed companies.

(iv) Offsets to expenses

If the issue is over-subscribed, there may be a considerable amount of funds available for placing in the money markets until the over-subscription moneys are returned. The money cannot be returned until the basis of allotment is arrived at and refund cheques are prepared and posted out which may take a number of days. It is customary for the interest earned on over-subscriptions to be retained by the company to defray the expenses of the issue. It is not unknown for a heavy over-subscription at a period of high interest rates to result in expenses being covered and an overall profit being made. Although there may be a suspicion in investors' minds that return of over-subscription moneys is delayed deliberately, the merchant and receiving banks are sensitive to possible criticism and do not themselves benefit from delay.

It is sometimes suggested that an attempt should be made to pay the interest back to unsuccessful applicants. Their funds generate the interest in the first place and they perhaps deserve a consolation prize for not achieving their desired investment. However, this possibility seems to be too burdensome for the organisers of issues to consider worthwhile.

(v) Who pays?

If the whole issue is devoted to raising new funds for the company, all the expenses incurred are payable by the company. If the prospectus involves solely the sale of existing shares, the underwriting costs will be borne by the holders of those shares. There is some flexibility in who bears the remaining costs, with some proportion normally borne by the company.

Where a new issue and an offer for sale are combined, the expenses of underwriting are shared in the same proportion as the proceeds. The administrative expenses involved in gaining the listing (such as printing and advertising costs and professional fees) may be borne wholly by the company going public, on the grounds that the listing is a corporate matter and has long-term benefits to the company. Alternatively, they may be split in the same proportion as the proceeds of the issue. Any transfer duty payable on the offer for sale shares is borne by the shareholders who sell those shares. The capital duty on new shares issued to the public will be borne entirely by the company.

CONCLUSIONS

The composition of the team of people involved in the issue is central to its success and the way the team is chosen is therefore a critical factor. The merchant bank will present an estimate of expenses at an early stage and suggest how these can be controlled. The availability of funds from the flotation makes the payment of expenses less frightening. After the expenses of the exercise have been estimated, the next items on the agenda tend to be pricing and timing of the issue.

CHAPTER 6

Timing and pricing

The launch of a new public company on the stock market is a delicate operation which requires favourable conditions for a successful outcome. Two of the most important elements are timing and pricing. A listing which is otherwise sound can fail if the timing of the launch is poor. Even if all other circumstances are auspicious, the market is not likely to accept an issue which is over-priced.

1   TIMING

The art of timing has been likened to astrology. The object is to divine when three factors which may only be approximately related to each other will swing into alignment. These are:

(i)   market cycles;
(ii) fashions in sectors; and
(iii) fortunes of the particular company.

(i) Market cycles

Stock markets tend to run in cycles of some years' duration. Periods of time when, on the average, prices are increasing are called 'bull' markets, while periods when they are in decline are dubbed 'bear' markets.

Flotations are likely to be concentrated in the later phases of a bull market, particularly when the level of market turnover is also high.

It is fairly obvious that companies would seek to issue new shares, or existing shareholders seek to dispose of some part of their holdings, when prices are high. It is less obvious why investors also tend to be more receptive to flotations during a bull market. They might be expected to consider prices expensive and to be suspicious that existing shareholders were trying to off-load their shares at or near the peak of the market. While some such feelings do no doubt exist, they seem to be outweighed by a mood of buoyant optimism which a bull market tends to bring with it. Investors are feeling confident and confidence spawns a willingness to experiment with new companies. Profits on existing holdings may be viewed as a bonus, available for trying something new. There may also be a shortage of sellers of shares in the more familiar companies. In these conditions, a pool of funds seems to be attracted to a series of new issues. As one closes, the over-subscriptions tend to be rolled into the next one.

It is important for those planning a flotation to catch the market while it is in a receptive mood. In smaller markets, the duration of this atmosphere may be quite brief. If conditions change, it may be a question not simply of adjusting the terms of the issue but of re-evaluating whether the issue can be undertaken at all.

(ii) Fashions in sectors

In addition to generally favourable market conditions, the success of a flotation is dependent on investors' current view of the sector in which a company is located.

The market can be fickle as regards which sectors it finds attractive. Previously favoured sectors can go rapidly out of style. Sometimes changes in basic economic conditions lie behind the market movements. For example, a drop in inflation, which can assist the industrial sector, may not suit property or financial shares. At other times, trends may reflect media attention or other ephemeral factors.

In view of the butterfly existence of a sector's popularity, it may be necessary to accelerate launch plans. However, the first company in a new sector to go public often plays a pioneering role, awakening investor interest and smoothing the path for others to follow. The pricing of the first issue is likely to be conservative. It may be more advantageous for the company going public to be a close follower rather than a leader.

Some sectors may be so depressed that it is unlikely that a flotation on any reasonable terms would be acceptable to investors. If an industry like shipping or steel is caught in the throes of a long-term crisis, even a good company in the sector may beat on the door to no avail.

(iii) Fortunes of the particular company

The final element in timing of a flotation is to identify a period when an upswing in a company's own fortunes coincides with its sector being in fashion and the market being in a bullish phase. The ideal time in the development of the company is when it can show a solid history of past performance and when a strong current year's profit can be forecast so as to achieve an attractive price for existing shareholders.

From a market point of view, there should be still the prospect of growth after the current year is completed. Markets are alert to an owner selling out a company in the peak year of its performance. The multiple at which the issue is pitched may prove misleading if earnings are reduced in the following years.

A balance should be struck between obtaining the best price for existing shareholders and leaving something for the market to go for. It may be argued that an enthusiastic response to the issue is, in any case, in the existing shareholders' interests if it results in a well-spread shareholder base with appetite for further investment and a good level of trading. This should prove of greater benefit to the company and its shareholders than engineering a one-time killing. Assuming the original shareholders retain the majority of their holdings, they should be more concerned with the market value of their remaining shares than with achieving the highest possible issue price.

II PRICING

The pricing of a new issue may be approached from a theoretical and a practical angle. It is necessary to build up from fundamentals an assessment of what the price 'ought to be' within a reasonable range. However, it must be recognised that over-sophistication can be dangerous. Discrepancies are inevitable between the theoretical basis and the realities of the market-place. In practice, investors have a choice between shares in the new company and existing shares. Pricing must be set with an eye to the alternative opportunities open to investors.

(i) Fundamental analysis

The starting point is to determine the appropriate basis for analysis. Care must be taken that valuation is not based on an assumption of a willing buyer/willing seller for the whole company, which will incorporate a premium for control. Value must be considered from the point of view of the buyer of a small number of shares in the market.

The principles of valuation which may be used are discussed in Part 1 of this book and some of them are quite elaborate. However, companies are principally valued for stock market purposes by reference to their future earnings and dividends and their net asset backing.

(a) Multiple of earnings and related methods

Earnings forecasts for inclusion in a prospectus rarely cover a period of more than one year, so that short-term factors predominate. However, in considering price, the merchant bank should ask for, and will normally have access to, earnings projections for some longer period depending on the company's own planning process and the nature of the industry. Such forecasts are used mainly to assess the quality of the company's earnings and are not published. The earnings used in the price earnings valuation formula will normally be the forecast earnings for the year currently in progress.

The projections which form the basis of earnings forecasts can be adapted to produce forecasts of cash flow to the company or to the shareholders in the form of dividends. Valuations can therefore also be carried out on the basis of discounted cash flow or dividends. Specific projections are rarely available beyond say three years, after which the usual expedient is to assume a constant growth rate. It should be appreciated, however, that, ignoring any differences in tax effects, valuations by reference to earnings, cash flow or dividends are all variations on the same theme. Any material differences in the results of valuations of the same company based on these three factors must be due to a difference in the assumptions underlying the calculations.

The main factors determining the multiple to be applied to the forecast earnings are expected future growth and financial and commercial risk. If cash flows are used then the discount rate will be set principally to reflect risk. The estimate of growth will be built into the cash flows themselves. As a matter of mathematics, if cash flows are not assumed to increase, then an identical valuation will be produced by using a discount rate which is the reciprocal of the price earnings ratio. For example, if cash flows are assumed not to grow and to continue indefinitely, a price earnings ratio of 8 and a discount rate of $12\frac{1}{2}\%$ will produce the same valuation.

If dividends are used, the discount rate will again be set by risk factors. However, it is very likely that cash flows to the company will be substantially higher than cash flows to the shareholders, i e dividends paid. Consequently the discount rate will have to be significantly lower if a valuation based on dividends is to be in the same range as one based on the company's cash flow. One justification for a lower discount rate is that the retention of earnings should produce higher growth.

For the purpose of a flotation, it seems unhelpful to base a valuation on dividends. The dividend yield on a share is likely to form only part of the investors' returns, the remaining and sometimes more significant contribution coming from capital gains in the market value.

(b) Net asset basis

An asset-intensive company, such as those in the property or shipping sectors, may be most usefully priced by reference to the valuation of those assets less liabilities. On a theoretical basis, it is possible to argue that the value should include a premium over asset value to reflect the skill involved in putting together a portfolio, arranging finance and presenting a convenient package for an investor.

In practice, the price in the market often reflects a discount from the underlying asset value. This is most easily observed in the case of investment trusts whose assets consist of other listed shares and where the market value of the portfolio is regularly calculated and published. Despite the liquidity of these investments and the fact that the prices of the shares owned by the trust may already reflect a discount from their own underlying net asset value, the price of the shares in the investment trust usually reflects a further discount from the total market price of its portfolio, say, in the range of 10 to 15%. The reason for this phenomenon is not entirely clear; it may reflect an investor preference for being as close to the actual asset as possible. While this effect is most easily calculable in the case of investment trusts, it seems likely that it applies generally to companies valued in the market on a net asset basis.

The level of gearing will also be relevant. The growth of companies which are capital intensive is likely to be significantly dependent on the skill with which loan finance is deployed. The ideal level of gearing is one which reflects management's ability to use borrowings to increase shareholders' returns while not approaching levels which could impose financial strain and cramp the company's commercial freedom.

It is of course possible to analyse a group into businesses which are best valued on an earnings basis and those which are best valued on an assets basis and then add the two.

(ii) Realities of the market

No matter what valuation may be placed on a company by a theoretical exercise, if investors can purchase what they regard as a comparable company at a cheaper price they will do so and ignore the new issue. For this reason, the price at which a company is floated is influenced at least as much by the multiples of existing listed companies which are considered to be comparable as by the theoretical valuation exercise. In addition, discreet soundings will be taken by the merchant bank and the stockbroker among their market contacts to establish what the market feels is a reasonable price range for the flotation.

(a) Comparable companies

Considerable time and effort will be spent in selecting the companies which can be legitimately used as the basis of comparison for setting the appropriate multiple of earnings (or, less frequently, discount to net assets) to be applied to the company to be listed. A price earnings multiple is essentially an artificial thing, created by dividing the market price, an observable fact, by the reported earnings per share which may be open to some interpretation but are nevertheless calculated on generally accepted principles. Dividing one by the other often produces a seductively plausible figure, such as 8.39 times. It only remains plausible, however, as long as nothing untoward happens to either of its parents. A loss-making company has a market price but no price earnings multiple. Anything which changes the market price or the reported earnings per share will also change the price earnings multiple. The question should be asked whether this is anything but a piece of mathematics.

If a new company fits neatly into a clearly defined market sector, the average multiple for that sector may be taken. However, a sector average is precisely that and may be biased by the rating of a few very large companies. A newly listed company is likely to be at the smaller end of the scale so that an average rating too heavily affected by big companies may be misleading.

Special factors may affect the multiples of individual companies in the sector. A price may be depressed after a disappointing recent announcement or be 'frothy' owing to possible takeover prospects. A company which has very low profits may appear to have a very high multiple; however, this may be better interpreted as the market's expectation of a recovery in earnings to a more normal level. Companies which are not comparable for one of these reasons, although they may be in the same market sector, should be discarded to leave a more relevant list.

Care must be taken not to confuse forecast with historic multiples. Usually a company going public will be forecasting strong growth for the current year and the pricing will be based on that forecast. Similar information is unlikely to be available on comparable companies, which may well be valued on the basis of results for the year past. If growth is expected in the sector, the historic multiples will be higher than one based on a forecast and an adjustment will be needed.

Once a valid comparison has been established it will usually be necessary to apply a small discount to the standard. The discount is to overcome the inertia factor and persuade potential investors to take the risk of investing in a new company rather than one which may be more familiar to them.

(b) Market soundings

There is usually sufficient grounds for disagreement on what is or is not a comparable company that even pricing on the basis of comparables has a degree of subjectivity. The merchant bank and stockbroker will therefore take soundings from their own colleagues and from close associates in the market to see whether an approximate consensus can be identified on what the pricing should be. The identity of the company will be disguised which confuses the issue somewhat but worthwhile reactions can be obtained. These opinions are of course themselves formed partly by fundamentals and comparables but will also include an element of personal interpretation and market feel.

In different markets, investors place different degrees of reliance on the factors underlying a valuation. In some markets, for example, investors prefer shares to be fully backed by net assets despite the fact that they are most appropriately valued by reference to earnings. The regulatory authorities may impose, officially or unofficially, certain guidelines such as a maximum price earnings ratio, a minimum discount of the share price to net assets, and a minimum dividend yield.

Part of the significance of the sounding-out process is that the people contacted will later be approached as sub-underwriters and possible subscribers for the issue.

(iii) Tender method of pricing

(a) Procedures

Rather than fixing the price in advance, it is possible to specify a minimum price and call for tenders. Under this procedure, the applicants themselves choose the price at which they wish to apply subject to a stated minimum. After applications have been received, a 'striking price' is fixed which generally is the price per share which realises the desired amount of money for the issue or sale of the fewest number of shares. Since it is conceivable that one applicant could tender for the whole issue at the highest price, factors such as spread of shareholders will also be taken into account. In this manner, the pricing decision is chiefly determined by the forces of supply and demand prevailing over a short period of time.

(b) Advantages

The tender method may appeal where the issue is not very large and there are no obviously comparable companies on which to base the price. A typical example might be a company with a new technology which is the first of its kind to be listed on the stock market. Existing shareholders may feel that pricing will be pitched too cautiously. The lack of similar listed companies means that underwriters are in uncharted waters. If the issue is small and a large over-subscription is expected after sounding out investor interest, vendors may feel they have little to risk and everything to gain by calling for tenders.

(c) Disadvantages and effect on 'stagging'

The tender method of fixing price is not always welcomed by potential investors who find a fixed price less complicated and more easily evaluated. It may also be considered that tenders reduce or eliminate stagging profits. Stagging is a term used for subscriptions by speculators often in excess of the holding they actually desire (in the expectation that applications will be scaled down) and with the object of selling at a profit as soon as trading begins.

The success of issues in some markets may be heavily dependent on the activities of the stags. A market view develops on whether an issue is conservatively priced, in which case it will be heavily over-subscribed, or slightly over-priced in which case the level of subscription may be very low indeed.

If the issue is priced at such a level that stags do not believe a profit is obtainable, arguments about the fundamental attractions of the company as an investment tend to fall on deaf ears. Even investors who believe such arguments may take the view that an under-subscription will result in a weak opening price, caused partly by selling from underwriters keen to limit losses on commitments they have been obliged to take up. If investors see a likelihood of obtaining shares in the market at a discount to the issue price, no amount of cajoling them to support the issue is likely to succeed. Some prospect of capital gain is in any case needed to compensate applicants for having funds locked into the issuing procedures rather than making purchases on market terms when trading begins.

CONCLUSION

A good timing decision comes from a correct assessment of the general state of the market, the popularity of a particular sector and the right stage of development of the company itself. Pricing owes something to fundamentals but more to market feel through identifying comparable companies and gauging market reaction.

If the pricing is acceptable to the promoters and the overall timing looks auspicious, the next step is to prepare a detailed prospectus and timetable for the issue.

CHAPTER 7

Components of a prospectus and timetable

The major administrative task in a flotation is the production of a prospectus document. While the precise contents of a prospectus vary from market to market, there tend to be 'building blocks' in common. In 'I Main components of a prospectus' below, the main components of these building blocks are summarised. Some components are critical and set the tone for the issue. Others may be laborious to draft or verify but rarely affect the overall outcome. Relative importance is not determined by the order in which they appear in the prospectus or the amount of text they are accorded.

In 'II Timetable' below, the time required to put together the prospectus is considered. Certain items, such as the accountant's report, provide basic information for other parts and so must be completed first.

I MAIN COMPONENTS OF A PROSPECTUS

The main components of a prospectus (based broadly on UK legislation) in the order which they generally appear are set out below, with brief comments on their importance.

(i) Description of the share capital of the company and a statement of the indebtedness of the group including contingent liabilities, guarantees and commitments

If the flotation is by way of new issue, the description of the share capital should include the effect of the issue of the new shares. The impact of any options outstanding, the exercise of any warrants and the conversion of convertible securities should also be set out.

Information on indebtedness has to be obtained independently from the banks concerned and this information takes time to collect and verify. Preparations should be made so that the figures are as current as possible, normally as at a date no more than a month before the date of the prospectus.

There is no one 'correct' level of borrowing. An apparently high level of gearing may deter some potential investors but assurances on the adequacy of working capital are given elsewhere in the document. If the flotation raises new funds for the company and one of the purposes of going public is stated to be to reduce borrowings, this should make good sense to investors. In general, however, reduction in borrowings is considered by the market to be one of the less exciting reasons for going public.

(ii) The full names of the directors of the company and a list of the other parties (chiefly professional firms) involved in the issue

This part is straightforward descriptive material, although it would be a mistake to under-estimate directors' ability to change even the most basic information presented about themselves. Written consent must be obtained from any professional firm whose opinion is given or who are quoted as experts for the use of their name in the form and context in which it is included.

(iii) History and business of the group, including background industry information and an explanation of 'what makes the group tick', with details of the main commercial factors governing its operations and future prospects

In order to give investors a general appreciation of how the group has evolved, there will be a few paragraphs prepared by the company's executives and edited by professional advisers which will summarise the origins of the business and its development to the present day.

The potted history is followed by a lengthy descriptive section, covering in general terms the various activities, countries, products and business conditions which are relevant to the operations of the company and its subsidiaries. Different product lines and divisions should be explained and a geographical analysis of production, sales and operating profit may be given. Commercial aspects such as retail network, agencies and distributorships, brand names, franchises, licences, patents and research and development capabilities should be discussed depending on the type of business. Critical relationships with customers should be mentioned. For example, could the supply of key components restrict output? Do sales to any individual customers represent a significant percentage of output of the group as a whole or of an individual product line or division?

This section provides the directors of the company with their main opportunity to get across the spirit and traditions of the company. Although the wording used, as is the case with the whole prospectus, is subject to strict legal scrutiny this section tends to be less dry than the remainder. A little pride in achievement is allowed to show through.

(iv) Directors, management and staff

Details should be given of the experience and areas of responsibility of the directors, distinguishing between executive and non-executive. Investors will also be interested to know something of senior management below the director level and be assured of the depth and professionalism of the management team in general. Any profit-participation or share-incentive scheme in operation or planned should be mentioned. Information on other employees may also be relevant particularly for groups with large labour forces. Some comment on labour relations may be helpful.

(v) Past results and forecasts of future profits and dividends

(a) Profits

The audited results and other financial information for a certain period, commonly five years, will be set out in the accountant's report. The report will include such notes as the auditors feel necessary to explain the figures in an objective way.

In the body of the prospectus, the directors of the company may wish to add their own comments and explanation of the past trend or of any special circumstances which might distort a particular year's figures. As well as giving background information, it is essential to anticipate any perception of weakness derived from the past record which could shed doubt on the forecast of profit. The major assumptions for the profit forecast will be listed and reviewed elsewhere in the prospectus by the auditors and merchant bank. Again, the directors may feel that the reader would be helped by further background comment in addition to the statement of the bare assumptions.

(b) Dividends

It is appropriate for the directors to make a statement of their policy on dividends. There is little reason for a private company to be concerned about consistency of dividend payments or indeed, depending on the tax position and requirements of the shareholders, about dividend payments at all. Consequently, the past record of dividends may be of little guidance to future policy.

Depending on the time of year when the company is floated, the first year's dividend payments may well be less than if the company had been a public company throughout the relevant financial year. The directors must therefore spell out not only their immediate intentions for the first period, but also how this may be validly scaled up for a full year's payment.

The amount of dividend to be paid will depend on a number of factors including the company's own need to retain funds for future growth. Very often a market will have fairly specific expectations of a dividend yield appropriate to a company in a particular sector in a particular market. Occasionally there is a 'target' yield in a market irrespective of the type of company.

The directors will wish to maintain future dividends at no less than the initial level. A dividend cut is widely interpreted as evidence of management failure, even in cyclical industries. The most widely used measure to assess whether a dividend can be maintained is the number of times it is covered by earnings. Some particularly stable component of earnings, such as rentals receivable under long-term leases or interest on bonds, may be weighted more heavily. A dividend cover in the range of one and a half to two times may be considered comfortable.

(vi) Balance sheet and interests in properties

The latest audited balance sheet of the company and the group with supporting notes will form part of the accountant's report. Directors may feel some commentary on the balance sheet and planned capital expenditure is helpful.

If a group is made up primarily of asset-intensive businesses such as property or shipping, it may be required and in any case be desirable to show up-to-date valuations of its major assets carried out by an independent professionally qualified valuer. If the valuations show significant differences from book value (either surpluses or deficits) an adjusted statement of net assets incorporating the valuations should be shown in this section. Any significant tax consequences of disposals at the valuation figures should also be shown.

It is not necessary for the valuations actually to be written into the books of the companies concerned. If they are, tax problems may arise and the charge for depreciation may increase, reducing reported profits.

(vii) Reasons for the issue, use of proceeds and statement of working capital

If existing shares are being sold to raise money for shareholders, no proceeds are received by the company. However, if new money is going into the company the reasons why it is being raised and the uses to which it will be put should be spelt out. In either case, a short statement is required from the directors stating that the group has sufficient working capital for its present requirements. This is usually interpreted to mean that detailed cash flow projections have been carried out covering a period of at least 12 months from the date of the prospectus. In this part of the prospectus, a few words are likely to represent several weeks of investigation and analysis.

(viii) Appendices

There will also be a number of appendices to the prospectus. These typically consist of:

(a) Accountant's report on the group

The accountant's report forms one of the main building blocks of the prospectus. Once the companies forming the basis of the flotation have been selected, it is the first significant piece of work to be put in hand.

The report will list the companies being examined and summarise the accounting policies used to prepare the accounts. The profit and loss accounts for past periods, commonly five years, will be shown together with notes. A statement of net assets of the company and of the group at the latest available date and, depending on requirements, for a number of years past will also be given, again with all relevant notes. Statements of sources and uses of funds and adjustments for the effect of inflation may also be included.

The formal report is addressed to the directors of the company to be floated and to the merchant bank. It is normally produced in draft form as soon as possible to highlight any potential snags in the flotation. At the same time, the accountants may be carrying out a more detailed investigation into the group for a 'long form' report, which is not for publication. Depending on the complexity of the group, the report for inclusion in the prospectus may take up to, say, three months to finalise.

(b) Summary of professional valuations

Professional independent valuations of assets may be required by law or by stock exchange regulations. The directors of the company may in any event decide that it would be desirable to show the financial position of the group taking into account revaluation of assets. In these cases, letters from the valuers giving the basis of their valuation and a summary of the results of their valuations will be set out in an appendix. In the case of a property company, relevant details of site and development areas, tenure, planning permissions and tenants' leases will be given, depending on the nature of the property. The feasibility of the flotation of a property company and pricing will depend principally on the valuation.

(c) Reports on profit forecast

Assuming a profit forecast is made, the assumptions underlying the forecast will be set out. The accountants will review the accounting policies and calculations for the forecast.

They will check that the forecast has been properly compiled on the basis of the assumptions made by the directors and that the profit does not include any items which arise owing to a change in accounting policies.

The merchant bank will discuss with the directors of the company whether the basis and assumptions used for the forecast are realistic and comprehensive. Following these discussions they will write to confirm that the forecast has been prepared after due and careful enquiry.

Letters from the auditors and merchant bank to this effect will be included in the appendix. The letters always state that despite the involvement of the professional firms the forecast is the sole responsibility of the directors of the company. This can make them feel rather lonely.

It may be argued that the assumptions listed in this appendix are virtually meaningless. They may be couched in sweeping terms and therefore unlikely to be fulfilled in all respects. They also tend to deal more with general conditions or trends in the economy, such as interest, taxation and exchange rates, than with specific commercial factors which have more meaning to a reader and a much more immediate effect on the company's business. It is countered that the most critical commercial factors cannot be set out without giving too much away to competitors.

(d) Statutory and general information

This appendix is prepared chiefly by the lawyers and deals with legal and regulatory points not already covered elsewhere in the prospectus. The main headings are likely to include the following:

— Details of incorporation of the company and share capital history including any reorganisation carried out in anticipation of the flotation.
— A list of the company's subsidiaries and associated companies giving share capital, date of incorporation and percentage owned by the group.
— Arrangements for underwriting including circumstances in which the underwriting contract could be cancelled and an estimate of the other major expenses of the issue, together with a statement of the net proceeds.
— Disclosure of interests. This is a wide ranging section and is basically intended

to cover details of shareholders' or directors' interests which might have some bearing on an investor's decision to invest. Obvious points include who the major shareholders are and the extent of their shareholding, whether any directors are selling shares, any service contracts the directors have and whether they are parties to any other contracts with the group. A number of other factors may be relevant, depending on the circumstances of the case. A rather cynical definition of what is material for disclosure is anything which one of the promoters does not wish to disclose. Some statement of the controlling shareholders' future business dealings with the group may be relevant at this point.

— Summary of relevant provisions of new articles of association. A company going public will adopt new articles of association which are available in full for public inspection. Relevant sections will be summarised in the prospectus. These will include clauses regarding voting rights of shares, procedures for changing the share capital and for transfer and issue of shares, any restrictions on the company's ability to borrow money and a summary of the directors' powers.

— Material contracts entered into by the company and its subsidiaries over some previous period, say the two years before the date of the prospectus. Some contracts may be sensitive from a commercial or other viewpoint. What is and is not a material contract is often the subject of one of the more lively debates to take place during the preparation of a prospectus.

(ix) Procedures for application

It is easy to lose sight of the fact that the main objective in the preparation of a prospectus is to facilitate applications. The procedures for application should be spelt out in as clear a manner as possible, even if they are fairly technical. These procedures will be covered both in the body of the prospectus and on a separate application form. The prospectus will cover procedures for applying for shares and the timetable for declaring results, posting out share certificates and the start of trading.

The application form will contain details of the minimum and other numbers of shares which may be applied for. A table may be included to help in calculations of the amount of money which will be required for each application. Procedures for cashing cheques and returning over-subscriptions will also be set out.

This section of the prospectus and the wording of the application form are highly standardised and familiar to professional investors. They can cause confusion for small investors or for people who do not regularly apply for new issues. If there is time, the receiving bankers or registrars will contact applicants who have submitted invalid applications to obtain clarification and make corrections.

II TIMETABLE

The precise period needed will vary with the regulations and practice of the particular markets being tapped and the circumstances of the company going public. The only general rule seems to be that it takes longer than expected. In constructing a timetable it is as well to build in some slack for unexpected delays and problems.

A factor which can upset the timetable is indecision by the shareholders and management of the company to be floated. A degree of indecision is inevitable since it is not until the executives concerned have a detailed appreciation of the costs and the work involved that they can take a final decision on whether a flotation is worthwhile. Very often it is not immediately clear which elements in a complex collection of businesses and assets should be included in the package for flotation. If a reorganisation is required, substantial costs may begin to be incurred before the merchant bank is committed to underwrite.

Management has to assess the risk of time and money being spent only for the flotation to be cancelled for market reasons which may have nothing to do with the company itself or the wish of the promoters to proceed. One method of limiting costs is to make any reorganisation conditional on a listing being obtained.

A decision on the elements to be floated must be taken before the accountants can be instructed to produce their report. It may prove desirable for the report to be carried out by or in conjunction with a firm which may not be familiar with the group. This will add to the time the report takes to complete. In addition, as accounts will not previously have been published, it is likely that some additional accounting work will be required beyond the programme which was previously followed.

In some jurisdictions, the stock exchange may require the audited accounts shown in the prospectus to be no more than six months old. Since it normally takes two to three months to prepare an accountant's report, this leaves a window of, say, three months between the time the report is completed and the deadline. This assumes that the accountants are instructed soon after the close of the financial period in question. If discussions about the elements to be floated delay the instructions to the accountants, the window will become even narrower.

Owing to the frequent experience of delays, it is desirable to build in contingency plans for a special audit to be conducted if the six months' stock exchange limitation on the age of the audited figures (or other time limit) runs out. If the company has relatively simple operations, such as a property company with a portfolio of a few large investment properties, a further audit may only take a matter of two or three weeks. In a major manufacturing or retailing concern, the requirement for a physical stock check among other factors may mean that elaborate preparations will have to be made if a further audit is needed.

While the accounting work is underway, it will be necessary for the lawyers to be instructed so that the basic legal work can be completed at approximately the same time as the accountant's report becomes available. If a valuation of assets is to be undertaken this work should also proceed in parallel.

Altogether it is rare for a prospectus to be published less than four months after the first major planning meeting. A typical timetable for a flotation based on the four-month period is set out below. Executives involved in the process normally query the amount of time allowed at first, only to find that in the event they have to scramble to meet the deadlines.

TIMETABLE

Note. 'I' means 'Impact Day', the first day on which the detailed terms of the issue are made known to the market and to the press. This is earlier than the date of the prospectus and considerably earlier than the start of trading in the shares on the stock market.

Date (in days)	*Event*
I – 120	First planning meeting held. Decision taken to proceed in principle. Merchant bank appointed. Estimated expenses discussed.
I – 110	(i) Package of companies/businesses/assets to be floated decided on. (ii) Accountants instructed and begin work. (iii) Lawyers instructed and begin work. (iv) Detailed timetable and list of responsibilities circulated to those involved.
I – 90	(i) Progress and possible problems reviewed with accountants. (ii) Property valuers instructed if appropriate.
I – 60	(i) Draft accountant's report, property valuation and profit forecast available. (ii) Basis of issue reviewed by company and underwriter.
I – 50	(i) Outline typewritten proof circulated to parties involved in the issue. (ii) Drafting and other work progresses.
I – 40	(i) Drafts of application form, share certificate, underwriting agreement and other documentation available. (ii) Receiving bankers, registrars and printers appointed.
I – 34	Drafting meeting to discuss documents before first printed proof is produced.
I – 30	Record date for borrowings and disclosures.
I – 27	First printed proof circulated, discussed by company and its advisers and sent for re-proofing.
I – 20	(i) Second proof circulated to advisers and other interested parties (including the stock exchange) discussed and sent for re-proofing. (ii) Confirm flotation date with stock exchange.

I − 13	(i) Third proof circulated, discussed and sent for re-proofing. Further proofs as required.
	(ii) Verification process commenced.
I − 6	Final proof prepared and circulated to all relevant parties. Final comments obtained.
I − 1	(i) Board meeting to approve prospectus and fix price.
	(ii) Underwriting proofs available.
IMPACT DAY	(i) Press announcement of issue.
	(ii) Sub-underwriting letters sent out.
	(iii) Bulk printing ordered.
	(iv) Underwriting agreement signed.
I + 7	(i) Prospectus signed and other formalities complied with.
	(ii) Prospectus advertised and distributed to the public.
I + 12	Application lists open and close.
I + 15	Cheques cleared.
I + 16	(i) Press announcement of overall results and basis of allocation.
	(ii) Underwriters' liability (if any) crystallised.
	(iii) Stock exchange grants listing.
I + 18	Trading in the shares commences.
I + 20	Letters of regret and refund cheques posted.
I + 25	(i) Documents of title posted.
	(ii) Funds released to company/vendors.
	(iii) Listing becomes unconditional.
I + 30	First day of settlement for dealings.

The details of the above timetable will vary according to local regulations. In particular, the arrangements for and timing of settlement of dealings can differ sharply from market to market.

In parallel with drafting of the documentation goes the preparation for the launch. Promotional and marketing efforts are becoming more elaborate. Assuming a successful issue, the promoters will start to consider what basis of allocation to adopt.

CHAPTER 8

Launch, allocation and the start of trading

As the time for the publication of the prospectus draws near, a detailed campaign leading to the launch of the company must be organised. The campaign has two aspects, general publicity and marketing efforts and the behind-the-scenes arrangements of a sub-underwriting syndicate. 'II Allocation' below, deals with how investors' applications are dealt with and, assuming an over-subscription, how the basis of allotment is determined. This at least has the consolation of being a problem of success. 'III Start of trading' below, covers the early days of trading. After the intense efforts of preparation, the first day of dealings is a more relaxed occasion.

I LAUNCH

(i) General publicity and marketing efforts

The objective of the publicity campaign is to increase the investing public's awareness of the company and its attractions as an investment. The more familiar the public are with the name of the company, the more comfortable they are likely to be with an investment. In some cases, for example a company with a famous brand name or a well-known retail chain, the name itself will have already been extensively advertised and this is a distinct advantage. However, the publicity may need to be redirected from the company's customers towards the investment community, from the glossy magazines towards the inky financial press, assuming these two constituencies do not overlap extensively.

As a general rule, companies seeking an initial listing are not likely to be very well known before flotation and carefully orchestrated promotional efforts will be needed. This may be done in various ways over the months before the launch. The promoters may engage the services of a public relations firm specialising in financial matters. A corporate advertising campaign may be undertaken. New products or services being launched by the company may be publicised more widely than usual. Opportunities will be taken to bring senior executives of the company to the attention of the public through speaking engagements and other public appearances. Profiles in the newspapers and interviews on radio or television will be engineered. If the company has a significant anniversary, moves its head office or opens a new branch, this may be made the occasion for more visible celebrations than would normally be the case.

As well as general publicity, the merchant bank may approach target investors with a detailed presentation of the company in advance of the issue. This can be quite a snappy affair, accompanied by charts, slides, sometimes a company film and other visual effects. This presentation may be given in a number of financial centres and has become irreverently known as a 'road show'.

At the time of publication, depending on the regulations of the market concerned, the prospectus is likely to be fully advertised in at least one prominent newspaper. A summarised version (referred to as abridged particulars) will appear in a number of other publications. In addition, there will be editorial comment on the company and merits of the issue. It would be entirely natural if those publications in which the prospectus is advertised consider that the flotation is a newsworthy event.

The use of radio and television for publicity purposes carries some potential dangers. It may not be possible to give all relevant details in the short time available and in an interview it is difficult to stick to a carefully prepared script. Off-the-cuff remarks may lead to information being presented or implied which has not been fully checked. If such information is given by the company's management or its advisers and cannot be fully substantiated it may have to be publicly withdrawn. This causes embarrassment for the individuals concerned and may damage the chances of a successful issue.

Coverage of the flotation is encouraged by holding a pre-launch press conference with plenty of time for a question and answer session. Senior executives of the company should be available to lend authenticity to the rehearsed presentations of the advisers.

Information which is presented to the press must be extracted from the prospectus and be fully consistent with it. Care must be taken when answering questions and entering into discussions that no additional information is released. Suggestions that the prospectus figures are deliberately conservative may be tempting.

It may prove helpful for management to organise a visit to the headquarters of the company or selected facilities for key institutional investors and brokers. The brokers then have sufficient information to put together a circular on the company if they consider it appropriate. They are unlikely to take the trouble to circularise clients with a negative reaction which generates no potential business so there is a reasonable chance that their recommendations will be positive.

Under stock exchange rules, a certain percentage of an issue (say 10%) may be reserved for priority applications from the company's employees. Management may take steps to publicise the procedures for application within the company. Some directors have felt so strongly that employees should be encouraged to participate that they have made arrangements either personally or with the company's bankers for finance to be available to allow employees to take up their allocations.

Companies offering a consumer product or service may give shareholders some special concession or discount. This may serve as an incentive for investors not only to apply for shares but to remain as long-term holders. Product loyalty may be increased by having customers as shareholders. Although sometimes dismissed as gimmicky and expensive, this tactic appears to be highly effective where the product or service is a suitable one.

As the level of investor awareness of an issue grows, a general view is likely to emerge as to whether the issue will be a success or a failure. This tends to be very much a self-feeding process. If applicants feel the issue will be over-subscribed, they will be inclined to increase their level of applications in anticipation of receiving less than the number of shares they apply for. On the other hand, if an issue is thought likely to be under-subscribed, investors may hesitate to apply at all, not necessarily because they dislike the company, but in anticipation of being able to buy the shares at a cheaper price after dealings start in the market. A good share is even better if it can be purchased at a discount.

(ii) Underwriting and sub-underwriting

Shortly before or just after signature of the underwriting agreement, the lead underwriter will normally offer the major part of the issue for sub-underwriting in the market. The numbers of sub-underwriters approached will vary but may exceed 100 in a large issue.

In some markets the sub-underwriting syndicate is organised directly by the lead underwriter, which is usually an investment or merchant bank. In other markets a stockbroker will serve as the intermediary to contact the sub-underwriters. One of the functions of the stockbroker to the company is to sound out in advance of the pricing of the issue the level of investment interest in the shares. Based on this research, the stockbroker will have already identified institutions who have expressed some intention to subscribe and therefore are a logical choice for sub-underwriting.

The sub-underwriting syndicate is normally comprised of other merchant banks, stockbrokers, investment and unit trusts, fund managers and other professionals in the market. These institutions may be investors themselves or may be partly, or wholly, intermediaries, passing on portions of their allocation to their own clients. In this way the risk of the issue being unfavourably received is widely spread through the market. Even if there is a disappointing level of public response, there will through the sub-underwriting syndicate be a reasonable spread of shareholders.

The company itself and its management is not usually involved in the sub-underwriting process. Indeed, often they may be entirely unaware who the sub-underwriters are. The promoters may of course express a desire for certain institutions or major investors to be included and these wishes would be taken into account by the lead underwriter.

Sub-underwriters receive a fee based on the money amount of risk they have assumed. The level of this fee depends on market practice and the length of time of exposure, but is commonly in the region of $1\frac{1}{4}$ to $1\frac{1}{2}$%. If they pass the risk on to their own clients they would keep some portion of the fee for themselves and re-allow the remainder to their clients. The split is standardised as institutions prefer to avoid criticism which might arise if different tiers of sub-underwriting commissions were circulating in the market.

If the lead underwriter has sufficient financial muscle and is confident enough about the company, market conditions and the reception of the issue, it may commit itself to sign the underwriting contract for the issue before it has formal replies from the institutions invited to sub-underwrite. A more cautious approach is to await the reaction of sub-underwriters before entering into a formal underwriting commitment although, of course, a withdrawal at this stage would be deeply embarrassing to the institution involved, is likely to enrage the client and would be widely known in the market. The promoters obviously prefer a firm underwriting commitment before any approach is made to sub-underwriters with the inevitable publicity leak. Sometimes a lead underwriter will encourage a certain vagueness about the precise stage an issue has reached during this sensitive period.

If the issue is fully subscribed, the sub-underwriters are released from their obligation to subscribe and are paid their fee. They do not normally receive any preferential allotment of shares and, if they apply, are treated on an equal footing with all other applicants. In special circumstances, particularly where the issue is very large and may be difficult for the market to absorb, sub-underwriters may be offered the incentive of being permitted some preferential allotment.

If the issue is under-subscribed, sub-underwriters will be called upon to subscribe for the shortfall pro rata to their commitments. Arrangements will have normally been put in place by the merchant bank to ensure that any applications generated by the sub-underwriter would be counted against their commitment should they be called upon.

The system of sub-underwriting has some inherent weaknesses. In a successful issue, sub-underwriters (except as noted above) are not preferred to any other applicant. Consequently they cannot 'protect' their clients' position, that is, guarantee them any allotment. This acts as a disincentive to develop a distribution network as compared to a system where investment banks know they have a certain number of shares available to sell to their customers.

If the issue is under-subscribed, the opening market price is likely to be weak and the sub-underwriters are not going to be thanked by their clients for 'stuffing' them with over-priced shares. If sub-underwriters retain the risk on their own book, the loss on a single unsuccessful issue can wipe out the fees received from ten successful ones. Only the capital profits from obtaining a preferred position in good issues can compensate for the losses incurred in bad ones.

The sub-underwriting system described above is based on UK practice or practice in markets based on the UK model. In the US, the underwriting syndicate functions much more effectively as a selling syndicate. Applications are generated by dealers who are granted concessions on price and reallowances rather than relying on a more direct appeal to retail investors. A longer period of time is allowed for selling and a preliminary prospectus is more widely circulated. It would seem that this system has some advantages.

II ALLOCATION

(i) Procedures for application

The procedure for application should be kept as simple as possible. Even minor complications can cause confusion and make the difference between whether a wavering subscriber applies or not.

The application procedures will be set out fully in the prospectus and again on the application form. The investor states the number of shares he is applying for and attaches a cheque for the cost of the investment. The total amount will be made up of the price for the shares, plus any associated costs such as taxes and brokerage. There is normally a minimum size for applications. In markets where a board lot system of trading is used, the minimum application will be for one board lot. Applications for greater than the minimum may be in some specified multiple of the minimum in which case the application form will include a table showing the amount payable for the numbers of the shares which may be applied for.

Practice varies as to whether all cheques accompanying application forms are presented for payment. Whenever an issue is under-subscribed, all cheques will be presented. In the case of a heavy over-subscription requiring a ballot, in some markets the ballot is held before cheques are cashed so that applicants who are wholly unsuccessful are not out of funds. This procedure also greatly decreases the number of refund cheques which need to be prepared and despatched. A reserve list is required in case cheques accompanying successful applications are dishonoured.

Applications from the public must normally be made within a few days of the publication of a prospectus. After the deadline for receipt of applications, the application list actually opens and closes in a very short period, sometimes only a few minutes.

Applications must be delivered to the receiving bank. This bank designates certain of its branches to process applications, which may be sent by post. Many, however, are delivered by hand close to the deadline to give applicants the chance to assess market reaction to the issue. Applications once made will be irrevocable during the period of issue.

(ii) Allocation

If the isssue is under-subscribed no problem of allocation arises. Valid applications will be allotted in full. Application forms will be passed on to the registrar by the receiving banker for drawing up the register of members on the basis of which share certificates will be prepared and despatched to the new shareholders.

If the issue is over-subscribed, a decision will have to be made on the basis of allocation. Applications may first be screened to eliminate multiple applications, that is, one person or group putting in many small applications in the hope of receiving more favourable treatment than if they had submitted one large one.

Following this screening, the registrar will classify the applications by size, showing the number of applications and amount of money in each category. This classification will then be reviewed by the company and the merchant bank with a view to producing an equitable basis of allocation, bearing in mind any preference the company may have for the profile of its shareholder base.

It is generally thought desirable to have a wide base of shareholders and for a preference to be given to the smaller applications. On the other hand, the success of an issue may be primarily due to a relatively few very large applicants. It is important that such people, who tie up considerable amounts of their funds, should not feel unfairly treated.

It is not possible to scale down applications if the scaling down will result in an allotment of less than the minimum application set out in the prospectus. Consequently, depending on the size of any over-subscription, a ballot may have to be held (normally done by computer) to determine allocation to the smaller applicants. A person who is successful in the ballot will be allotted his application in full if it is for the minimum amount. Other applicants for the minimum size will not be allotted any shares.

Once an application reaches a size where a percentage scaling down will result in a holding of more than the minimum amount, this procedure is usually adopted.

Under listing regulations, it is often permissible to reserve 10% of the issue for employees of the company. Employee application forms will be coloured differently and are handled separately from other applications, usually by the company secretary.

(iii) Applications and allotment under the tender method

Applicants state the number of shares they wish to apply for and fill in the price per share they are prepared to pay. The company may state or have in mind the minimum amount it wishes to raise. The maximum number of shares to be issued or sold is also stated. Once the applications have been received, a price will be fixed, called the 'striking price', at which sufficient applications have been received to cover at least the amount intended to be raised.

The striking price will not necessarily be the highest price at which sufficient applications are received to cover the target amount. Factors such as number and distribution of shareholdings will also be taken into account because of the need to establish a satisfactory market in the shares.

Applicants who tender at below the striking price receive no shares and their cheques are returned to them.

All the shares will be sold or issued at the striking price. Applicants who tender at or above the striking price may be subject to a ballot or may be scaled down. In some issues, applicants at prices above the striking price are favoured. The application form may also allow applicants to apply at whatever striking price is set, leaving the actual price blank at the time of application.

If the issue is underwritten, it will be underwritten at the minimum price for the issue stated by the company.

III   START OF TRADING

Once the basis of allocation has been decided, the registrar can begin to produce the share certificates. Because of the large number of share certificates involved, this process may take some time. In some countries, trading starts immediately after the basis of allotment is announced for deferred settlement. Temporary documents of title may be issued which can be renounced to a third party when the holding is sold without the payment of transfer duties.

If trading is on the basis of immediate settlement, dealings in the securities are not permitted before all shareholders are expected to have received their share certificates. Two clear trading days are allowed for receipt after the registrar can certify that certificates have been despatched. Large shareholders may prefer to collect their share certificates direct from the registrar.

Because of the considerable gap in time between the publication of the prospectus and the commencement of official trading, there sometimes is an informal market in anticipation of official trading which is referred to as the 'grey market'. Trading in the grey market may begin even before the issue has closed with prices obtainable being widely although unofficially reported. If the grey market price is above the issue price, this may be a factor contributing to the over-subscription of an issue. This process is open to some abuse.

At the opening of official trading, turnover is likely to be very high. A number of shareholders may well have subscribed for an issue in the belief that the issue price has been set conservatively so that an immediate dealing profit will be available. This process is referred to as 'stagging'. Stags are normally very short-term holders and will seek to sell out either in the grey market (without knowing their precise allocation) or in the official market as soon as trading commences.

Large applicants who have been scaled down may be seeking to top up their allocations. Many institutions set a minimum value for their holdings in order to control the cost of monitoring them. The clash of the stags aiming to realise a profit and the institutions looking to build up their holdings can make for an active two-way market in the shares on the opening. After say the first two weeks of trading, levels of turnover will normally fall.

Opinions vary on what constitutes success of an issue in terms of trading. Promoters who have sold shares are sometimes devastated if the market price falls below the issue price, taking it as a personal insult which their financial advantage only partially soothes. Some managements feel they have done a good deal for the company (as opposed to its new shareholders) if they hit the peak with their flotation timing. A very heavy over-subscription and high stagging profits are obviously irritating to vendor shareholders. Merchant bankers (being modest fellows) are probably happiest with a modest over-subscription and a modest premium on the first day of dealing.

It is interesting to compare the register of shareholders of a company at its first annual general meeting as a public company with the initial register compiled by the registrars after the flotation. The number of shareholders sometimes halves in this period.

If the controlling shareholder of the company has been a buyer, the shareholding base of the company will have contracted although the price may benefit. It is standard procedure for the merchant bank to ask for assurances that the promoters and other major existing shareholders will not sell their holdings into the market for a period of, say, six months after the flotation. Where the original shareholders, whose base cost for the shares may be very low compared to the issue price, do unload their holdings into the market, the price of the shares may be depressed for a considerable time.

CHAPTER 9

Alternative methods of gaining a listing

The process of obtaining a listing through a full scale flotation or initial public offering is subject to the moods of the market and uncertain of success up to the moment of announcement and underwriting. Alternative methods of achieving a listing which avoid some of the uncertainties are therefore worth considering. The two main methods are:

(i) Taking control of an existing listed 'shell' company.
(ii) Spin-offs and other methods of achieving a sufficient spread of shareholders for a listing to be granted without offering shares to the public.

I SHELL COMPANIES

A listing may be obtained by means of gaining control of an already listed company, usually small and inactive. Control is secured either by purchase of a major block of existing shares or by an agreement for the issue of substantial numbers of new shares. A majority of representatives of the new shareholders is appointed to the board. The assets or business for which listing is desired are then sold into the company for cash or shares.

This procedure is sometimes referred to as 'reverse' takeover or a 'back-door' listing. The company used is referred to as a 'shell' company. Depending on circumstances, the stock exchange in question may require a suspension of trading in the shares until full details of the reorganisation proposed have been published.

(i) Advantages

The advantages of using a shell company are as follows:

(a) Size/type of assets to be injected

It has, on occasion, proved possible to obtain listings via a shell company for assets or businesses which would not meet all the criteria for a full scale flotation or which might not for the moment prove attractive to investors. For example, a business which has only been in existence for a relatively short time might not have a sufficient track record to form the basis of a standard flotation. A property development might take some years to come to fruition and until it did there would be no prospects of dividends. A special situation might be too speculative for investors in general.

There would appear to be some inconsistency in this experience. The attitude of the regulatory authorities in different jurisdictions varies and, within markets, has changed from time to time and case to case. One view might be that anything done to improve the prospects of dormant listed companies is good and should be encouraged. If the company remains inactive and is eventually delisted, the public shareholders will be penalised. A contrary view holds that such benefits are outweighed by the potential dangers of allowing a listing for businesses which might not otherwise be able to achieve this status. If a business is not suitable for listing on its own, what is the logic for allowing it to be listed via a shell? This view holds that the acid test should be what is acceptable to underwriters and the market when their own money and reputation is at stake.

(b) Control of circumstances

The procedure for a full scale flotation is relatively rigid and lengthy. Because of rules calling for audited accounts not more than a certain number of months old (often six months) and documentary and regulatory requirements, there may only be a limited number of months in a year when it is practicable for a company to go public. If a company is not able to obtain a place in the queue from the stock exchange during these months, plans for a flotation may have to be postponed.

Bunching of issues is likely as a consensus emerges on favourable conditions and timing. An issue can easily be crowded out. Market conditions which are beyond the control of the company may delay the launch. Complications in the legal or accounting work may also force a delay. Once a delay has occurred it may be several months before the procedure can be completed or even restarted. If the mood breaks, the new issue market can be virtually closed and the chance lost.

With a shell company, the timetable and feasibility is much less subject to the requirements of third parties. Once control of the shell has been obtained, the question of injection of assets can usually be decided without significant permissions needed from outside authorities although the proposals will normally be put to a vote of independent shareholders. The timetable is also more flexible. There is no deadline for accounts. No flotation price has to be set and sometimes no funds are raised. There is no highly publicised under- or over-subscription. The market will react to the proposals after they are announced and the price will adjust to them.

(c) Speed

Although the procedures for a shell company operation take several months to complete, the impact on the market is felt as soon as a full announcement of the terms of the proposals can be made, providing no suspension of trading is necessary.

Practice varies in different markets as to the length of time it may be necessary (if at all) to suspend trading in the shares of a shell company at the time proposals are announced. However, provided that intentions of the parties can be clearly and fully stated at the outset, any suspension in the trading of the shares may be a brief one. The effect is therefore that the shares of the shell company are likely to be re-rated in the market almost immediately, on the basis that the transaction will proceed.

Although the transaction may not in fact be completed for a number of months, the controlling shareholders already have a vehicle which reflects what is intended. This is not the case with a full scale flotation where trading in the shares cannot begin until the end of the whole operation. The months of planning before trading begins can be a frustrating experience and opportunities may be missed in the interim.

(d) Cost

Depending on the circumstances, it may be possible to achieve a listing at a lower cost by using a shell company. However, although many of the costs associated with the production of a full-scale prospectus will be avoided or reduced, a premium over the net asset value will normally be required by the shareholders relinquishing control, reflecting among other factors the convenience of a shell company and the amounts of costs saved. A premium at the upper end of the market range is likely to render a shell company operation more expensive than a flotation.

(ii) Disadvantages

The main disadvantages are likely to be:

(a) Difficulty of obtaining control of a suitable shell

Negotiating for control of a shell company can tax the patience of the most persistent suitor. Although there may be existing major shareholders with whom negotiations can be conducted, they are often unable or unwilling to make final decisions on the sale of a controlling stake. The fact that someone wishes to buy their dormant company may be the very factor which convinces them to keep it.

(b) History of the company

The reason that a shell company has become a shell may be traced to something that has gone badly wrong in the past. Large losses may have been incurred, the aftermath of which may include law suits, receivership or other events which serve to taint the name of the company. As accounts may have not always been efficiently kept, there is the danger of unrecorded or undisclosed liabilities and other claims and contingencies. These are all the more likely to surface once it is realised that a new party has made a financial commitment to the company or injected new assets or capital, which it will wish to preserve.

A purchaser may to some extent be able to protect himself through the terms of a sale-and-purchase contract, if one is signed. The vendors are likely to argue that, as the company is public, the basis of the transaction is the same as any market purchase of listed shares and resist further documentation, particularly giving warranties. Although this argument has some theoretical merit, a shell company is by definition a 'failed' public company and retains some of the character of a private company, despite its listing. Its major shareholders will certainly know more of its affairs than the average shareholder of a public company. Some additional documentation including limited warranties is a fair compromise.

(c) No funds are raised

An important result of a flotation once it is underwritten is the guarantee of funds to the company or its existing shareholders. No funds are raised through the simple purchase of a shell company or by the injection of assets. The raising of new equity must be tackled separately.

(d) Lack of marketability

A full scale prospectus achieves a very high degree of visibility and if successful, a large shareholding base for the newly floated group. A shell company is not likely to have many shareholders (perhaps a few hundred) and almost no marketability. If a general offer is required to all shareholders after the acquisition of control, the position may be worsened in the first instance owing to acceptances of the offer. Any improvement of marketability and widening of shareholding which is required by the authorities or desired by the new controlling shareholders must be undertaken as a separate exercise. This can prove a difficult and tedious process.

(iii) Identifying a suitable shell company

A suitable shell company will have the following characteristics:

(a) Size

The company is being sought for its listing and not for its existing business or assets. It should ideally have a low level of issued share capital and assets. If the company has a large authorised share capital, this may save capital duty at a later stage (depending on local taxation rules) when further issues of shares are made.

(b) Simplicity

Investigation will be simplified if the company has no or few subsidiaries. The assets of the group should be as straightforward as possible, for example, holdings of cash, marketable securities or investment properties. If the company or any of its subsidiaries operate active businesses, it may be preferable for them to be sold out of the group to the previous controlling shareholders as part of the transaction. The shareholders will be able to fund these purchases from the cash they receive from sale of their shares.

(c) Availability

It is highly desirable that there should be one existing controlling shareholder who can be approached as regards a possible transaction and who can give a commitment before any public announcement is needed. It is also an advantage if this controlling shareholder is a substantial party whose integrity can be relied upon and from whom, subject to negotiation, worthwhile warranties about the financial position of the shell company can be obtained.

(iv) Procedure: general offer, assets to be injected and marketing of shares

(a) General offer

Control of a public company is defined differently in different markets. If control of a company is obtained, or if a substantial block of shares is purchased and a subsequent issue of shares gives one party a controlling position, a general offer may be required to be made to the remaining shareholders. The offer, if required, will be in cash or with a cash alternative at the highest price paid for the shares. The offer documentation is likely to emphasise information on the new controlling shareholder and his intentions for the future direction of the company.

On the face of it, the offer may be attractive to minority shareholders. They may be influenced by the decision of the major shareholder to sell and follow his example. In the past, they may have been 'locked in' by lack of trading in the shares and wish to take the opportunity to dispose of their investment. In order to obtain control of the shell company, the purchaser is likely to have paid a premium over net assets. The offer price will therefore be at a premium to the net asset value.

The new shareholder must guard against possible delisting (and therefore total frustration of his plans) if the offer is overwhelmingly accepted. Careful attention to the assets to be injected and to marketing plans for the shares is therefore needed.

The existing controlling shareholder of a shell company may agree not to sell any of his shares and allow control to pass by way of injection of assets for the issue of new shares. In this case, the requirement for a general offer (if any) may be waived by the relevant authorities provided that the issue of new shares has been approved by the shareholders of the shell company in general meeting. Any shareholders with a conflict of interest must not vote.

(b) Assets to be injected

The assets to be injected should be identified by the new controlling shareholder before he acquires control of a shell. The practice of acquiring a shell and then thinking of what to put in it frequently has unfortunate results.

The suitability of the assets or business to be injected should be assessed against the desired position of the company after it has made the acquisitions. The factors to be considered include asset backing, earnings and dividend paying ability. The fundamentals of the enlarged group should be attractive to the investing public. An accountant's report will be required on any active businesses being injected and an independent professional valuation will be needed of any major assets.

If assets are purchased from the new controlling shareholders by the company at around this time, particularly for cash, care must be taken not to infringe regulations preventing the company giving assistance in the purchase of its own shares. Ideally, the party taking control should be able to demonstrate that they could finance the acquisition without any subsequent transaction with the company.

(c) Marketing of shares

Purchasing control of a shell company achieves a listing but does nothing of itself to improve marketability or raise funds. Improvements in marketability and fund-raising must be undertaken as a separate exercise by the new controlling shareholders. Methods used are as follows:

Placing through brokers. The new controlling shareholders may seek to develop their links with the broking community. They may provide background information for circulars on the new group and its prospects. It is in a broker's interest to circulate clients if the circular provokes sufficient market interest to generate commission on purchases and sales of the shares. Sometimes the new controlling shareholders will undertake to make lines of shares available to the market to ensure that the interest aroused can be satisfied in reasonable size without an immediate price rise and tightening of the market.

Rights issue. After obtaining control, a rights issue may be announced on relatively attractive terms. To facilitate a broadening of the shareholder base, the new controlling shareholder may elect not to take up some or all of his rights. Shares will be available for placing in the market or for other shareholders through excess application forms (if permitted by stock exchange rules) or alternatively they may be taken up by underwriting institutions. If the company's plans are favourably received by the market, new shareholders can be expected to buy so as to be eligible for the rights issue.

Further acquisitions. The shareholding base may be widened by acquisition of further assets or companies from third parties for new shares. If the vendors do not wish to retain the shares it may be possible to arrange a vendor placing through a merchant bank or stockbroker.

In general terms, whether these measures will succeed will be heavily dependent on the quality of assets injected into the shell company and the reputation of the new shareholders.

II SPIN-OFFS AND OTHER METHODS

A spin-off is a technique which can only be used in this context by an already listed group.

(i) Procedure

The steps involved in a spin-off are as follows:

(a) Separation

The business or assets which are to be spun-off must first be put into a separate subsidiary, if they are not already held in this form. This achieves legal separation. However, there may be substantial inter-company borrowings or other financial dealings which must be unwound or put on an arm's length basis. Care must be taken that the company is strong enough financially to survive on its own. Management must also be independent. Transitional arrangements may be needed for such matters as shared computer facilities, insurance and employee benefits.

(b) Distribution

The shares of the subsidiary are distributed pro rata to the shareholders of the holding company. The shareholders do not pay any consideration for the shares they receive but may be liable for transfer duty when they are registered in their name. The receipt of the new shares is not likely to be taxed as income in the hands of shareholders. On a subsequent sale, some tax liability is likely to be incurred.

The articles of the holding company may not always provide for this kind of distribution. If they do not, or if the relevant clauses are ambiguous, a shareholders' meeting will be needed. It may be desirable in any case.

The distribution, like any dividend, requires sufficient distributable reserves to be available. The amount of reserves needed are equal to the book value of the shares to be distributed.

If sufficient reserves are not available or if the distribution would absorb so much of the reserves that future cash dividends would be prejudiced, it is possible to proceed by way of a reduction of capital. This requires a meeting of shareholders and legal confirmation. It is facilitated if the holding company has no creditors or if the creditors can be safeguarded in some way, for example, by a bank guarantee.

It is possible to offer the shares of the subsidiary for purchase by the shareholders of the holding company by way of rights rather than distributing them. This is not a popular method, perhaps because it appears to shareholders that they are being asked to buy something which they already (if indirectly) own.

(c) Obtaining a listing

A listing for the company is applied for on the basis that there is already a sufficiently wide spread of shareholders and no separate marketing exercise is required. A company which has been spun-off from a larger group will have initially the same shareholders as that already listed group. The spread of shareholders must therefore by definition be adequate to obtain a listing for the shares of the newly spun-off company. This type of listing is said to be obtained via an 'introduction'.

Despite the fact that there may be no sales of shares undertaken, the requirements to provide information to the market must still be fulfilled and a full prospectus document produced.

One of the uncertainties of this type of operation is the price at which the shares will initially trade. As there has been no pricing or underwriting and no previous trading, the price can only be estimated by reference to the financial information published about the company and by comparison with similar listed companies. The group undertaking the spin-off will not normally hazard any indication of the likely price at which trading will commence.

(ii) Advantages

(a) Rationalisation of group structure

A spin-off may be employed by a conglomerate or other group which concludes part of its business is so different in commercial or financial needs that it should be managed and owned outside the group. Sometimes the technique is used when the financial future of a member of the group is uncertain. A spin-off may be preferable to jeopardising the whole group by supporting the company or incurring the odium of having a subsidiary go bankrupt. Rather than the business being sold to an unrelated party, which may in any case be unrealistic at a reasonable price, ownership is transferred to the shareholders of the parent company via a spin-off.

(b) Increase in market value

After the spin-off, shareholders will have two distinct investments, one being their original holding and the other a proportionate holding in the newly spun-off company. This gives them greater flexibility and may, by appealing to different investor preferences, increase the combined market value of the two holdings over the market value of the original one. The attractions of the newly spun-off company might have been buried in the complexities or problems of the parent group and so not given full weight; or the company may be in a 'glamour' sector and on its own can attract a premium rating from investors who wish to have an investment wholly in that sector. Sceptics might of course query why the company became part of the original group in the first place.

(c) Creating a listed vehicle

A spin-off is a useful technique for a group which wants to create a listed vehicle for some specific purpose, such as starting a new line of business or investing in more speculative situations than its normal activities. Instead of buying a shell company, it may create one by setting up a subsidiary, putting some simple assets (perhaps cash, property or securities) into it and then distributing the shares to its own shareholders. The new company might not otherwise be eligible for a listing or not worth the trouble of a full marketing exercise. The alternative would be to buy a shell company, but the spin-off avoids the need to identify a suitable shell and paying a premium for control.

(d) Defence tactic

If a takeover is threatened, a spin-off may be used as a defence tactic to increase the market value of a group, put a 'crown jewel' beyond the reach of an aggressor or simply muddy the waters.

(iii) Other methods

Various other methods may be adopted to achieve a sufficiently wide spread of shareholders for a company to be granted a listing via an introduction without any further marketing of shares.

(a) Private sales and private placements

Well-established businesses may have become public companies and achieved a considerable spread of shareholders through private sales and placements without actually becoming listed. Application for listing may be made subsequently.

(b) Share exchange

A new company may be incorporated to take over an existing listed company via a share exchange. This may be desirable if it is not possible to be certain of the financial position of a shell company. Rather than using the shell as the holding company, a new holding company is put on top of the shell. The advantage of this structure is that any assets or businesses to be injected can be controlled by the new holding company rather than by the shell. The financial damage of any claims can then be limited to the shell company and kept isolated from the rest of the new listed group.

Imagination is the only limit to other methods which can be utilised to give a new company the same spread of shareholders as an existing company and on this basis to apply for a listing. Shares in a new company may be offered (usually with a cash alternative) as a minor part of the overall consideration for the shares in a listed company. Liquidators have been approached in effect to transfer the listing of a company in liquidation before it is de-listed in exchange for a payment to creditors plus a distribution to the shareholders of a small percentage of the shares of the new company. This comes close to handing out shares to people in the street to achieve a sufficient number of shareholders.

CONCLUSIONS

Because of strict rules, cumbersome procedures and expense, alternatives to obtaining a listing via a full prospectus issue are eagerly sought. Parties who wish to gain a listing primarily to have a listed vehicle to further their expansion plans may feel a shell company gives them a greater degree of flexibility. Companies frustrated by market conditions or timing constraints but which otherwise would be suitable for a full listing may also use this route. Parties with access to an existing listed company can explore spin-offs and other variations as the basis for an introduction.

CHAPTER 10

Rights issues

Once a listing has been obtained, a company may raise further capital by issuing securities without such extensive documentation as is required for the initial listing. As information is published about public companies, investors are considered to be aware of it or to be able to inform themselves if they wish. Existing registered shareholders of a company will receive regular information about its fortunes, including the interim and final accounts.

As a general rule existing shareholders have a prior claim (or pre-emptive right) to distributions made by the company. This right may be based on law, the articles of the company, stock exchanges regulations or market practice. It may be argued that issues of new shares or equity-linked securities, particularly on terms which reflect a discount to the market price, affect this right and consequently should be offered first to existing shareholders. Issues made in this way are termed 'rights issues'.

In the UK, issues of new shares for cash (except in relatively rare circumstances) have by law to be made by way of rights. In countries where market practice is influenced by the UK, this requirement may be founded on stock exchange regulations rather than law and be subject to certain quite common exceptions. For example, it may be possible to issue a limited percentage of a company's issued share capital, say 10%, to outside investors for cash without participation by existing shareholders. In the US, it is common to find the articles of association of a company permit shares to be offered for cash to outside investors via public offerings.

There are two main arguments in favour of the rights issue procedure. First, it provides a shareholder with a means of ensuring that his percentage holding in the company is not diluted, at least not by issues of new shares for cash. Second, he receives the benefit of any discount in the price at which the new shares are issued compared to the prevailing market price.

Existing shareholders are a very logical source of new equity for the company as they have already made a deliberate decision to invest in it. On the other hand, it may be argued that a public offering of shares is a quicker and simpler procedure, allows more direct participation by major institutions and consequently is a more efficient way of raising further equity.

The basis and technical aspects of rights issues are considered in the following section. Pricing and underwriting are covered in 'II Market aspects: pricing, underwriting and trading' below, and timing and costs in section III.

I   BASIS AND TECHNICAL ASPECTS

(i) Size

The basis of the rights issue is expressed as the number of new shares (or other securities) a shareholder is entitled to subscribe for in relation to an existing holding. A one-for-four rights issue is an issue where a shareholder can subscribe for one new share for every four shares he currently holds. In a one-for-four issue, a holder of 1,000 shares could subscribe for 250 new shares, making his total holding 1,250 shares.

The basis of the issue is governed by the amount it is desired to raise. A standard amount to raise by way of rights would be approximately 20% of the company's current market capitalisation. Except in special circumstances, larger issues might be considered to make unreasonably heavy calls on shareholders to increase their investment. Allowing for a normal discount on pricing, to raise 20% of the market capitalisation requires an issue of, say, one-for-four or three-for-ten, that is existing shareholders will be offered three new shares at the rights issue price for every ten shares that they currently hold.

If the issue is a relatively large one a partly paid formula may be used. Shareholders may be asked to pay, for example, 50% on acceptance and the balance some months later. The final date is usually before the end of the company's financial year to prevent partly paid shares appearing in the balance sheet. During the time that they are partly paid, the shares will be separately traded. Shareholders who do not pay the second instalment on the due date are liable to forfeit their shares.

(ii) Type of security

The most common type of rights issue is a further issue of ordinary shares ranking equally in all respects with the existing ordinary shares. The equal ranking is required to avoid confusion in trading in the shares which would arise if ordinary shares with differing entitlements were in the market. In fact, it is unlikely that the stock exchange will allow dealings at all unless the new shares when fully paid rank equally with the existing shares.

The likely area of difficulty is as regards dividend payments. If the money raised by the issue is received after the end of (or part way through) a period for which a dividend is declared, it is not obvious how the new shares should rank for this dividend. To reduce this problem a rights issue may be announced simultaneously with final or interim results. In this case, only the existing shares rank for the dividend in respect of the period just ended but both existing and new shares rank for all subsequent distributions.

While new ordinary shares are the securities most frequently issued by way of rights, other kinds of securities may be employed. The security will gain a listing because it is issued by a company whose shares are themselves listed and will be held, if everything goes smoothly, by approximately the same investors as the ordinary shares. On occasion, preference shares, deferred or preferred shares and unsecured or convertible unsecured loan stock are used instead of ordinary shares. It is possible to make a rights offering of shares in another company, if a suitable block of investments is held by the company making the rights offer.

(iii) Fractions and odd lots

The use of a round number for the basis of an issue (such as three-for-ten) will reduce the number of fractions of a share which arise on a rights issue. As it is not possible to allot a fraction of a share, the fractions which would arise are aggregated and the resulting shares sold for the benefit of the comany. This involves a small penalty to the shareholder.

A further inconvenience may arise in markets where a board lot system of trading is used. Investors will tend to hold their shares in complete board lots. The basis of the rights issue will almost certainly result in an odd lot being issued to them which may have to be sold at a discount to market price. To minimise losses, the company may make special arrangements with designated stock-brokers to facilitate trading in odd lots for a limited period of time.

(iv) Documentation

The documentation for rights issues is considerably simpler than for a flotation. The reason is that shares are being offered to existing shareholders in an existing listed company. It can therefore be assumed that the potential subscribers are already reasonably well-informed about the company. The documents shareholders receive in connection with a rights issue are:

(a) An explanatory circular from the company

The main requirements are to up-date the information on the financial position of the company, including its borrowings and commitments, to say why it is making the issue and to explain clearly the terms, procedures and timetable.

(b) A provisional allotment letter

This sets out how many shares have been provisionally allotted to the shareholder to whom it is addressed. The shares are said to be provisionally allotted because allotment is subject to the payment of the rights issue price per share. The form also describes the procedures and timing for paying the amount due, for selling the rights and for splitting them, if the shareholder wants to subscribe for some and sell the remainder. The provisional allotment letter serves as the document of title for trading in the rights shares before the amount due is paid.

In most jurisdictions, rights issue documents must be filed with the relevant authorities before despatch.

(c) Excess application form

In some markets shareholders will receive a form which allows them to subscribe for additional shares over and above those which they have been provisionally allotted. If some shareholders do not take up their rights, these shares will be allotted to shareholders who make excess applications prior to any call being made on the underwriters. In some markets, this procedure is considered to penalise shareholders who do not either take up or sell their rights and is not permitted. In such markets rights not taken up are aggregated and sold in the market if possible, with the proceeds being distributed to the shareholders whose rights they were.

(v) Accounting aspects

(a) Earnings per share

In the long term, the effect on earnings per share will depend on the use to which the new capital is put. Unless the company needs new equity simply for survival, it is unlikely that the directors would invest funds raised via a rights issue in projects which were not expected ultimately to increase the earnings per share. In the short term, the company may be taking advantage of favourable market conditions and have no immediate use for the funds. At the time of the issue, the increase in earnings attributable to the issue is normally calculated by assuming the funds are used to repay debt (reducing the interest charge) or are put on deposit.

For reporting purposes, earnings per share for a year in which a rights issue has been made are based on actual earnings for that year divided by the weighted average number of shares in issue (not the actual number in issue at the year end). The weighted average takes into account two factors: first that the rights shares have only been in issue for a proportion of the year; and second that there is a 'bonus' element in the rights issue. Conceptually, the issue is split between an issue at full market price and a bonus issue. The number of shares in issue at the beginning of the year is grossed up for the purpose of the calculation by a factor equal to the market price before the issue divided by the 'ex rights' price.

(b) Assets per share

Book net assets per share will be increased or decreased depending on whether the rights price is at a premium or a discount to book net assets per share.

II   MARKET ASPECTS: PRICING, UNDERWRITING AND TRADING

(i) Pricing

Unlike setting the price for an initial flotation, rights issue pricing owes little to fundamental analysis or the rating of comparable companies. The pricing of a rights issue is based on the market price of the shares of the company at the time of the issue, adjusted for the expected effect of issuing new shares at below market price.

Shareholders must be given a reasonable incentive to buy the new shares, their alternative being to buy existing shares from the market, not in a merely comparable company but in the company itself. Consequently, the rights issue must be made at a discount to the market price. A fairly standard discount can be observed in most markets, required for the issue to be underwritten by a merchant bank or other financial institution. This institution will wish to spread its risk to sub-underwriters who will in turn look to the discount to protect them from market fluctuations. The amount of discount which is necessary to attract market support depends on the volatility of the market concerned and the length of time during which the sub-underwriters will be exposed. The standard discount varies from about 15% to about 25% on the 'ex rights' price.

An adjustment to the prevailing market price has to be made to reflect the fall which will occur (other things being equal) owing to the issue of new shares at a discount to the market price. In addition, most rights issues are made in conjunction with the final or interim announcement when a cash and possibly also a bonus share dividend will be paid. It is important therefore to include any ex dividend and ex bonus effect. In most cases, the new rights shares will not rank for the dividend or bonus issue as these relate to a financial period which has already finished. Taking all these factors into account, the apparent discount between the market price before the issue and the issue price is not as great as it appears. An example of how to calculate the ex rights price and the discount at which the issue is pitched is as follows:

A company's current share price is $5. Its financial year coincides with the calendar year. With the announcement of its result for the past year, the company declares a final dividend of 30 cents and bonus issue of one share for every ten shares held. It also announces a rights issue of three new shares for every ten shares held at a price of $3 per share. The new rights shares do not rank for the final cash dividend or the bonus issue. The bonus shares do not rank for the cash dividend or the rights issue. The method of calculation of the ex rights price and rights issue discount is as follows:

Current market price per share	$5.00
Less final dividend per share	0.30
	$4.70

Ex bonus adjustment:
10 existing shares at $4.70 per share plus 1 free
share results in a weighted average price of $4.27
($47 divided by 11)

Ex rights adjustment:

	No of shares	Market value ($)
10 existing shares ex dividend and ex bonus at $4.27 per share	10	42.70
3 new rights shares at $3.00 per share	3	9.00
	13	51.70

Weighted average price
('ex rights' price) $3.98

($51.70 divided by 13)

Rights issue discount is:
1—(rights price divided by price ex cash dividend, bonus and rights)
1—(3 ÷ 3.98)   24.6%

This compares with an 'apparent' discount of 40%, based on the $3 rights price and the $5 market price before the announcement of the results and the rights issue.

The level to which the market price 'ex rights' settles will depend not only on the terms of the rights issue but on the results and the tone of the announcement itself which accompany it. If the company appears to be doing well and a good profit and dividend forecast is made, shareholders will naturally be encouraged to invest more money. If the reasons for making the issue carry the promise of growth to come, this may meet a better response than if funds are required, for example, to reduce a high level of borrowings. The share price, far from falling as the mathematical ex rights calculations predict, may actually rise owing to the 'announcement effects' and the belief that the rights issue is a sign of an aggressive management and an exciting future.

(ii) Underwriting

Although rights issues are usually underwritten, there is no absolute requirement for underwriting. An alternative strategy is for a company to make an issue at a 'deep discount', offering shares to its shareholders at such an attractive price that the risk of an alert shareholder not taking up his rights is virtually nil. Even if some shareholders do not respond, their rights can be easily placed in the market or will be taken up by other shareholders through excess applications, where this is the market practice.

The main advantage of a deeply discounted issue is that it enables the company to avoid paying underwriting fees. A possible disadvantage is that the drop in the market price occasioned by the rights issue will be a good deal steeper than it would have been with a conventional issue.

In practice, directors seem reluctant to abandon the comfort of an underwriting. This may be in part due to the unfamiliarity of management with the procedures involved as equity issues for the average company are an infrequent occurrence. They will therefore seek the guidance of a merchant bank at an early stage and the merchant bank will have an overall financial advisory role as well as being the underwriter. Unless they have severe doubts about the attractions of the company's shares, it is likely that the merchant bank will steer the company in the direction of an underwritten issue. They may well believe this is the best way to ensure that the company achieves its objectives. In addition, the transaction will be potentially much more profitable for themselves.

Some managements are reluctant to adopt the deep discount method as they consider it results in shares being issued too cheaply. However, it may be argued that provided the existing shareholders take up the issue, the price at which the issue is made is not relevant. Any benefit in the price will go to existing shareholders pro rata to their shareholdings and therefore their interests are not harmed. Conceptually, a rights issue at a deep discount could be considered as partly a conventional rights issue and partly a bonus issue combined into one.

It may be argued that the drop in share price after a deeply discounted issue may in some way affect confidence among investors who do not understand the procedure or who are not following the company closely, but notice the share price drop. If the company has warrants or convertible securities outstanding, the adjustment of the exercise or conversion price may not necessarily fully compensate them for the dilution of their interest, depending on the market conditions at the time.

It is possible that these arguments may be too academic for a practical management's taste. A commonsense view is that the company should issue the shares as close to the market price as possible. This often leads to a spirited argument on price with management deaf to underwriters' pleas that a high discount is irrelevant to shareholders and that the issue should not be priced too finely.

In some sense a low discount must be of some value to shareholders. If the shares are not taken up, the underwriters will have to subscribe for them at a higher price. They will therefore have to contribute more money to the company, or the same money for less shares, than they would have if the discount had been higher.

(iii) Trading

In the case of an initial flotation, a leak of information is not market sensitive as no securities of the company are yet traded. A rights issue on the other hand (assuming the company is already listed) is likely to affect the price of the shares and therefore elaborate security precautions are taken. These may include the use of code names and drafting meetings held on neutral ground.

Rights issues provide that the rights themselves are tradable 'nil paid', that is before any payment of the amount due has been made. The rights will have a value reflecting the difference between the market price of the shares and the rights issue price. This enables shareholders who do not wish to subscribe for more shares to sell their rights and thus recoup any loss in value after the shares are traded ex rights. One possible market strategy is for a shareholder to sell sufficient of his rights to enable him to subscribe for the remainder.

Dealings in the market in the rights 'nil paid' are likely to be very active owing to adjustments of shareholders' desired holdings and to the activities of speculators who may be attracted by the geared nature of the investment. The price of the rights will vary much more in percentage terms than the price of the underlying shares. A major indicator of whether or not an issue will be fully subscribed is the level of activity in trading in the rights and whether a reasonable premium exists up to the close of trading.

It is important to find out the attitude of any substantial shareholder in advance. A major shareholder not taking up his rights may sour the whole issue unless a good reason can be given. One possible reason is to allow scope to widen the spread of shareholders.

If a major shareholder sells his rights continually in the market, this is likely to depress the price of the 'nil paid' rights and jeopardise the success of the issue. It is preferable for the merchant bank or stockbroker in charge of the issue arrangements to be instructed to place the shareholder's rights in an organised way as soon as possible after trading commences.

III   TIMING AND COSTS

(i) Overall factors

The number of rights issues made is closely correlated to the level and turnover of the stock market. Directors prefer to make issues when the market price of the company's shares is high, perhaps considering that this is in some sense 'cheap money' for the company. Shareholders on their part may be more inclined to support their company with fresh capital when the share price has been going up. They may therefore be happy to subscribe for new shares even at prices which are historically high.

It is a common experience that funds may not necessarily be required by a company at a time which coincides with the peak of the market. However, a management may be well-advised to adopt a long-term view of the amount of new equity which is desirable and take advantage of periods of market strength to raise funds smoothly. If a company delays until it has an urgent requirement for new equity, there is a danger that the market mood may have changed. There may be a reluctance on investors' part to provide funds when they are really needed as the need may be perceived as a sign of weakness. The market prefers to feel it is backing winners, even when they have no real need of additional capital, than nursing lame ducks back to health.

(ii) Timetable

The detailed timing of a rights issue will vary with local market procedures. It is usual to give shareholders a fairly long period (say 3 weeks) to decide whether to subscribe for the new shares and to make their own funding arrangements, if necessary. This period also allows a reasonable opportunity for trading in the market.

The starting point for an issue is to establish the shareholders who are entitled to receive it. This involves a record date being announced. Sufficient time should be allowed for shareholders who have not held their shares in registered form to make the necessary arrangements to receive the benefit of the issue.

If there is insufficient authorised share capital to allow for the rights issue, an extraordinary general meeting of the company will be required to agree to an increase. Depending on the articles of association of the company, the period of notice required for the meeting may cause some delay to the timetable. It is important that no trading in the rights shares takes place before the meeting. If for some reason the increase in authorised share capital was turned down, the issue could not proceed and any dealings would have been on a false basis.

A sample rights issue timetable for which an increase in authorised share capital is required is set out below. The precise timing will vary by as much as three weeks depending on the practice in different markets.

Note. I means 'Impact Day', the first day on which the detailed terms of the issue are made known to the market and the press.

Date (days)

I − 30	(i)	Decide in principle to proceed and whether profit forecast will be made.
	(ii)	Instruct merchant bank, accountants and lawyers.
	(iii)	Begin drafting rights issue documents.
	(iv)	Record date for indebtedness.
By I − 10	(i)	Financial position of company reviewed and basis of issue decided.
	(ii)	Printed proof of rights issue documents prepared, circulated and discussed.
	(iii)	Record date for issue (depending on local dealing rules).
I − 7		Further proofs and drafting meetings as required.
I	(i)	Board meeting to approve issue. Underwriting agreement signed.
	(ii)	Press announcement released.
	(iii)	Sub-underwriting completed.
	(iv)	Print order given.
I + 1		Posting of explanatory circular with notice of meeting.
I + 15		Extraordinary general meeting held.
I + 16		Posting of provisional allotment letter and, where appropriate, form of application for excess shares.
I + 19		Dealings in rights shares (nil paid) commence.
I + 37		Last day for acceptance and payment for rights shares.
I + 38		Underwriters and sub-underwriters informed of their liability (if any).
I + 50		New share certificates despatched.

The dealing arrangements for the rights shares nil paid and fully paid will vary with local market practice as regards dealing and settlement and whether renounceable temporary documents of title are used.

(iii) Costs

The costs of a rights issue are substantially less than for a new flotation owing to the lesser degree of investigation and documentation required and the simpler procedures.

The major expense is for underwriting, assuming the issue is made at a conventional discount. Most markets have fairly standard rates for underwriting which seem resistant to competitive pressures. The rates range from about 2% to about 4% of the amount raised by the issue. They may be increased if an unfamiliar or previously unlisted security is used or if the timetable of the issue involves a longer exposure than standard, for example because of the need to hold an extraordinary general meeting. An extra two weeks' exposure may cost the company an additional fee of $\frac{1}{4}$%.

As new securities are being issued, it is likely that there will be capital duty at the rates prevailing in the relevant market.

The other main expenses will be for accounting and legal work, based principally on time spent. The charges of the registrars and receiving bankers and for the printing and distribution of the documents will depend on variable factors such as the number of shareholders.

The average costs of rights issues depend on size. Some costs (principally professional fees) are largely fixed but the majority are variable. In addition, smaller issues may be perceived as more risky and consequently the percentage underwriting charge may be increased. On average the cost may range from a minimum of $3\frac{1}{2}$% of the funds raised for a large issue by a well-known company to about 7% of the funds raised or more for a speculative, rarely traded concern.

CONCLUSIONS

Rights issues have been a reliable source of new equity funds for already listed companies. Shareholders who have already decided to buy shares in a company are likely to agree to increase their investment by a reasonable amount when offered further shares at a discount to the market price. Management may, however, be well advised to approach shareholders when the company is doing well rather than waiting until funds are urgently needed.

Rights issues require a circular to shareholders to inform them of the terms of the issue and update them about the affairs of the company. They also allow a fairly long (say three weeks) gestation period for shareholders to trade in their rights and decide whether to invest. For these reasons, offering new shares direct to institutions and other investors may be a more streamlined way of raising new equity. Methods of issuing new equity which do not involve existing shareholders are discussed in the next chapter.

CHAPTER 11

Placings and other issues of shares and equity-linked securities

Shares and other equity-linked securities of a company are likely to be issued to third parties (that is investors who are not existing shareholders) in two types of situations. The first one, referred to as a placing or public offering, involves the issue of shares for cash. As discussed in the previous chapter, restrictions may exist on a company's ability to issue new shares for cash in this way. In countries such as the US, it is common to seek shareholders' permission to take advantage of the public offering method.

Placings are also used in the situation where a holder of a large block of shares wishes to reduce or dispose of his holding in one transaction rather than by a series of sales in the market. A single transaction allows him to be certain of the amount realised. From the point of view of the company and the other shareholders, it is desirable to avoid a constant 'tap' of shares on to the market which is likely to depress the share price.

There are no problems of control and dilution involved in the issue of non-equity linked securities such as bonds. This type of issue is primarily carried out via the placing method.

In the second section of this chapter various reasons for issuing new shares besides raising cash are discussed. Shares may be issued to existing shareholders by means of a bonus or capitalisation issue or be used as an alternative to the payment of cash dividends. They may also be issued as the result of the exercise of options. A common reason to grant options over new shares is to establish an employee incentive scheme. Convertible securities involve the granting of an option, as do warrants, frequently attached as a 'sweetener' to a fixed income security.

Equity or equity-linked securities may also be issued in exchange for other shares, to acquire assets or to extinguish liabilities. Such issues may be followed by a placing for cash by the parties who receive the new securities.

I PLACINGS FOR CASH

(i) Procedures

When a placing is used, existing shareholders are not given the opportunity to purchase the securities but instead the shares are sold to third parties. Placings are normally organised by merchant banks or stockbrokers, or the two acting in combination. Depending on the size of the placing, a widespread syndicate of 'placees' may be formed with institutions ranked by the size of their participation.

Placings may be made with the investment funds of merchant banks or other venture capitalists at an early stage in a company's development, before the shares are actively traded or a listing is obtained. This type of transaction is referred to as a private placement, meaning that there will be no attempt at this stage to interest the general public in the shares. The investors will be principally major clients of the merchant bank or other institution organising the private placement. Companies which accept an injection of capital from such sources should recognise that they will come under considerable pressure from their new shareholders to go public as soon as practicable. Such investors look to achieve a degree of marketability for their investment within, say, three to five years.

The directors and management of the company whose securities are being placed may be involved to a greater or lesser degree. If an existing block is being placed it is possible that this will be carried out without the co-operation or even the knowledge of the company concerned. If the vendor has kept the company informed the company may arrange to release some statement of current trading or prospects in support of the placing. Where the company is raising new capital, a placing letter will normally be prepared providing up-to-date financial information and explaining the background to the placing. If a stockbroker is helping to organise the placing, it may have available a recently prepared circular on the company which can be used to encourage investor interest.

A placing or a series of placings can serve to establish a wide enough spread of shareholders to apply for a listing via an introduction. A placing can also be used as the method of marketing the shares at the time when a company goes public. In some countries, stock exchange authorities frown on this practice, as it favours selected clients of the underwriters and stockbrokers. Public investors may not have a genuine opportunity to get in 'at the ground floor'.

(ii) Timing

Because of the sophistication of the participants (normally institutions and other major investors), a placing can be carried out very quickly. It may be completed within one trading day or even a few hours. This assumes that some preparatory sounding out will have been done by the organisers of the placing. Such preparations can be carried out without committing the company to the placing or making any public announcement.

One of the advantages of a placing is that a company and its advisers are not locked into a particular timetable. Timing can be adjusted to correspond to the state of the market. The company and its advisers can await favourable conditions to launch the operation.

Placings are most common in periods of strong institutional demand for securities. These tend to coincide with periods of high market activity overall. In such conditions, the ability to pick up a substantial block of securities at a fixed price may be valuable to institutions. The alternative is to carry out a programme of market purchases over a short period of time which may have the effect of pushing up the price against the purchaser.

(iii) Pricing and market reaction

If the securities to be placed are already listed, pricing is set at a discount to the prevailing market price on the assumption that the placees would have the alternative of buying the shares in the open market. In normal circumstances, a discount of around 10% to the market price will be sufficient. Because of the short time taken to complete a placing, the discount is not required to cushion a long period of exposure as in the case of a rights issue, where shareholders may be given three weeks to make up their minds. In circumstances where there is a strong institutional demand for the shares, the placing price may be very near the market price. In difficult conditions, a higher discount may have to be offered.

The advisers handling the placing will also take into account the level of market trading in the shares and the recent price movements. A sharp rise in the price of the securities to be placed shortly before the placing operation may be viewed with some scepticism.

Placings can give rise to some confusion in the market. Companies and their advisers may be reluctant to announce a placing until it has been successfully completed in case any problems are encountered and the placing is called off. This may have the effect that rumours arise concerning a market operation being underway about which clarification from the company is delayed. In addition, some participants in the market will have been offered shares and will be aware of the situation whereas others will not. In the case of a placing of existing shares, there may not be an obligation to make an announcement at all which can lead to a prolonged period of doubt as to what has actually happened. Management of companies in which a placing is occurring with their knowledge should keep in mind the confusion which may arise and try to minimise it to the extent possible.

(iv) Costs

The costs for a placing are in general lower than for a rights issue, particularly if no substantial documentation is required. As a placing involves considerably fewer numbers of investors than a rights issue, the variable costs at least will be substantially less.

The placing may be underwritten, in which case normal underwriting fees will apply. Alternatively, the placing may be handled on a best efforts basis in which case a brokerage or placing fee of say around 1–2% of the value of the securities would be charged.

The discount to the market price at which a placing is made will be considerably less than for a comparable rights issue, say 10% against 25%. However, whether this in some sense saves money for the company (in the case where new capital is being raised) is arguable. In a rights issue the benefit of the discount goes to the existing owners of the company whereas in a placing this benefit, although smaller, goes to third parties.

(v) Placings of debt securities

Issues of bonds and unsecured loan stocks are an important source of funds to the corporate sector. The depth of this market varies widely from country to country.

As a general rule, the more institutionalised the market is, the more feasible significant issues of corporate debt become. Institutions such as insurance companies and pension funds have long-term liabilities to their clients which may be matched by the long-term fixed obligations of a corporation when it issues debt. Most individuals have no such quantifiable long-term requirements against which the inflows from debt securities can be conveniently matched.

The corporate debt market becomes highly active at periods when corporate treasurers perceive long-term interest rates to be cyclically low. The pricing of debt securities is chiefly determined by the running yield and yield to maturity of comparable issues. The rights of the bond holders will be set out in a formal document and summarised in an information memorandum available to the market.

II   REASONS FOR ISSUING NEW SHARES BESIDES RAISING CASH

(i) Bonus issues and share dividends

(a) Bonus issue

A bonus (or capitalisation) issue does not involve any payment by shareholders. The issue is effected by transferring amounts from share premium account and/or reserves and applying them in paying up further issued share capital. As with a rights issue, the size of a bonus issue is expressed in relation to an existing shareholding (for example one-for-ten). In theory, the bonus issue should make no difference at all to the market value of an investor's holding. If for example, the price prior to a one-for-ten bonus is $1 per share, ex bonus it should adjust to $0.91 so that the new total holding of 11 shares is identical in market value to the previous holding of 10 shares.

There are a number of reasons why bonus issues have a degree of popularity. Some directors feel that issued share capital should be kept roughly in line with net worth. As retained profits and other reserves grow a proportion is capitalised via bonus issues. This has the effect that they cannot be paid out as cash dividends. In some markets, shareholders pay at least as much attention to the level of bonus issue as to cash dividends and are pleased to see the number of shares they hold increase.

Despite the fact that the value of shareholders' investments should be unchanged after the issue, it appears that in some markets there may not always be a full adjustment. This may be partly due to investors' fondness for bonus issues. However, it seems likely that the announcement of a bonus issue is taken as the directors' expression of confidence in satisfactory future growth. This impression will be strengthened if the announcement of a bonus is accompanied by a statement that the directors expect that cash dividends on the enlarged share capital can be maintained at the same per share figure. In such circumstances, experience suggests that share prices may recover towards the 'cum bonus' price quite rapidly.

(b) Share dividend

A company may offer its shareholders new shares as an alternative to receiving a cash dividend. The new shares will be paid up from the amount of cash dividend the shareholder foregoes. The articles of association of a company do not always permit shares to be issued in this way. A change to the articles may be required therefore if a company wishes to introduce such a scheme.

If a company operates a share dividend scheme, shareholders are allowed to choose whether to receive their dividend in the form of new shares or in cash. The price at which the new shares are issued is normally based on the average market price for a period ending a few days before the shareholder must make his decision.

Companies have found share dividend schemes a useful way of conserving cash while maintaining an attractive level of dividend. For some shareholders, there may be tax advantages in receiving their dividend by way of shares, which may not be counted as income until sold, rather than in cash. Major shareholders may find such an arrangement a convenient way of keeping their holdings topped up. In a rising market, shareholders will make a gain by taking shares rather than the fixed cash amount.

(ii) Options, convertibles and warrants

(a) Options

A company may grant options over unissued shares as part of a share incentive scheme for employees. Such a scheme may well be limited to the more senior employees who are considered to have some influence on the results of the company. The options are usually issued at a fixed price corresponding to the market price at the time the options are granted. The scheme should be approved by shareholders and is normally limited to a relatively small (say under 10%) percentage of the current issued share capital of the company.

(b) Convertible securities

Convertibles may be issued either when a company wishes to issue equity but can only do so by giving new investors a preferred position or when it would prefer to issue debt but wishes to reduce the fixed servicing costs. Experience suggests that on balance most convertible securities are eventually converted into equity so that the company should probably regard itself as making a deferred equity issue.

Conversion is likely to take place not necessarily when the market price of the shares exceeds the conversion price but when the income from the shares which would be received on conversion exceeds the fixed income from holding the convertible. The company can therefore exercise some degree of influence on the time investors will convert.

The terms of a convertible security will usually contain a clause enabling the company to force holders to convert in certain circumstances. The most common of these are after a substantial percentage (say 75%) of the convertible holders have converted their stock or if the market price of the underlying security exceeds the conversion price by a given margin for a certain length of time.

(c) Warrants

An issue of loan stock or bonds with warrants is the equivalent of an issue of convertible stock with the convertible 'package' split into two separate elements. Investors who prefer a fixed income component and those to whom the much more speculative nature of the warrant appeals can tailor their investments accordingly. Warrants are thus a useful device for 'sweetening' an issue at no immediate expense to the company. Their issue is, in effect, off-balance sheet as there will be no sign on the face of the accounts that warrants exist. A reference will, however, be contained in the notes and by showing an earnings per share figure on a 'fully diluted' basis.

As warrants are often long-dated, the threat of dilution may overhang the share price for a period of years. In some countries the stock exchanges consider that for this reason the amount of warrants outstanding should be kept fairly small in relation to the total issued share capital.

(iii) Takeovers and acquisitions of assets

The company may issue its shares in exchange for shares of other companies. This may be part of the takeover of full control of another company. It is also possible to issue new shares in exchange for assets, for example to acquire a business or a property.

There are a number of advantages in using shares as all or part of the consideration for acquisitions. As the company does not have to pay out cash, larger acquisitions can be tackled or smaller ones financed in a more flexible way. The vendor may also consider that he is not entirely disposing of his interest and may hope for some capital appreciation in the shares he receives rather than concentrating on the money amount he obtains. The personal tax position of vendors may also be improved. The acquiror must, however, guard against a weakening of control in the enlarged group. He must also bear in mind the effect of dilution on existing shareholders if a premium price is being paid for the acquisition.

On occasions, companies may agree to issue shares to each other in such a way that a cross-holding is created. The reasons for this may be to consolidate control or to raise capital in due course via a subsequent sale to third parties of the shares received.

At times of financial stress, it may be possible for a company to use an issue of shares to cancel a liability. This, however, requires that the creditor in question is prepared to see the ranking of his claim decrease in return for the chance of future growth by becoming a shareholder. The effect on the balance sheet of cancelling debt in exchange for equity can be very dramatic as liabilities decrease at the same time as net worth increases. For this reason, a cancellation of debt in return for new preference or ordinary shares is a common feature in difficult corporate debt restructurings.

While it may suit the company to pay for shares or assets by means of a new issue of its own securities, it may not necessarily be convenient or acceptable to the vendors to retain the shares which they receive. In these circumstances, a vendor placing may be arranged as an integral part of the transaction. In a vendor placing, the shares issued to the vendors of the assets are immediately placed on to third parties who have been lined up by the company or its financial advisers in advance. The third parties will normally be institutions who are already shareholders of the company or who through existing contacts with stockbrokers or merchant banks are known to be receptive to taking a significant investment. As is the case with a normal placing, timing can be very rapid. A vendor placing would normally be underwritten or carried out on a fully committed basis since it is unlikely that the vendors will accept any other terms in such circumstances.

Part 3

Takeovers, mergers and disposals

Introduction

Part 3 of this book deals with takeovers, mergers and disposals. This Introduction is intended to explain some basic terms and concepts and to present an overview of the topics covered in the individual chapters.

Why takeovers are made (see ch 12 below)

The reasons why takeovers are made are examined under three headings. The first is commercial and deals with such aspects as increase in market share, growth, synergy, security of supply and diversification. Acquisition of a business in the same field (a 'horizontal' acquisition) will increase the combined group's market share. This type of acquisition is the most easily justified in terms of 'fit' but may fall foul of anti-monopoly legislation. Growth can be achieved economically and swiftly by acquisition but should not become an end in itself.

Synergy is the theory that two plus two can equal more than four. This proposition is a major argument that merger and acquisition activity benefits the economy as a whole. An acquisition primarily undertaken to secure supplies or sales is called 'vertical'. Particularly in a process industry, it is convenient to bring all the stages of operation under the control of one group but it can complicate business relationships.

Diversification, or spreading the risk, can be justified on a commonsense level – do not keep all your eggs in one basket. It is also the subject of increasingly sophisticated analysis. Acquisitions which fall into this category are called 'conglomerate' to distinguish them from horizontal or vertical integration.

The second heading is financial. An 'asset stripper' will concentrate on obtaining a discount to a company's net asset value, intending to recoup the purchase price from the sale of assets. Another financial objective may be to increase earnings per share following the acquisition. If an acquiror buys a business less highly rated on the stock exchange than their own by way of a share exchange, earnings per share of the enlarged group will rise. This strategy requires ever more and bigger acquisitions to sustain it. It also depends on the acquiror's price earnings ratio not being averaged down following the acquisitions. The opposite effect, when earnings per share declines as a result of a transaction, is called 'dilution'.

An acquiror may be able to reduce the gearing of the combined group by buying a cash rich company. A company with highly rated paper will attempt to buy assets for shares, increasing its asset backing per share and creating a platform for a further stage of growth.

Personal ambition is a major factor in making acquisitions. Personal commitment may be necessary to push a deal through at sticky moments. Some acquisitions are 'customised', to obtain a management team, a stock exchange listing, access to tax losses or important operating licences.

Acquisition search: developing criteria, generating opportunities and preliminary screening (see ch 13 below)

The multiplicity of motives for acquisitions spills over into the planning process, complicating the development of criteria. Once the criteria have been set, the company needs to ensure that it makes effective use of all available market channels to generate opportunities. This process often throws up a bewildering range of half-formed ideas. Discipline is required in preliminary screening if analysts are not to be overwhelmed by the wealth of possibilities.

Criteria can be looked at under the same general headings as objectives, that is commercial, financial and customised. In addition, size and the availability of finance will be critical. Commercial criteria include type of industry and the attitude of the management and workforce. Financial criteria can be set in beguilingly precise numbers but a degree of flexibility is essential. Whether paper is acceptable may be relevant. If an acquisition is for a specific purpose, the criteria more or less set themselves. An upper size limit should be set – few companies can take over General Motors. Below a certain size on the other hand, an acquisition may just not be worth the effort. Size can be judged by reference to various factors, including price, turnover, capital which will be tied up and profitability. Finance will be more readily available for asset rich companies or those with a highly predictable cash flow.

Opportunities are generated internally and externally. Executives working in an industry will know more about it than outside professionals. Constructive use of this pool of knowledge should be encouraged. In addition, a company may establish its own merger and acquisition unit. External sources include advertising and the use of intermediaries. Merger brokers operate aggressively in the field. Experienced merchant bankers see a constant flow of opportunities across their desks. A merchant bank should be able to offer a package of finance to back its proposals. A close relationship with a merchant bank or other acquisition professionals has proved an ingredient in the growth of many business empires.

Preliminary screening boils down to a more rigorous and practical application of criteria to the range of opportunities which have been generated. A 'nose' for a realistic proposal can save significant waste of time. Screening should take into account the overall impact of an acquisition on the acquiror's business. The factors include increased official scrutiny which may result, the after-shock of a contested battle and the extent of the risk of the acquisition to the organisation as a whole.

Acquisition analysis: collecting and evaluating information (see ch 14)

A certain amount of information may be obtained from public sources on an anonymous basis. However, the information required by regulations to be available for public inspection is limited in scope and may be considerably out of date.

Except where a bid is expected to be contested, the target company itself will in due course be approached for information. This approach should be handled with kid gloves. Information requested should be kept to a reasonable minimum to avoid antagonising the vendors. This also prevents the acquiror's analysts being overwhelmed by figures. The information requested should be tailored to the key characteristics of the business being examined. The really critical points are often quite small in number. A battery of questions directed at a particular aspect is likely to tip the acquiror's negotiating hand. Sensitive topics may be left to be covered by a warranty in the sale and purchase agreement. If they are made the subject of probing questions, the vendor may feel he is before an inquisition.

A sample questionnaire is included in ch 14 below. When requesting any of the items the acquiror should ask himself whether the information would make any difference to his decision to proceed or not.

If the information confirms that the acquisition is of interest in principle, the next step is to set a price range and decide on the type of consideration. Value in the context of an acquisition is not absolute and will be influenced by the acquiror's objectives. An asset stripper will need a significant discount to open market value on a willing buyer, willing seller basis in order to cater for a substantial programme of rapid sales. Vendors may be expected to sell at a cyclical peak in earnings so that an apparently reasonable price earnings ratio may prove illusory. On the other hand, a purchaser may increase the estimate of the target company's earnings to take into account savings from rationalisation after the merger.

In the case of conglomerates, it is likely that adding together valuations of each constituent business will produce a higher figure than one overall valuation based on net assets or earnings. This is legitimate provided that each business can stand on its own and could conceivably be sold as a separate unit.

The share price of a listed company is only an approximate guide to the price which may be needed for a successful acquisition. Market price relates to smallish transactions and so contains no premium for control. To overcome investor inertia, some premium, say at least 20%, must be offered unless the market price has some 'froth' in it. Shareholders may be reluctant to sell in any event at a price less than they originally paid for the shares.

It is useful to set an upper price limit for an acquisition before negotiations begin. Although some flexibility is desirable to cater for fresh information becoming available as it often does during a bid, the dangers of being carried away 'in hot pursuit' are acute.

Acquisition analysis is usually based on long-term expected results. An acquisition which appears attractive on this basis may nevertheless not have an immediate beneficial effect on the published accounts of the acquiror. The market, on the other hand, tends to judge a management over the short term. If earnings per share are diluted following an acquisition, the market may not necessarily appreciate the longer-term benefits in view.

A package of different forms of payment, particularly the use of convertible securities, may help to alleviate this problem. An example of how this works in practice is given.

Other factors to be taken into consideration include goodwill, pre-acquisition profits and the effect of the acquisition on the balance sheet and gearing of the enlarged group. Borrowing restrictions and covenants based on other financial ratios will need checking.

Structure of offer and terms of payment (see ch 15 below)

The task of gaining control can be approached from various different angles. It may prove advantageous to purchase a major asset directly rather than the company which owns it. If a company is purchased, its worth, particularly in the case of a private company, may lie more in shareholder loans than in share capital. It is important to ensure that the entire shareholders' funds are purchased. Care is needed if shareholder loans have not borne interest and the price is calculated on earnings.

If a company has financial problems, effective control may be acquired by purchasing bank or other third party loans without the need to acquire shares. It may be possible to negotiate conversion rights to be attached to such loans. If the equity does subsequently prove of value, the acquiror's interests are protected. Control may also be obtained by subscribing new shares, thus strengthening the capital base of the company, rather than the purchase of existing shares. This route may avoid the need for a general offer in countries where an offer might otherwise be triggered under a takeover code.

If a purchaser decides to take the route of buying shares in a company, he should still consider whether he needs to buy the entire share capital. The advantage of having 100% control is principally that it eliminates any need to provide information to outside shareholders and protect their interests. If he controls 100%, the acquiror has unfettered access to the target company's assets and cash flow. On the other hand, the funds required are obviously decreased if less than 100% is purchased. A listing for the shares may be continued. The loyalty of management, employees and customers may be more easily retained. Partial control usually involves a holding of over 50% but in the case of a widely-held company a level as low as 20% may confer control. At the lower levels, an option to buy further shares becomes particularly valuable.

There are a number of ways of paying for an acquisition. Cash has the great merit of simplicity. It can be raised from existing surplus resources of the company supplemented by bank borrowings. Cash resources may be topped up by issues of securities particularly 'junk' bonds. Junk bonds have been popular in the case of leveraged buy-outs where a group of investors is put together for the purposes of acquiring a company. Where management is involved this type of operation is commonly called a management buy-out. Tax implications and presentational aspects may also affect the decision as to whether to fund a bid in cash. In some jurisdictions, legal problems may arise if it could be argued that a company is giving assistance in the purchase of its own shares.

Payment may be made on a deferred basis rather than for immediate settlement. A purchaser may need assistance in completing the transaction in the form of vendor finance. Deferred payment may also serve as a disguised reduction in price where the nominal amount paid is a sensitive issue. A deferred payment structure allows for a period of investigation before all payments are handed over. It also allows for adjustments in price to be made where the total amount payable is related to future performance.

Securities of the acquiror may be offered as consideration. Ordinary shares of the acquiror are the most straightforward choice, but may have to be underwritten. Specific requirements of the acquiror or the vendor may result in a new class of shares being issued with special rights to meet the situation, for example, high dividend income or a dividend linked to the results of the business being acquired. Debt securities can also be useful where additional income is required. These are most appropriate where the acquisition is asset rich. The debt may be made convertible into ordinary shares. Warrants may be included in the package as a sweetener.

Approach, negotiations and opening the attack (see ch 16 below)

The time when analysis stops and the initial approach is made is a critical phase. A clumsy approach may do irretrievable damage. It is well worth careful thought being devoted to identifying the right tactics. There may be some parties connected with the target company who are more sympathetic than others. An acquiror should be alert to a possible conflict of interest between shareholders who may simply be interested in the highest offer and management who are concerned for their jobs and power base. The use of an intermediary whose interest lies in reconciling the objectives of buyer and seller may be productive. With a public company, special efforts to maintain secrecy will be required. Pressure may mount from the authorities for an announcement before the parties are ready.

Negotiations depend on the skill of the participants to a large degree. Knowledge of the party on the opposite side of the table is fundamental. A front line negotiator, however experienced, must rely on a support team.

A recommendation of the terms of the offer by the target company's board is probably the single most critical factor for success. It can be regarded as having a value of its own. To obtain a recommendation it may be necessary to keep something in reserve so that the vendors feel they have won some concessions in return.

In the heat of negotiation, it is difficult to resist paying too much to clinch a deal. Limits set beforehand are useful safeguards. A seller on the other hand may play the reluctant bride and try to create a sense of rivalry even where no actual rivals exist. He may for tactical reasons appear willing to negotiate whether or not he is in fact prepared to do so. The acquiror must assess whether the negotiations are progressing or are simply a play for time.

In the case of a private company, there is little alternative to continuing the negotiations or abandoning the transaction. Where a public company is being considered, the option exists to appeal to shareholders over the heads of the existing directors and management. As in any frontal assault, this course of action requires a certain amount of courage. The main weapon is price. There will no doubt be a price which is attractive even to loyal shareholders. The timing should be designed to catch the target at a moment of weakness for itself and at a period when the bidder can make positive comments about his own business. Hopefully, potential rivals may be pre-occupied with other projects.

Purchases in the market in advance of the bid and during it will help to create a springboard. Rapid purchase of an effective controlling stake is known as a 'dawn raid'. The acquiror must take care not to fall foul of local rules governing accumulation of such stakes and of bidding up the target company's share price against itself.

The offer document addressed to the target shareholders will be used as a platform for criticising the target company and emphasising the attractions of the offer and trumpeting the virtues of the offeror. The components of the offer should be tailored to suit the preferences of the shareholders of the target company as far as they can be ascertained.

The art of self-defence (see ch 17 below)

There are three types of counter measure which may be taken against an unwanted bid. The first, good housekeeping, covers areas which a competent management would attend to in any case. Second, there are measures which have a commercial basis but whose primary purpose is to repel an unexpected bid. Third, there are short-term expedients adopted to counter a specific hostile bid after it has been announced.

Good housekeeping is a continuous process. It includes monitoring the company's share price and trying to keep it in line with the underlying value of the company. The single most effective deterrent against an unwanted bid is a share price which fairly reflects the profit potential and asset backing of the company. As the company's shareholders will be the ultimate arbiters in a takeover battle it is important for management to know who they are, communicate with them and monitor significant changes. All announcements should be reviewed carefully with a view to their public relations impact. The directors should avoid giving any 'hostages to fortune' in the statements they release. Management should from time to time put themselves in the shoes of an aggressor and consider what steps he might take to rationalise the company after an acquisition. Incumbent management should not wait to initiate appropriate action as they know the company's potential better than any outside party.

Measures adopted primarily to repel an expected bid take some time and preparation to put in place. Changes to the procedures for holding meetings or electing directors can make it more difficult for an aggressor to succeed in taking control. Obstacles can be built into the financial structure. Defensive shareholdings can be created by voting pacts, placing blocks in friendly hands or by cross-holdings. Valuable assets can be sold or placed out of the reach of an aggressor. Acquisitions can be made of businesses which are not attractive to a bidder or which make the group too large for him to swallow. The bidder can be bought off through greenmail. A threatened company may open negotiations with a more congenial partner.

After an offer is announced, it can be opposed in various ways. New information can be released to demonstrate for example that the existing management is doing a good job and that the price offered is too cheap. Such information frequently involves a profit and dividend forecast and a revaluation of assets. The terms of the bid can be attacked and so can the bidder. The bid can be criticised for the level and type of consideration. It can be claimed to be opportunist since this is likely in some sense to be true. The motives of the bidder can be impugned.

Various other spoiling tactics can be employed. They are available equally whether the bid is good or bad. The laws and market regulations concerning takeovers can be invoked, with claims of violations of procedures and inadequate disclosure. Anti-monopoly rules may be brought into play and time limits skilfully manipulated.

In the closing stages of a bid, perhaps the most critical factor is whether the market price is at a premium to the offer. A programme of share purchases by friends of the target company may be helpful. Extensive advertising and public relations exercises may be mounted through the media. Stockbrokers and other professionals may be enlisted to lobby major shareholders. Appeals to shareholder and customer loyalty, and even patriotism, may be made. As a last resort, a management in distress may seek a 'white knight' to rescue it from the clutches of the hostile bidder.

Formal procedures and techniques (see ch 18 below)

An acquisition of a private company can only be carried through by negotiation with directors or major shareholders. The articles of association of private companies usually contain pre-emption rights and restrictions on the transfer of shares. Even a willing seller (and the intended purchaser) must take these into account if the transaction relates to less than 100% of the company.

The transaction will be documented by a sale and purchase agreement. This is made up of a number of fairly standard sections. One common area of difficulty is the extent of the warranties about the company being sold which a seller will be expected to give to the purchaser.

A business which has encountered financial difficulty may come under the control of a receiver or liquidator. In order to separate a continuing business from the problems of the past, a new subsidiary may be set up and the relevant assets 'hived down'. This will allow the purchaser to buy a business which starts with a clean sheet. It is unlikely that a receiver or liquidator will give warranties.

Management buy-outs have become a major area of acquisition activity. Originally a division or small subsidiary of a larger group which was under-performing would be the most likely target. More recently, the capital available for such operations has increased considerably and major public groups have been bought out. A typical transaction will have a multi-tiered financial structure with high gearing inevitable if the management group and equity partners wish to retain voting control.

A much wider range of options is open when a public company is the target. An acquisition of a significant stake may be possible through a dawn raid. A partial offer may be made for less than 100% of the share capital. A full bid may be made by way of a public offer, or, in some jurisdictions, a legal procedure called a scheme of arrangement. A scheme is an all or nothing procedure which has advantages in terms of saving transfer duty and speed in reaching 100% control. It is more cumbersome overall and requires the recommendation of the target company. 100% of the target company may be acquired under a public offer if acceptances are received from a minimum number of the shareholders to whom the offer is made.

Whether a partial offer, full offer or scheme of arrangement is employed, extensive documentation is circulated to shareholders on behalf of the acquiror. These documents cover areas laid down by regulation such as financial and legal information and disclosures of interest. Comments from the chairman of the offeror or offeree are also included and a letter from the merchant bank arguing the pros and cons of the offer. If shareholders' meetings are required the notices will be attached to the letter.

Role of professionals and technical aspects (see ch 19 below)

Mergers and acquisitions require a combination of skills to bring about a successful conclusion.

The prime movers are often merchant banks who have taken the lead in building up large departments of full-time professionals specialising in merger and acquisition work. They are actively involved in generating ideas and putting up proposals. They may assist with valuations and advise on the type of payment. They often play a role in the negotiating process.

In markets where a takeover code operates, the merchant bank monitors compliance, submits draft documents to the secretariat and discusses contentious points with them. Changes of tactics and market conditions give rise to revisions in the detailed rules although a number of important principles have remained basically unchanged. An experienced merchant bank will be familiar with the areas likely to cause difficulty and aware of the authorities' general approach to them.

The merchant bank normally has the role of co-ordinating the input of all parties involved in the production of the offer document to be sent to the target company's shareholders. The offeror looks to the merchant bank for assistance in putting together the financing of the offer, either directly by underwriting or loans or through its market skill in putting together a syndicate.

An accountant's report commissioned by the purchaser on the target company's business is often a basic building block. A request for an investigation may meet various degrees of resistance from the vendor. In compiling the report the accountants will highlight any items of potential under- or over-valuation and comment more generally on the adequacy of systems and the competence of management. They will be on the look-out for one-time adjustments to the accounts which could, for example, produce unrepresentative earnings used as a basis for pricing.

The accountants will be best placed to advise on the effect an acquisition may have on the acquiror's balance sheet and profit and loss account. Technical matters to be reviewed include the cost of acquisition in the acquiror's books, goodwill on consolidation and the extent of pre-acquisition profits.

In an acquisition of any complexity, legal advice will be required at an early stage. Procedural matters such as the conduct of meetings may be a critical element in deciding on tactics. Many lawyers are skilled negotiators and play a leading role in negotiations as well as providing advice behind the scenes. If a heads of agreement is used at a preliminary stage, drafting is almost inseparable from negotiating.

The sales and purchase agreement is a major responsibility of the lawyers involved. When a public offer document is prepared, the lawyers will have an overall brief to ensure rules and regulations are complied with and that proper disclosure is made. If the takeover is by way of a scheme of arrangement, the legal requirements will determine the procedure and timetable for the entire transaction.

A number of tactics, particularly in defence, are the province of the lawyers. Legal moves to repel or delay an unwelcome bidder are a major part of any well-organised defensive campaign. Offers and defences require a plethora of approvals by boards and individual directors which it would normally be the responsibility of the lawyers to organise correctly.

Tax advice is of critical importance. The correct structure for an acquisition can make the difference between a transaction which is highly rewarding and one which is marginal. Tax aspects include transfer duty when shares or assets are bought or sold, capital duty when securities are issued, tax on the income stream generated by the acquisition, tax on the eventual sale of the investment, the tax liabilities of the company being acquired and the tax position of the vendor shareholders. Tax advice may be provided by the accountants or lawyers working on the acquisition or may be given by tax specialists.

Where an acquisition involves listed companies, the involvement of a firm of stockbrokers is likely to be necessary. From time to time professionals from other fields will be called upon for assistance. With large numbers of specialists involved, the role of co-ordination becomes as difficult as it is important.

Disposals (see ch 20)

It is logical for a management to spend as much energy and enterprise on identifying and preparing for disposals as it does on acquisitions. This rarely proves to be the case. Acquisitions are associated with growth and achievement. Disposals carry a connotation of decline and failure. Employees are worried about their own positions. A major task therefore is for management to encourage a positive attitude towards disposals.

One of the prerequisites for a rational approach to disposals is a fair system of measuring performance. Management accounts may include allocations of costs and income which do not provide an appropriate basis for considering a disposal.

When a company has been identified for disposal, it should be groomed so as to appear in the best light possible to a purchaser. The purchaser will look at key factors and statistics. The seller can anticipate this analysis and prepare answers for the questions which may arise.

Successful sales depend critically on timing. It may be advantageous to sell the company at a period when it appears to the purchaser that there is still something to go for. At this point in the cycle, finance may also be more readily available. Information must be provided to the purchaser but sometimes to supply everything asked for is counter-productive. Creating an auction-room atmosphere and encouraging a little rivalry can do wonders for the price achieved.

Intermediaries have an important role to play. They allow the principals to be flexible without fear of showing weakness. A skilful intermediary will make both parties feel he is on their side. A realistic vendor will realise that he may have to assist a purchaser with financing. A willingness to take some of the vendor's shares helps promote a feeling of partnership.

If a company is forced to make a disposal to raise money, one of the more promising assets of the group may have to be selected. Market perception of the vendor's financial position will be critical and skill is required in achieving the desired image. Other reasons for sales include defence against an unwanted takeover, a buy-out by a group organised by management and streamlining a company for flotation.

CHAPTER 12

Why takeovers are made

To gain an understanding of the processes involved in merger and acquisition activities, it is necessary to have some appreciation of the driving forces which lie behind them. Most of these forces are rational and it may well be that no acquisition of significant size, at least in a public company, is likely to proceed unless it is capable of rational justification. However, mergers and acquisitions form an area of business activity where the emotions and instincts of those closely involved play a major part. Why a particular deal is being progressed in a particular way becomes a complex matter. Anticipating the next move becomes as much a matter of psychology as of logic.

The reasons for making acquisitions are probably as numerous as people who make them. However, motives can be usefully grouped under three headings:

I   Commercial;
II Financial;
III Customised.

Very often of course there will be elements of all three present in a particular acquisition.

I   COMMERCIAL

Many acquisitions are designed to strengthen the commercial position of the company. This may be looked at from a number of aspects.

(i) Increase in market share/reduction of competition

An acquisition of a company in the same general line of business will increase the acquiror's market share in that sector. At the same time, the acquiror may strengthen its market position in another way by eliminating an active competitor. Acquisitions of this type (called horizontal) are the most easily justified by the acquiror in terms of 'fit'. A target company in the same line of business is likely to have a broadly similar structure and organisation. Its business should be fairly easy for the acquiror to understand and assimilate. Specific executives may be known to management. The industry grape-vine will probably have alerted the acquiror to any significant problems that may exist and some which no doubt do not. After the acquisition, there may be obvious cost savings through the elimination of duplicated functions or by economies of scale.

The opposite side of the coin is that mergers of this type are the most likely to attract official scrutiny. This is particularly so in jurisdictions where, and at periods when, anti-monopoly regulatory bodies are strong or fears of unemployment are high.

The very reasons which make this type of acquisition attractive, principally reduction in competition and the elimination of duplication leading to redundancies, are the factors which can most readily unite opposition groups.

(ii) Growth

Management has the responsibility for determining the future direction and policy of the business. The development of a new product range or entry into a new technology or geographical area can be achieved more quickly and perhaps more effectively by acquiring an existing business than by starting from scratch. In sectors which have a depressed stock market rating it may also be possible to acquire assets and facilities through an acquisition at a lower price than the cost to build comparable 'green field' facilities. It must be borne in mind, however, that it is rare for the assets acquired to be precisely what the acquiror would have wished or in the condition it would desire.

Growth can become an end in itself, perhaps because it is taken as a proxy for dynamic management. In the short term, whether growth is simply growth in assets and sales or whether it is also growth in profitability can become obscured. Comparing the year-by-year performance of a fast-growing group on a consistent basis is a difficult task.

(iii) Synergy

It has been frequently argued that in certain circumstances a complex business is worth more than the sum of its parts, in other words, two plus two can equal more than four. The thrust of this argument is that by putting organisations together the performance of the components can be enhanced and their potential increased by feeding off each other's strengths. Examples might be a company with a good product range combining with a company with strong marketing and distributing capability or a research-oriented company combining with a traditional manufacturer. Size alone can confer benefits, for example when negotiating with suppliers, customers and financiers.

In practice it has been difficult to demonstrate that these theoretical advantages have been realised. It is fairly easy to show that costs have been reduced following a horizontal merger. Benefits from synergy tend to be less tangible and more difficult to quantify particularly when accounting systems may not have been designed to capture the relevant information. Despite this, synergy remains one of the most important theoretical bases used to justify mergers and acquisitions because it opens up the prospect of benefits to the economy as a whole. Synergy is therefore an important counter to arguments in favour of restraints on merger activity.

(iv) Security of supply and sales

Critical business relationships exist with suppliers and customers. In some industries, for example textiles and petroleum, the relationships are so close that it is difficult for the functions of supply, production and marketing to be conducted on a totally arm's length basis. There is therefore a tendency for these activities to be controlled inside one group. An industry where this type of merger has occurred is called 'vertically integrated'.

It should be said that what is presented as compelling business logic at one time seems later to owe much to herd instinct. An increased availability of a previously scarce raw material, for example crude oil, decreases the importance of a guaranteed source of supply. Although vertical integration brings more aspects of the business under top management's control, it also complicates the allocation of profits and costs. The performance of executives in charge of a particular division cannot be properly evaluated and monitored if key variables are out of their hands. Initiative may be stifled as freedom of action of the various parts of the organisation are constrained by the interests of others.

(v) Diversification

Management may seek to reduce risks by acquiring a portfolio of assets or companies rather than being dependent on one product or industry. To combine in one group businesses which are not equally affected by prevailing economic factors and cycles should produce a more consistent overall performance than to be heavily dependent on one business. Complex analysis may seek to demonstrate this statistically, backing up the commonsense belief in not keeping 'all your eggs in one basket'.

Groups consisting of businesses which do not bear particularly close commercial relationships with each other are called conglomerates. It has proved difficult to demonstrate that conglomerates have achieved a superior performance through reduction of risk. Their rise seems to have been partly a product of 'merger mania' and of the philosophy that a good manager can manage anything. However, the practical difficulties of controlling very diverse groups may have cancelled out the theoretical benefits of diversification. Conglomerates built up of disparate parts have at a later stage of their development tended to rationalise their activities. Management pick out certain core businesses, spinning off or disposing of 'non-core' companies.

II FINANCIAL

It is rare that the commercial attractions of a potential acquisition will be so compelling that the acquiror decides to buy at any price. It may happen on occasion if a very big group wishes for example to gain access to a new technology, but normally there must be an attractive financial basis. Financial attractions may be considered under a number of headings:

(i) Bargains

Few people can resist a real or perceived bargain. This is as true of companies as anything else. When bargains occur in the corporate field, it is usually due to some element of weakness. The weakness may be in the company itself because of declining profitability or liquidity problems. The weakness may lie with a controlling shareholder under pressure to sell. In the case of a public company, the market rating may be poor for some reason not directly connected with the company, for example the sector being out of fashion with investors.

Potential acquirors may have identified a company as an opportunity and be patiently waiting for the right moment. Bargain prices are often dependent on opportunism. A company which is ready to strike holds a distinct advantage. A popular moment to bid for a public company is after disappointing results have just been announced and before a recovery can be forecast.

(ii) Discount to asset value

This is probably the most popular and most reliable financial basis for an acquisition. Aggressive individuals or organisations have been labelled 'asset strippers' because they make no disguise that this is their primary motivation. However, eminently respectable companies may also make asset backing the primary focus of their analysis.

Analysis will be concentrated on the balance sheet of the target company. Book values will not be accepted as accurate assessments of present market value but each item will be scrutinised for potential appreciation and for losses. Liabilities and contingent liabilities will be examined. Many sources of information will be tapped. Some figures may be rough estimates or even guesses, so a considerable margin for error must be allowed. Allowing room for negotiation, a situation may not be of real interest unless the estimate of revised net asset value is, in the case of a public company, at least 50% higher than the prevailing market price.

The type of company which tends to attract most attention is one with substantial fixed assets and yet a lacklustre profit and dividend record. Over a period of time the company may come to be valued principally in relation to its profits and dividends rather than its asset backing. This situation is likely to reflect uninspired management in general.

It sometimes happens that assets become more valuable if put to some alternative use in an area in which the current management may have no expertise. Management may be adequate as regards the traditional business but not alert to some change in the outside environment. A classic example is a business operating a department store on a site which becomes ripe for redevelopment. Acquirors with expertise in a relevant area may be able to derive more benefit from a particular asset than its existing controllers, however well they run their traditional business. Certain intangible factors such as tax losses may only be valuable in the hands of someone capable of ensuring profits are earned in the relevant entity.

(iii) Increase in earnings per share

A company may increase its earnings per share by issuing shares to acquire another company rated at a lower price earnings multiple. A simplified example would be as follows:

Assume: (a) An all-share offer by the acquiror for 100% of the shares of the target company.

       (b) The terms are based on the market prices of the shares of the two companies.

	Acquiror		*Target*
Latest earnings	100		50
Number of shares in issue	1000		1000
Earnings per share	0.10		0.05
Multiple on which shares are rated	12 times		8 times
Share price	1.20		0.40
Market capitalisation	1200		400
Terms of offer (based on respective market prices)	1 new share	*for*	3 existing shares

Combined group

Enlarged issued share capital	1000 + 333	—	1333
Combined earnings	100	50	150
New earnings per share	(150 divided by 1333)		0.1125
Multiple on which shares are rated	(*assume acquiror's rating unchanged*)		12
New share price	0.1125 ×	12	1.35
New market capitalisation	1333 ×	1.35	1800

The increase in earnings per share, from 0.10 to 0.1125, is a simple question of mathematics, following from the assumption that the terms of the share exchange are based on respective market prices. (This is in fact an over-simplification, as normally a premium over market would have to be paid for the target.) The increase in the market price of the acquiror after the offer from $1.20 to $1.35 depends on whether the combined group remains rated at the multiple of the acquiror prior to the offer, that is 12 times. If it does, or at least holds at above the weighted average multiple of the acquiror and the target (weighted by size of earnings), the market capitalisation of the combined group will be higher than that of the two companies separately.

An aggressive company may have gained for itself a high market rating on the expectation of rapid growth in profits. These expectations can be fulfilled, at least in the short term, be acquisitions on terms such as those illustrated in the example. Indeed, they may be self-fulfilling for the moment in that the ability to grow by acquisition (apparently proved) may be part of the reason for the premium rating. However, unless the acquisitions are very skilful ones, the rating of the acquiror will in due course suffer as the proportion of earnings contributed by lowly-rated companies increases. In addition, the size and number of acquisitions at low ratings needed to maintain this strategy over a period of time becomes ever larger, leading to its collapse unless the acquiror and/or the companies acquired are also capable of achieving organic growth.

In the case of a cash offer, a similar effect will be achieved if the return from the business acquired at the purchase price is higher than the funding cost. The funding cost in the short term (as it will affect the reported earnings) could be considered either to be the cost of debt incurred to finance the purchase or, if surplus cash is used, the interest foregone on the cash deposits. In the longer term, if acquisitions are funded purely by cash or borrowings, the increased gearing is likely to require further equity issues.

(iv) Gearing

An acquisition by means of a share exchange of a company which has low borrowings or surplus cash is likely to reduce the financial gearing of the enlarged group. In an extreme form, the acquiring company may issue shares to purchase an investment trust or other company with highly liquid assets. This type of transaction may be seen more as a disguised equity issue than a true acquisition.

An acquiror may take the opportunity to change the balance of its capital structure. The terms of an acquisition may include the issue of unsecured loan stock or convertible securities in addition to ordinary shares and cash. By juggling with the proportions of such elements in the total consideration, the acquiring group can increase or decrease the proportion of long-term debt in its balance sheet and adjust its overall gearing.

(v) Opportunity to issue highly rated paper

In the growth cycle of an aggressive listed company, there tends to come a period when it attempts to issue its shares to third parties in return for assets. The market rating of a share in the short term is likely to be set by expectations of profit growth. Maintaining rapid increases in profits requires an additional accumulation of assets to be amassed to form a basis for a second phase of growth. The management of a company may therefore take the opportunity to issue paper at a time when its market rating and share price are high but its asset backing low. Whether this strategy succeeds in producing the profits necessary to sustain the share price will depend on the potential of the assets acquired and the acquiror's ability to manage as well as to 'wheel and deal'.

III   CUSTOMISED

In addition to the commercial and financial aspects, specialised factors may be involved in the selection of an acquisition target. Empire building, to increase power or protect it, can be a powerful motive. Sometimes acquisitions are made to secure scarce resources, for example the services of a particularly talented manager or a licence which would be otherwise unobtainable.

(i) Ambition

Prestige and compensation in an organisation may depend more on size than results. Acquisitions are the quickest way of building up the size of the group.

An element of 'small town boy makes good' may come into play. An individual who has built up his company reaches a stage where he seeks to acquire more established and well known organisations. Sometimes these are companies he has admired in the past or had to ask for help during his rise.

A successful acquisition often brings with it extensive publicity. Certain noted corporate raiders and their advisers have become national figures for a time. The exposure may mainly be a matter of ego. However, it can also be justified in terms of increased corporate and management visibility. This may lead to improved ratings in the stock market and a larger number of acquisition opportunities being presented by brokers.

A high degree of determination on the part of an individual or group is usually necessary to bring an acquisition to a successful conclusion, particularly if it is contested. During the course of an acquisition, occasions almost always arise where the parties concerned are ready to call it off. In these circumstances, the motivation and drive of a particular individual can be a critical factor.

(ii) Defence

It is commonly believed that the bigger the group is, the harder it is to swallow. Companies therefore sometimes attempt acquisitions principally in order to grow too big to be taken over by a feared rival. In addition, the more complex a group is, the greater is the likelihood that regulatory authorities or some other interested parties will find grounds to raise objections to a takeover. A company in a sensitive area, for example communications and broadcasting, may be particularly favoured as an acquisition partly for this reason.

Companies espousing this philosophy should be wary of creating their own downfall. Ill-conceived acquisitions can lead to criticisms and disaffection from shareholders. Weakening the financial position of the group through expensive purchases ultimately plays into an acquiror's hands.

(iii) Management

Some acquisitions are made primarily to obtain the services of a manager or management team who have proved themselves competent at running a particular type of company or handling a particular type of crisis. Sometimes the specialised professional expertise or contacts of individuals are what is sought. An example would be the purchase of a stockbroker or insurance agency by a bank. In such cases, an important task is for groups of people with a different approach to conducting business to learn to work together effectively.

(iv) Stock exchange listing

Control of companies may be sought which have little or no assets or business but which are listed on a stock exchange. Once control has been obtained, the acquiror will typically inject a business or assets into the company. Depending on the nature of the assets and the length of time they have been held or operated, a listing is obtained which might not have otherwise been possible.

(v) Tax losses

Companies which have been unsuccessful may have accumulated considerable losses for taxation purposes which may in certain circumstances be utilised by an acquiring group. Usually the company is valued on the basis of a discount to the amount of tax which will be saved. The feasibility of such an acquisition depends critically on the tax regulations in the country concerned and the current interpretation of them.

(vi) Licences

A licence, for example to conduct a banking business or operate a TV station, may be more easily obtained by acquiring a company which already holds such a licence than by a fresh application. Care must be taken to ensure that a change of control in the company acquired does not jeopardise the continuity or validity of the licence. If it is practical, this matter should be cleared in advance with the authority responsible for granting the licence or regulating companies which hold it. This may not always be possible for tactical reasons, in which case any agreement should be conditional on the appropriate clearance being obtained.

This chapter has discussed the main motives for making takeovers. The motives are divided into commercial, financial and customised. An acquisition which is undertaken for a specialised purpose may also have a commercial basis and be capable of justification in financial terms.

CHAPTER 13

Acquisition search: developing criteria, generating opportunities and preliminary screening

The multiplicity of motives for takeovers discussed in the last chapter spills over into the next stage. To conduct an effective search it is necessary to develop relevant criteria. Criteria which have proved useful are discussed in 'I Developing and setting criteria' below. When the criteria have been established, procedures are needed for generating suitable proposals. Imaginative management can widen the range of opportunities which arise internally or are presented by the market. This aspect is discussed in 'II Generating opportunities' below. A preliminary screening of potential targets is required to prevent analysts being overwhelmed by too many options. Screening candidates is partly a matter of rigorous application of the criteria and partly depends on an ability to see the main implications of an acquisition before detailed analysis commences. This topic is dealt with in 'III Preliminary screening' below.

I DEVELOPING AND SETTING CRITERIA

A clear statement of management's objectives in looking for acquisitions should suggest suitable criteria. The more precisely the objectives can be stated, the more definite will be the criteria for an appropriate acquisition.

In the previous chapter, the reasons why takeovers are made are discussed under three general headings:

(i)   Commercial;
(ii) Financial;
(iii) Customised.

Criteria can be considered under these same headings. Other types of criteria apply whatever the motive for an acquisition. The main ones are:

(iv) Is the acquiror biting off more than he can chew?
(v)   Can the acquisition be financed?

(i) Commercial

If an acquisition is being considered principally for commercial reasons, typical criteria are likely to include the following:

(a) Type of industry/activity

Acquisitions intended to increase market share must be in areas of activity closely related to the acquiror's existing business. If the objective is growth in a general sense, companies engaged in different areas would be considered. Frequently, a company is prepared to consider a potentially more difficult acquisition in a business with which it is thoroughly familiar. If an acquisition in a new area, it must be capable of 'standing on its own feet'. A loss-making company or a company with management problems might not be considered whatever its other attractions.

If the acquiror is seeking benefits related to synergy, it will concentrate on the fit of business. A strong manufacturer may be looking for an organisation with a widespread marketing and distribution network. A company seeking to secure supply of a key component or additional sales outlets will focus specifically on these areas.

The last type of commercial motive discussed in ch 12 above was diversification. By definition, this will involve the acquiror actively seeking a business with significantly different characteristics from its own, perhaps in a totally unrelated industry.

Criteria related to type of industry and activity may be defined in a positive or in a negative way. A company may take a positive decision to emphasise high technology or overseas markets. On the other hand, a company may decide it will in no circumstances consider an acquisition in say property or shipping. This type of rule should not be allowed to degenerate into dogma. A ruling which is soundly based when established should be reviewed periodically as business conditions change and the company itself evolves.

(b) Management and workforce

Acquisitions undertaken primarily for commercial reasons are vulnerable to the reactions of management and workforce. Unless a reasonable degree of co-operation can be established, many of the anticipated benefits may not be realised in practice.

Acquirors may decide that they will not consider an acquisition of this type unless management has been proved to be competent. They may also seek assurances that the majority of the senior executives are willing to stay.

The attitude of the workforce is perhaps less likely to be one of outright opposition but nevertheless problems can occur. If the acquiror has not previously had to deal with a unionised labour force, he may be unwilling to acquire a company whose workers are organised in this manner. Lack of experience in negotiating with unions may act as a deterrent. The acquiror may also be apprehensive about the spread of unions to his own organisation.

(ii) Financial

If an acquisition is intended principally to improve the financial position of the acquiror, strict financial criteria will be applied. Financial criteria are amongst the most difficult to establish in a way which does not prove to be counter-productive. If the returns required are set too high or applied too strictly, an ideal acquisition target may be defined which in reality is never encountered.

Few people can resist a bargain. However, a management which insists on buying companies at below market price may find that they make no acquisitions. When they do finally succeed in concluding a deal, the results may be disappointing. The emphasis on apparent cheapness can cause business weaknesses to be overlooked.

Asset strippers aim to acquire companies at a discount to net assets. Allowing room for negotiation, a target may not be of real interest unless the discount is substantial, say one-third. Although it may seem that only a forced seller would accept such terms, there is scope for a good deal of disagreement in buyers' and sellers' estimates of what assets are actually worth.

If increase in earnings per share is paramount, it is unlikely that a company currently making losses will even be considered. Many companies are prepared to give an acquisition say two years to recover to a position of reasonable profitability. Unless some latitude is allowed, an acquiror will rule out the possibility of making a potentially attractive acquisition at the low point in a company's fortunes.

Some acquisitions are used to improve the gearing of the enlarged group. In this case a company which is already highly geared or one which is facing substantial capital commitments is unlikely to be considered.

If an acquiror's strategy is to issue highly-rated shares or other paper, the willingness of vendors to accept such paper may make an acquisition attractive which would not meet normal criteria. If a vendor has a pressing need for cash, this is likely to rule out the use of paper except in circumstances where a vendor placing can be arranged.

(iii) Customised

In addition to financial and commercial aspects, other more specialised factors are often involved in acquisitions. This will make setting criteria a simpler process. For example, if a company is being acquired for its management, stock exchange listing, its tax losses or a licence it holds, then the criteria more or less set themselves. If an acquisition is being made as a defence against a takeover threat, it can be judged purely by its effectiveness in this respect. One extremely important factor will be sheer availability at short notice.

In circumstances where motives include subjective elements such as empire building, criteria are unlikely to be set in an organised way. The motive may not be fully realised by the decision makers themselves, far less openly acknowledged.

(iv) Size

There are likely to be fairly obvious limits to the size of a possible acquisition. Even in the era of junk bonds and leveraged buy-outs, there is little sense in the average company drawing up a complex scheme to take over General Motors.

It is also useful to set a cut-off point at the lower end of the scale. There is a large fixed element in the time and expense in evaluating an acquisition. The acquisition must be of a certain minimum size to justify the effort involved. A series of small acquisitions ties up management time without making a significant difference to the performance of the group.

Size may be defined in different ways. A trading company may have an impressive turnover figure without a large asset base. A company with a big balance sheet if it is in financial difficulties or is heavily geared may not be expensive to buy.

An acquiror may wish to consider maximum and minimum size criteria under various headings:

(a) Purchase price

What is the most a company is prepared to pay or can afford to pay? This figure may depend on the possibility of using paper as part of the consideration.

(b) Turnover or value added

These may be the most useful indicators of how substantial a business is being considered. Care is required as some companies may have a high turnover with little value added whereas others may have a smaller turnover but with value added representing a significant proportion.

(c) Assets, liabilities and capital requirements

The most immediate impact of an acquisition is frequently on the balance sheet. Key ratios may come under pressure. An acquisition must be judged not only in terms of its initial effect (including the price paid) but taking into account any additional capital which may be required. Weakness in capital structure or heavy capital commitments may have been part of the reason the company was vulnerable to a takeover in the first place.

(d) Market share

There is a school of thought which believes that controlling a substantial proportion of a particular market is the best guide to whether a company can survive and prosper in the long term. A company with a toehold in its market may be eliminated if a period of intense competition is encountered. An appropriate minimum criterion for percentage market share will depend on the industry structure.

(e) Profitability

Most companies making acquisitions establish a minimum rate of return which the target should be capable of generating. The minimum hurdle rate of return may be reduced if the acquisition is in a familiar business or increased if it operates in high risk areas of the world. Some discretion must be exercised as to the year in which this target return is intended to be achieved.

(f) Number of employees, diversity of markets served and spread of business

A further way of measuring size is by reference to the numbers of people employed and the numbers of markets served or products produced. This may be taken as a proxy for the complexity of the business as a whole. The more complex an acquisition, the more likely it is that something will go wrong.

(v) Can it be financed?

It is of little use planning to buy a business the aspiring acquiror cannot finance. Managers who have been successful in building up businesses by acquisition try to finance each proposal to a large extent on a project basis, minimising the call on the financial resources of the holding company and avoiding giving its guarantee. Some types of acquisition can be financed more easily than others. This depends partly on the characteristics of the target company and partly on the requirements of the vendors.

A company with valuable fixed assets or a predictable surplus cash flow will be more easily borrowed against. Businesses which have a high proportion of goodwill in the price paid and are subject to abrupt market changes or cycles will not commonly be considered by financiers to provide good collateral. The acquiror is likely to have to fund such acquisitions substantially out of its own cash flow.

A desire not to miss any possible opportunity can lead to a reluctance to define criteria too closely. This is particularly the case when acquisitions are being sought for financial or opportunistic reasons. Precise definitions may be seen more as closing down attractive options than a useful sharpening of focus.

In the case of acquisitions undertaken primarily for commercial reasons, it is productive to avoid the 'we-are-interested-in-everything' approach, which can amount to a failure to set a policy at all. Too much reliance may be placed on advisers or brokers presenting suitable proposals. No outside party can tell a management what type of acquisition they should seek. Management must itself define its own objectives and set criteria which are consistent with them.

II GENERATING OPPORTUNITIES

Once a management has set its criteria for making acquisitions, it must develop procedures for generating suitable proposals. The criteria selected can then be applied to narrow down the range of opportunities the market presents. One important principle is to identify opportunities before they have become stale. Experience suggests that attractive acquisitions are progressed quickly. Those that have been in the market for some months are rarely worth the trouble of analysis.

It may be useful to divide sources for acquisition opportunities into two categories, those which are generated internally, that is by the staff of the company through their private contacts or through their executive function in the company, and those which are generated by or through external professionals in the merger and acquisition field.

(i) Internal sources

(a) From non-specialists

The senior staff of a competently run business know more about that area of business and the major participants in it than an external professional. Consequently, the best ideas for acquisitions within a company's existing sphere of business will often come from the staff themselves. Management should try to provide some forum or channel of communication so that ideas can be put forward and discussed, with some credit and involvement in analysis going to the originator. As executives may be more conscious of brand names and marketing networks than corporate organisations, assistance in providing information on the corporate structure of the industry may stimulate the flow of ideas.

(b) Merger and acquisition unit

In addition to opportunities identified through involvement in a particular business field, the company may also establish a specialist merger and acquisition unit. One of the functions of this unit will be to search publicly available information to find targets which fit the criteria which have been laid down. Except in a very major conglomerate, such units are unlikely to be entirely independent or engaged solely in merger and acquisition work. They may be located for example in the treasurer's or controller's departments or within a corporate planning function. Such arrangements promote economical use of manpower. However, the approach of the staff will be coloured by the environment in which they find themselves. They will be more effective if they act in an independent entrepreneurial way to locate the widest range of opportunities.

(ii) External sources

(a) Advertisements

Companies rely on external sources to supply or prompt many of their acquisition ideas. One obvious source of possibilities is simply to advertise for them. In practice, unless the type of acquisition is a standard one, sellers will be reluctant to reply to such an open approach. It seems that a modification of Groucho Marx's law applies, that you would not wish to buy a company whose owners answer your advertisement.

(b) Intermediaries

The role of the intermediary is well established in the merger and acquisition field. Intermediaries may be experienced businessmen and negotiators. Often they are senior accountants or lawyers with expert knowledge of certain industries. Others are pure merger brokers whose modus operandi is to match buyer and seller without necessarily knowing much about either. Investment and merchant banks have access to a continuous stream of proposals through their professional and client contacts. They can offer a package of services, including provision or introduction of suitable financing and the placing of securities in support of an acquisition.

Many significant business empires have been built up through a close association with one or more merchant banks. The development of a personal relationship is fundamental. As a merchant bank becomes familiar with the philosophy of an acquiror, it can increasingly anticipate his reaction. If the group becomes a significant client, the merchant bank will take the initiative in presenting proposals in order to keep the client relationship active. A merchant bank is not as transaction orientated as a merger broker but will still seek to get a transaction moving as quickly as possible. A client who is known to react swiftly and is prepared to pursue opportunities in spite of the inevitable uncertainties will soon gain a favoured position.

Receivers and liquidators are a productive source of potential acquisitions. Unlike many sellers, they do not have any emotional attachment to the businesses or assets it is their responsibility to realise. They are frequently under time pressure. Not only are they firm sellers but they may be willing to accept a discount on the open market value in return for speed, certainty and simplicity of the transaction.

Relationships with outside professionals are usually conducted at a senior level. A company may also promote contact between its analysts and the junior staff of merchant banks to create an additional channel of information. Merchant bank executives are usually allocated on a client basis and competition to present good proposals to clients is fierce. Which client sees which opportunity first may be a matter effectively settled at a fairly junior level, allowing the more senior executives to remain above the fray.

III PRELIMINARY SCREENING

Once the criteria have been developed and opportunities generated, the preliminary screening process, which may partly be carried out by computer, comes down to a rigorous application of the criteria. In seeking suitable acquisitions, it is possible to go down a large number of blind alleys. Promising proposals can fall down at the eleventh hour leaving nothing but a good deal of wasted time and the frustration of having the prize snatched away. Experience can assist the company's staff in developing a sense of what type of proposal is realistic. From the outset, they should adopt a questioning attitude as to whether a proposal has the ingredients necessary for a successful outcome. If a proposal does not make good commercial sense to all the participants, it is likely to be only a matter of time before it founders.

A number of subjective factors play a role in the preliminary screening process.

(i) Commercial

There may be unanticipated commercial consequences arising from an acquisition, particularly in an industry where vertical integration is involved. An arm's length commercial relationship between supplier and customer frequently proves easier to handle than the relationship between parent and subsidiary.

Rival suppliers may feel that a competitor who becomes a member of the group will always receive favoured treatment.

If an acquisition takes a group into an area in which its own customers are active, the business put at risk may cancel out the expected benefits of the acquisition. Existing participants in the industry may feel that their supplier is trespassing on their own preserve. The resultant loss of business may make the uncertain benefits of entering a new field too costly.

(ii) Management

An acquisition may be intended to secure the expertise and business generating abilities of its management. However, loss of independence and changes in working environment may result in disenchantment with a large group. In a service business, for example advertising or insurance brokerage, the members of the firm acquired may be very capable of leaving to set up on their own. Although it may be possible to impose certain restrictions on them for a period of time by means of service contracts or other agreements, this can result in the almost equally unsatisfactory position of a senior management with no real commitment to their job.

(iii) Matters of judgment

The intangible aspects of taking a company into an area in which it has no previous experience should be examined at an early stage. Acquisitions of companies in sensitive areas such as broadcasting and gambling can lead to official scrutiny of a group which may not have had to deal with regulatory authorities in this manner. Companies engaged in material litigation can absorb significant amounts of senior management time. Entry into overseas markets by way of takeovers of domestic companies may spark off a xenophobic reaction.

Management should assess whether an acquisition can be concluded on an agreed basis or whether it will be contested to the bitter end. A contested takeover can provoke a counter-attack on the acquiror's financial position, management performance and business ethics. Unless an acquiror has the stomach for this kind of infighting, contested takeovers are best avoided.

Another test to apply at the screening stage is the extent of the down-side risk of any acquisition. Management should ask themselves what is the worst that could happen in a 'disaster' scenario. Owing to a great reluctance to cut losses on high profile acquisitions, a management may be drawn into supporting a difficult situation far longer than it should. In extreme circumstances, an acquisition may threaten the survival of the whole group. This type of target clearly needs a different type of evaluation from the more run-of-the-mill project.

CONCLUSION

Setting criteria, generating opportunities and carrying out preliminary screening overlap to a considerable extent. They are themselves closely linked with and derived from the reasons for making acquisitions in the first place. It is possible to approach this aspect of mergers and acquisitions by attempting to set such precise criteria that they virtually pick out acquisition targets and dictate whether they should be pursued to the next stage. However, this approach, while logical, may produce too rigid a system which results in a failure to identify and take advantage of attractive acquisitions. The approach suggested in this chapter has been to set criteria based on the objectives of the takeover programme. The generating of opportunities is left as a separate exercise. In this way, a wide range of choice is initially presented. A preliminary screening process is then required to apply a more rigorous application of the criteria. The analysis should be extended to take into account matters of judgment as discussed above.

This procedure is far from perfect. A significant gap can develop between the specified criteria and the actual desired characteristics of an acquisition. The planners and analysts may put up a series of proposals only to find that management reaction to them is largely unpredictable.

When a promising candidate has been selected and survives the preliminary screening, the next step is to collect more detailed information and begin in-depth financial analysis.

CHAPTER 14

Acquisition analysis: collecting and evaluating information

Once a target company has been identified, the next step is the collection of information so that a more detailed financial analysis of the company may be carried out. This analysis forms the basis of the assessment of valuation and what price should be paid and whether it should be paid in cash or shares or some other more complex package. The effect on earnings per share and gearing are highly relevant to this decision.

A cynical acquiror will always assume that there is some good reason why a company is for sale. One objective of the analysis will be to identify any weakness which has led to a company becoming 'in play'.

A poor acquisition can have consequences which are not limited to the initial price paid. There is a strong tendency not to admit that an acquisition has been a mistake and instead of cutting losses to 'throw good money after bad' by trying to improve a hopeless situation. The health of the whole group may be affected, even companies with no direct relationship to the struggling acquisition. The best chance of avoiding a damaging acquisition is when the initial analysis is carried out. Minds are open and there is no vested interest in the decision.

I COLLECTING INFORMATION

Analysis can only be as sound as the information on which it is based. Information on acquisition targets may be derived from a number of sources.

(i) Publicly available information

Under the provisions of company law in most countries, a company is obliged to file certain information for public inspection. The information normally includes details of the authorised and issued share capital, the list of registered shareholders and the current directors. Certain basic financial information may also be provided.

Information held on file for public inspection tends to be up-dated annually. A fairly generous time limit is allowed for the provision of the required information. It frequently happens that the latest publicly available information is considerably out of date, especially as authorities do not always have the time to chase up prompt filing by the very large number of companies which have been established.

Some comment and analysis may be obtained from press cuttings if the company is one which has attracted public attention. Credit analysis companies and similar organisations are another potential source. In addition to searching publicly available information, such organisations may have carried out interviews with selected suppliers, customers and creditors of the group. Trade and marketing associations may be able to supply literature on products and other commercial aspects of the company.

Companies which have a public listing must produce annual accounts and publish results periodically, usually twice a year and sometimes quarterly. Supplementary information may also be required. They may provide additional information to stockbrokers as the basis of reports which are circulated semi-privately. If the company has been engaged in any major transactions such as raising capital in the public markets or taking over another company, other relevant documents will have been issued containing more details than appears in the accounts.

In many jurisdictions, transactions involving land are taxed and must be registered in such a way that the details are made public. Similarly, a public register of charged assets may be kept to enable creditors to assess the financial risk they run in dealing with the company. From these two registers, key information on the fixed assets of the company and the extent to which they have been charged to support borrowings may be obtained.

The acquiror may be relying on public sources because he does not wish to alert the target to his intentions. Drawing on the various sources described above does carry some risk of a leak occurring. Although public sources can be consulted anonymously, an alert observer may notice that a particular file is frequently out for use. A company whose management is nervous of a threat may quickly realise that questions are being asked in trade associations. The acquiror may be able to shield his own identity by having his enquiries carried out by a third party. However, the more extensive the enquiries become, the more difficult it will be to prevent rumours starting that someone is 'sniffing around'.

(ii) Asking the target company itself

Except in the case of a bid which is expected to be opposed, after an acquiror has done what homework he can based on public sources, the next step would be to approach the target company to open negotiations. If the initial approach meets with some response, it will be followed by a request for information.

The moment at which many negotiations founder is when a company which may be attracted by a proposal first realises the extent to which it will have to bare its soul. It is therefore important that the request be handled tactfully and restricted to relevant information which can reasonably be made available. This also helps prevent an acquiror from being overwhelmed by a mass of information. The danger of not seeing 'the wood for the trees' is a real one when substantial analysis has to be carried out from scratch, often under time pressure.

The key characteristics of a business can often be identified beforehand. The information requested should be designed to highlight these characteristics. An acquiror should ask the question 'what am I buying?' and tailor the information requested to allow him to answer that question. Sometimes the really significant points in a particular transaction may be quite limited.

When an important aspect has been isolated, questions must be phrased in a careful way. Intensive questions on a specific point may tip a negotiating hand, emphasising to the other side points the acquiror considers of significant value. Questions on major assets or profit trends will come as no surprise, but if the acquiror is interested in something more unusual, a battery of questions is bound to alert even an unwary target company to a factor they may have overlooked.

Some requests may cover areas such as the directors' own personal dealings or highly sensitive commercial aspects. In these cases, checks may only be needed of a negative kind, to establish that nothing untoward has happened. If this information proves hard to obtain, it may be possible to 'skin the cat' in other ways, for example by including warranties on the relevant points in the sale and purchase contract.

A list of the items which might be included in a request for information is shown below. It should be borne in mind that not all items will be essential in every case.

In specialised cases, a different emphasis may be needed. The acquiror should ask himself 'if I knew this piece of information, would it make any difference to my decision?'

QUESTIONNAIRE

(a) Statutory/legal

1   Memorandum and articles of association.
2   Authorised and issued share capital, including details of voting and dividend rights.
3   Details of capital convertible into shares and of any warrants or options outstanding.
4   Terms of any trust deeds or major loan agreements.
5   Details of any litigation or material claims.
6   Minutes of recent board meetings.

(b) Financial

7   Latest audited accounts for the company, group, individual subsidiaries and, where appropriate, associates for as many past years as is useful.
8   Copy of the consolidation schedule used in drawing up the consolidated accounts.
9   Profit and cash flow budgets or forecast for the current and, if available, subsequent years and projected balance sheet.
10 Statement of borrowings and cash position and capital commitments, guarantees, leases and other financial commitments. Details of any significant foreign exchange exposure.
11 Monthly management accounts for the current year.
12 List of properties and other major fixed assets with current valuations, and, if relevant, a schedule of tenancies and insurance coverage.
13 Details of any tax losses and of assets with book value higher than their tax written down value.
14 Details of any intangible assets such as trademarks or patents.
15 Details of pension or provident fund scheme. Is it fully funded? Is it overfunded?

(c) Market statistics (if listed)

16   Summary of monthly or weekly share price movements, price earnings ratio, dividend yield and net asset backing over say the past 12 months.
17   Analysis of level of turnover in shares and buying cost to major shareholders.
18   Details of major shareholders and spread of shareholdings.

(d) Directors, management and employees

19   Names of directors, their business background, their involvement in the group and their shareholdings.
20   Details of contracts of service.
21   Organisation chart.
22   Numbers of employees, where located, typical training or qualifications and union involvement, if any.

(e) Commercial

23   Description of business and products and services.
24   Sales/marketing organisation and procedures, trade or conference memberships, import or export quotas, licences and distribution agreements or agencies.
25   Geographical spread of production and sales.
26   Level of research and development expenditure, new products, competitive position, payment reputation.
27   Details of any organisation, affiliated or not, on which the company's business critically depends. Top ten customers and the percentage of sales they account for.

It should be emphasised that to slap down a standardised list of questions is one of the surest ways to kill an acquisition proposal. A selective approach will elicit a more positive response from the vendor and start the acquiror's analysis off on the right track.

II   EVALUATING INFORMATION

The evaluation phase falls into two parts. The first is setting a price based on an objective valuation of the target company, adjusted for refined analysis of the circumstances of the case and the horse trading aspect of what is needed to do the deal. The second is assessing the impact of the acquisition on the published profit and loss account and balance sheet of the acquiror and adjusting the components of the offer accordingly.

(i) Setting the price

When sufficient information has been obtained and assuming the acquisition remains of interest in principle, the next task is to decide what price to pay. The major methods of valuation have been discussed in Part 1 of this book, and in broad terms, can be applied to the valuation of a company in the context of an acquisition. However, particular aspects assume different degrees of importance and relevance. An important principle to be borne in mind is that value is not absolute and, like beauty, can be in the eye of the beholder.

Major aspects to be considered are as follows:

(a) Net asset value

The approach to assessing a company's net asset value should be adapted to the strategy of a bidder after the acquisition is completed. If an essential part of his strategy is to realise significant sums in cash over a short period, it is necessary to be sure that assets earmarked for disposal are valued on a quick sale basis. The market may be aware that asset sales are likely after the acquisition. This will affect the vendor's bargaining position and the price realised.

Different views may be taken of a stake in an associate company. A purchaser who is in a position to control the company (perhaps because of an existing stake) may attribute a higher value than would a passive investor.

(b) Multiple of earnings

The quality of earnings of an acquisition target should be scrutinised by reference to the factors discussed in Part 1. However, the acquiror may be able to identify areas of cost savings should the acquisition be completed. Some upward revision in earnings estimates may be legitimate as part of analysing the consequences of the acquisition.

The purchaser of a company which is available for sale should be wary that the company may have reached a cyclical peak in earnings. Many purchasers assume that the price earnings multiple on which an acquisition is valued will decline as future growth comes through. However, in cyclical industries the price earnings multiple at the purchase price may well increase. Similarly, if an acquiror is striking at an opportunist time of depressed earnings, it must obviously not be too surprised if its own analysis shows the purchase to be on a rather high immediate multiple.

(c) Cash flow basis

Calculating the return on the purchase of a company by discounting an expected stream of cash flows can involve the assumption that cash generated is reinvested at the same rate of return. This may not be the case if the acquisition target is a business where the proceeds are unlikely to be reinvested, for example a mine or a quarry which is being worked out or a 'cash cow', ie a business which generates cash and does not require significant funds to be reinvested. It may be necessary to modify normal internal rate of return methods, so that funds reinvested are assumed only to earn the average return on capital of the acquiring group. This may well be lower than the return expected on the acquisition, especially if the acquisition is attractive principally for financial reasons.

In evaluating cash flow, it may be that cash generated by the acquisition will include other elements besides operating cash flow, such as sales of fixed assets. A company which has been run by an inactive management is likely to have some fat in working capital. For example, stocks and debtors may have been kept at higher levels than necessary. If such funds can be released, they can be regarded as a legitimate part of the cash generated from the acquisition.

(d) Composite

In conglomerate groups, it is likely that a valuation which looks at each part of the business separately may be higher than a valuation simply based on group earnings or consolidated net assets. Some parts of the group may generate substantial profits but have a low book value. Some assets with a high book value may for the moment be generating little or no income. A simple valuation of the consolidated group may gloss over this aspect.

If this basis of acquisition is to be accepted, the seller must be prepared to adopt an approach equivalent to a controlled liquidation or at least a partial break-up of the group. If the purchaser is not willing to accept this, he may be better advised to let the existing management handle the asset sales and buy only the parts of the business which interest him.

(e) Share price

If a company is quoted, it is of course possible to base the valuation on the market price. Indeed, this is the most natural starting point in many ways. However, it must be accepted by a purchaser that the share price is a price for a small number of shares and may have little relevance, depending on the circumstances, to the price which is necessary to achieve control of the whole company.

The simple force of inertia will require the offeror to pay a premium over the market price. If a shareholder can buy and sell in the market at a certain price there is no need for him to take the trouble to consider the terms of an offer. A premium over market is therefore necessary simply to get shareholders' attention. The level of premium will vary with circumstances, but, as a rule of thumb, might be considered to be in the region of 20% to 40%.

Attention must also be paid to the target company's price history. While negotiations are in progress or investigations are being made, leaks or rumours may occur which are likely to cause a rise in the share price. This 'froth' may result in a price which settles at a small discount to the market's guess of where a bidder might eventually pitch his offer. In these circumstances, the purchaser may assess the price which may have to be paid on the basis of the share price prevailing before the rumours started. If the rumours prove false, the price is likely to fall back to the previous level.

It may also be useful to look at the price history over a number of years, particularly the peaks and the levels of turnover in the shares at those peaks. The offer price may look attractive compared with current values. Shareholders have a habit of remembering the price they originally paid. If that price was higher than the offer, they may be reluctant to take what they would still consider to be a loss. The share price lows may be useful for calculations to show the attractions of the offer. On the negative side, they may indicate substantial possible tax liabilities for shareholders deemed to have made a disposal under the offer.

The general techniques of company valuation apply to valuing an acquisition but with a sharpened focus. An assessment should also be made on a strictly practical basis of the price it is thought necessary to secure control of the company. If this price is significantly above an objective valuation, strong warning signs should be registered against proceeding.

Especially in a situation which is likely to be contested, it is useful to set an upper limit before negotiations begin and while cold logic and rationality still prevail. In the heat of a contested battle when victory becomes more important than price, it is easy to lose sight of the objective value. A maximum price formula established in advance is the best safeguard against living to regret an expensive acquisition. It is legitimate to allow some flexibility, as during a contested takeover, the target company will frequently release new and more favourable financial information, on which the acquiror may be able to justify a higher valuation.

(ii) Implications on acquiror's published results and deciding the forms of payment to be offered

The purpose of the valuation phase of the exercise is to arrive at a soundly based price range and an assessment of what price it may be necessary to pay to succeed, which may be above or below valuation. It is necessary then to examine in what forms the acquiror can or should provide the consideration required.

The valuation placed on an acquisition is in effect a summary of results covering a large number of periods.

Typically, the acquisition may look expensive in the early years and more reasonable later on when problems have been solved and improvements to performance have come through. Shareholders tend to judge management over the short term. A company which ignores this may itself become a takeover target.

(a) Effect on earnings per share

In devising the terms of an offer a major objective is that the earnings per share of the acquiror should be increased following the acquisition. The opposite effect where earnings per share are decreased is called 'dilution'.

In the case of an acquisition for cash, the immediate cost may be simply the interest foregone on short-term deposits or investments in which surplus liquidity has been deployed. If the acquisition is funded by borrowings, the interest cost on the debt incurred will be evident.

Where an acquisition is small or expected to grow quickly, it may be possible to offer the target company's shareholders new shares in the acquiror without significant dilution to the acquiror's shareholders. Often, however, this is a luxury which the acquiror cannot afford, since a premium over market price will have to be offered to the target company's shareholders whereas the acquiror's shares will be issued at market price. The position will be worsened if the market price of the acquiror comes under pressure following the announcement of an offer.

To soften the impact of an acquisition the acquiror may offer a more complex package of consideration than shares alone. Particularly in countries where taxation is assessed on a group basis, offering cash or loan stock as a proportion of the consideration is likely to improve the acquiror's earnings per share figure after the acquisition. This is because the earnings yield on the acquisition (the earnings divided by the purchase price) is likely to be higher than the after tax cost of debt.

Convertible loan stock may be a useful ingredient. The coupon payable on convertible loan stock will be lower than on a straight loan stock owing to the value of the conversion rights, whereas the conversion price may be set at a premium to the current market price of the shares. The immediate impact on earnings is therefore beneficial. Regulations may require earnings per share to be shown on a post conversion basis in the accounts. With a judicious mixture of types of consideration and a reasonable conversion premium, the effect on earnings per share can still be favourable even on a post conversion basis.

(b) Example of tailoring the terms of an offer to avoid dilution

An example of how this type of package works is set out below. The example is an extension of the example shown in ch 2 above which illustrated that earnings per share will increase by using highly rated paper to acquire businesses with a lower rating. The example below demonstrates that even if (as often happens in a bid) it is necessary to pay a premium over market price so that the acquisition is not necessarily made on an advantageous price earnings ratio, nevertheless by introducing other elements into the terms an increase in earnings per share can be achieved.

Assume: (a) An offer by the acquiror for 100% of the shares of the target company, partly in shares, partly in loan stock.
(b) The terms are based on a total value for the target company of 500.
(c) The acquiror's shares are issued at market value.
(d) The convertible loan stock is convertible at a 10% premium to current market value of the acquiror's shares.

	Acquiror	Target
Latest pre-tax profits	133	67
Tax at 25%	(33)	(17)
Latest earnings	100	50
Number of shares in issue	1000	1000
Earnings per share	0.10	0.05
Multiple on which shares are rated	10 times	10 times (at offer price)
Market capitalisation	1000	500
Offer terms		
40% in shares		200
40% in 7% Convertible Loan Stock (CLS)		200
20% in 10% Unsecured Loan Stock/cash (ULS)		100
		500

	Pre-conversion	*Post conversion*
Effect on earnings per share		
Pre-tax profits of target	67	67
Less: interest on CLS	(14)	—
interest on ULS	(10)	(10)
	43	57
Less: tax at 25%	(11)	(14)
Earnings from target	32	43
Earnings from acquiror	100	100
Total	132	143
Shares of acquiror in issue	1000	1000
Shares issued for acquisition	200	200
Shares issued on conversion to CLS	—	180
Total	1200	1380
Net earnings per share	0.110	0.104

In the above example, the cost of debt at 10% is in nominal terms the same as the assumed earnings yield on the acquiror's shares which is also 10%. However, because interest payments are allowable for tax, an improvement in earnings per share from 0.10 to 0.11 is achieved. An equally important factor is the assumption that the coupon on convertible loan stock will be 7%, significantly lower than on the straight loan stock. After conversion, an improvement in earnings per share is still registered. This is partly because of the tax relief on the interest payment on the straight loan stock and partly because it is assumed that the conversion price for the convertible loan stock can be set at a premium to the current market price of the shares. This results in the issue of fewer shares than if shares have been issued at the outset.

(c) Goodwill

If a company is acquired at a premium over the 'fair' value of its assets, on consolidation an item of goodwill will be thrown up in the balance sheet. It is likely that the group's auditors will insist that this figure be written off over a certain period of time. In this case, the earnings contribution from the acquisition will be decreased by the write-off of goodwill each year. Although this has no effect on cash flow, it may significantly alter the published earnings of the group. This factor is discussed in more detail in ch 10 above.

(d) Balance sheet and gearing: purchase for cash

If a company is bought for cash, the existing equity base of the acquiror must be large enough to support the business acquired as well as its own. In effect, the shareholders' funds of the target company have been repaid in cash, increasing the gearing of the enlarged group.

To the extent that the acquired company has existing borrowings or immediate capital requirements, the gearing of the enlarged group will be further increased, possibly to dangerous levels. The acquiror must confirm that the terms of its own loan capital permit the acquisition on the basis proposed. Covenants to maintain a specified level of net current assets or debt to equity ratio may come under pressure. In addition, the transfer of control of a company can sometimes trigger repayment of its debts. Against this, the company acquired may have surplus liquid assets or assets which can be sold to counter the apparent increase in gearing.

In the case of a share exchange, gearing will not automatically be increased. Whether the gearing of the combined group will be higher or lower will depend on whether the company being acquired has financed a higher or lower proportion of its assets with borrowings than the acquiror.

The type of assets of the company being acquired must also be considered. A service company with little asset base may not add significantly to the new group's borrowing power. However, an asset rich acquisition may enable new funds to be raised even if the assets themselves are not immediately saleable.

It is sometimes possible to arrange for an issue of new share capital to existing or new shareholders in anticipation of an acquisition or immediately following one. At the time of an acquisition, considerable documentation will be available about the company. It may provide a suitable opportunity to arrange for further equity to be raised as a separate exercise and leave the offer in cash. This allows the overall capital structure of the enlarged group to be strengthened without making the terms of the offer itself more complex.

As mentioned above, a purchase of a company at above the fair value of its assets may give rise to an item of goodwill in the consolidated balance sheet of the group. In the calculation of gearing, goodwill is generally regarded as an intangible asset and may be deducted from the net asset figure, increasing the gearing of the enlarged group.

CHAPTER 15

Structure of offer and terms of payment

In most acquisitions, there will be scope for some flexibility in three critical areas which are discussed in this chapter.

(i)   What is the most appropriate method of gaining control of a particular target? It may not always be necessary to purchase the company to achieve the objective.

(ii) What level of control is desired? Sometimes it will be essential to obtain 100% control; at other times it may be the last thing an acquiror wants.

(iii) What options are open in paying for control? Payment can, for example, be in cash or securities and may be made on an immediate or deferred basis.

I   METHODS OF GAINING CONTROL

The task of gaining control can be approached from various different angles depending on the reasons for the acquisition, the resources of the acquiror and other more technical factors.

(i) Assets or company?

If the reason for making an acquisition is primarily to control a major asset and not for the business, it may be feasible to purchase that asset rather than the company which owns it. The factors to consider include the following:

(a) Simplicity

The complications of acquiring an asset are less than those of acquiring a company. If a company is acquired, it is necessary to investigate all its assets and liabilities, including contracts it may have entered into and other actual or contingent obligations. On the other hand, it is usually possible to buy an asset such as a property or a ship by itself, without any entanglements.

(b) Finance

Banks may be prepared to finance a higher percentage of the purchase price where they can take a direct charge over the asset than if their security is at one stage removed, through shares in a company. Interest costs may be lower, reflecting the bank's perception of lesser risk. Security documents are likely to be shorter and in a more standard form, decreasing legal fees and management time required.

(c) Taxation

Taxation implications may exert a deciding influence on the matter.

In some countries, tax on the transfer of an asset is greater than tax on the transfer of shares. Negotiations may be complicated, if the purchaser of an asset is liable for all the transfer duty. In a transaction involving shares, buyer and seller usually split the duty payments equally.

The vendor's profits or income tax liability may be affected if the asset is sold rather than the company. On the other hand, if the purchaser buys the company, he must be aware that the cost of the asset in the company's books for tax purposes may be much lower (for example, because values have risen with inflation) than the value which is reflected in the price paid for shares. A provision for contingent tax should be included in the calculations of the value of the company.

This approach will not be possible where the attractiveness of an acquisition depends on the business connections of the company such as its suppliers, customers and other commercial relationships.

(ii) Shares and shareholder loans

A private company may well be established with a small share capital and subsequently funded by loans from shareholders or other related parties. This method has the advantage of minimising any capital duty on the issue of new shares. It is also more flexible as the advance can be repaid without any question of reduction of capital or the need to have sufficient distributable reserves to declare dividends.

If a company capitalised in this way is being considered, it is important to ensure that the entire shareholders' funds are purchased and not simply the share capital. Calculations of value must be carried out on a consistent basis. Very often it is convenient not to charge interest on shareholder loans. This means that if the company is valued on an earnings basis, the valuation will correspond to the entire shareholders' funds, whether they are made up of share capital or loans or both. No question of repayment of loans to shareholders in addition to the purchase price can arise. On the other hand, if the loans have been treated on an arm's length basis and interest charged, then an earnings-based valuation will relate simply to the worth of the issued share capital. The repayment of any shareholder loans and the interest rate which they are to bear are matters to be considered separately.

In some countries, there may be no or a lower rate of transfer tax on the assignment of loans. There may therefore be considerable tax savings available by purchasing shareholder loans in such a way that the value attributed to the share capital of the company being acquired is reduced.

Particular care must be taken when a bank or financial company is being acquired. Part of the funding arrangements and deposit base may be tied to, or depend on, the outgoing management and shareholders. If, as is usual, a premium is being paid over net asset value, partly to reflect the value of the deposit base, it must be clear what deposits are likely to be withdrawn following the change of control. This is not only a question of value but of liquidity. The worst possible start to the acquisition of a financial institution is to suffer a loss of confidence and a run on deposits after a change of control.

(iii) Obtaining control via loans

It will sometimes be the case that a company's shareholders' funds have become largely irrelevant. Where a company has encountered financial difficulty, the lenders to the company may have the effective control due to the erosion of the company's equity base. Depending on the terms of the loans, it may be possible to acquire control by buying the benefit of the loan rather than by buying the shares. For example, the terms of the loan may give the lender the right to take security over assets through a floating charge and to put in a receiver/manager to run the business. This would allow the prospective purchaser to control the company's affairs while an investigation is carried out as to whether deeper involvement is wise. This can substantially reduce the risks involved in a purchase where quick action may be required to prevent liquidation of the company.

The terms of the loan may, by agreement of the board and the shareholders of the company, be amended to include the right of conversion into equity. Alternatively, the prospective purchaser may be granted options to subscribe new equity in due course, thus enabling the acquiror to control the share capital if the equity proves to have a value. In the meantime by purchasing the benefit of a loan, the acquiror can signal to the market that he is not committed to stand behind the obligations of the company. On occasions, a purchaser who becomes a major shareholder of a company is seen as having taken moral responsibility for the company overall. This can lead either to embarrassment if the company is subsequently allowed to fail or to financial loss if the purchaser feels obliged to support it.

(iv) Obtaining control by subscription of new shares rather than purchase

If control of a company is available for purchase because of a shortage of capital, it is sensible to consider obtaining that control by an injection of new capital rather than a purchase of existing shares or loans. The company being acquired will no doubt require financial support in any case. It is more attractive for the purchaser to kill two birds with one stone by subscribing for sufficient new shares to obtain majority control while at the same time providing cash to the company. If shares are bought from existing shareholders, cash goes out of the system. The financial position of the company is not improved unless there is an agreement for the shareholders receiving the cash to support the company in some way. Because no existing shares are purchased, the new controlling shareholder may be able to obtain a waiver from making a general offer to all shareholders which would otherwise be required when control passes under the terms of the takeover code, in countries where a code operates.

This procedure requires that existing shareholders are willing to retain their shares while being diluted by the new party. This may not be unrealistic as the original shareholders frequently prefer not to sell at a moment they may feel is the nadir of the company's fortunes.

(v) Management control

Sometimes control can be obtained at a management level in a way which achieves the 'acquiror's' purpose without any acquisition being made. A majority on the board of directors may be secured through a proxy fight without significant purchases of shares. The mere threat of a takeover bid or proxy fight may persuade the board of a company to accommodate the wishes of a third party.

This method is only really effective if control is desired to achieve a specific objective rather than for the overall financial benefits of owning the majority of the shares in a company. For example, a property developer eyeing a company with a large land bank may be perfectly content to secure a joint venture agreement over the development of that land. To acquire the company and assume responsibility for its business and employees is an unnecessary complication. The whole benefits of control to the developer can be achieved through one agreement.

II LEVEL OF CONTROL DESIRED

If an acquiror has decided to purchase a company rather than its assets, he should then consider whether he wishes or needs to control all the share capital of a company. On some occasions, a lesser amount will be sufficient.

(i) 100% control

The major advantage of owning the entire share capital of a company is flexibility in what can be done after the acquisition has been completed. Assets can be transferred or sold without having to consider the interests of minority shareholders. Funds can be channelled more easily to wherever they are needed. Future projects, business and costs can be allocated without the need to be fair to outside equity partners. Banks who have given financial support to fund an acquisition may place proportionately greater security value on the entire share capital of a company than on any lesser percentage.

If the company being acquired is a public company, the retention of minority shareholders may prove particularly burdensome. Some transactions will require the approval of shareholders in general meeting. The report and accounts and other documents have to be published and sent to shareholders. The annual general meeting has to be held in public, allowing questions to be raised by outside parties. Material transactions with the controlling shareholder may be criticised by minorities. The controlling shareholders themselves will be unable to vote on such transactions. If the minorities are hostile or become very small, the outcome of such meetings may be difficult to forecast.

As a consequence, it frequently happens that controlling shareholders eventually decide to buy out small minorities. This is done principally to reduce the level of disclosure required, to minimise administration costs and to consolidate the management of the company fully with its parent.

(ii) Partial control

There are a number of reasons why an acquiror may not wish to purchase 100% of the share capital of the target company.

(a) Cost

One obvious advantage of a partial purchase is that the total consideration to be paid is correspondingly lower. In some cases, it may simply not be possible for an acquiror to fund a purchase of 100%.

(b) Commitment of management and other parties

Even if finance is not a constraint, it may be desirable to leave key parties such as the management team with a share in the business in order to provide them with a reason for staying on and an incentive in running the business. A purchaser may be particularly concerned at the prospect of losing senior executives soon after a takeover when its own capacity to replace them is likely to be low. The retention of a shareholding in outside hands also helps to preserve the image of independence. This may be desirable in the case of a group with a long tradition and a loyal customer base.

(c) Gaining or retaining a listing

If the target company is publicly quoted, its listing may have been one attraction in making the acquisition. To retain the listing, it will be necessary to demonstrate that there remains a sufficient spread of shareholdings in public hands to ensure an adequate degree of marketability. In this case, it is advantageous if certain shareholders agree from the outset not to accept an offer or not to accept it for the entirety of their holdings.

The new controlling shareholder of a listed company may wish to retain the listing for essentially the same reasons as persuade shareholders to take a company public in the first place. The most relevant reasons in the context of an acquisition are to be able to use paper for future acquisitions through the newly acquired vehicle and to raise loans against the security of the shares. Unlisted shares are unlikely to be as acceptable to vendors of companies as consideration or to banks as security.

Partial control usually relates to holdings of over 50% of the share capital. The issue of voting at general meetings is not in doubt at least on matters which require a simple majority. In the case of a company with a wide spread of passive shareholders, effective control may be gained at a much lower shareholding level than 50%, provided that the new shareholder is able to obtain board representation and the appointment of key executives. This is reflected in the takeover codes of countries where such codes operate. The level of shareholding at which a general offer for a public company is required varies considerably but can be as low as 20%.

Partial control may be backed up by an option to purchase further shares (possibly all the remaining shares) at some later date. The attraction to a purchaser is that further time is allowed for investigation and increased familiarity with the company before a commitment to go the whole hog is made. An option can also serve as a method of deferred purchase while eliminating the possibility that the vendors will sell their remaining shares to a third party.

In such cases, the option price may be subject to increase (or decrease) depending on the performance of the company in the intervening period. This may be seen as an attractive feature to both acquiror and vendor at the time of the transaction. The acquiror may consider that the sellers are not washing their hands of the company and have an incentive to achieve profit growth. On the other hand, the vendors may feel that they do not entirely forego the future potential by agreeing to sell now.

III TERMS OF PAYMENT

There are a number of different ways in which an acquiror can consider financing its acquisition. Sometimes this will require negotiation with the vendors; at others, negotiations will be with third party financiers so that the vendors receive the same type of consideration irrespective of how the acquisition is financed.

(i) Cash

Cash has the great merit of being simple, understandable and hard to argue with. The attractions of cash are likely to be most apparent to the seller but some noted takeover exponents consider that cash payment imposes a useful discipline on the buyer also. A number of factors need consideration.

(a) How can cash be raised?

If an acquiror has sufficient liquid assets, it may simply pay for an acquisition out of its own funds. For an acquisition of a significant size, an acquiror is likely to wish at least to supplement its own resources by external funding.

The most common source of finance is bank lending. Credit lines may have already been negotiated, although they may not necessarily be available or suitable as acquisition finance. As a major acquisition is outside the ordinary course of business, the company should brief its bankers beforehand or, if confidentiality forbids this, at the earliest stage possible. Most acquisitions need longer-term finance than the company's normal requirements. The acquiror may wish to negotiate with its bankers for extended maturities.

If bank finance is required, the question of security for the borrowings will arise. In some countries, legal problems can occur if a company could be considered to be giving assistance in the purchase of its own shares. This is a point on which detailed legal advice is required. Unless the acquiror is very lightly geared or the acquisition is a small one, repayments of bank borrowings to fund a cash bid are very likely to come, at least in part, from the cash flow (including asset disposals) of the company being acquired. Even under the strictest interpretation of the legislation, it seems that the company acquired could pay very substantial dividends to its new parent to service loans, provided it has sufficient distributable reserves.

Funds can also be raised for acquisitions by the issue of securities to institutions and other third parties. The issue of high yielding bonds ('junk bonds') has become an important source of financing acquisitions in the US. Such bonds are attractive to investors as they typically involve high fees and yield considerably more than would be normal for a standard bond issue.

The payment of the high coupons and the repayment of the principal depends significantly on funds being released from disposals of the assets of the company being acquired. If the disposal programme does not proceed to schedule, if economic conditions worsen or if the acquiror has misjudged the value of the assets in the first place, the worth of 'junk bonds' could be brought into question. They represent the replacement of a significant part of the acquisition's equity by debt obligations of the acquiror company. This implies that it is possible to run the enlarged group with a significantly lower level of equity than was the case previously. This strategy does not leave much margin for error.

(b) LBOs and MBOs

In a leveraged buy-out, a group of parties come together to acquire a company funded principally with loans intended to be repaid out of asset disposals. Where management is involved this type of operation is called a 'management buy-out'. As a practical matter, it is likely that management involvement will be necessary in order to gain the confidence of the lending or other investment institutions. Their risk would be extreme if a highly geared group were intended to be run without the assistance of existing management or other people with very similar experience who could develop an informed and detailed plan to show how the loans could be repaid.

Many leveraged buy-out operations begin to look like a controlled liquidation, at least of a part of the business. Indeed, the main logic underlying such transactions is that there exists a profitable core of businesses to which a group can be stripped down, freeing up significant, perhaps not fully productive assets, for disposals.

The same logic suggests that at least one party to the transaction has under-valued the assets involved. The vendor may be a large conglomerate who during a period of growth acquired a series of businesses without subsequently being able to manage them actively or understand them properly. Management can become frustrated that administrative controls deprive them of the flexibility to make decisions and of the availability of funds for expansion. This may lead to a decline in the business and the demoralisation of management which results in under-performance. Indeed, once management begins to contemplate a buy-out there is little incentive to improve performance in advance of it.

Freed of the shackles of an unsympathetic parent, the business may indeed recover. If the problems are more deep-seated than appears, a resurgence of management enthusiasm may not be sufficient by itself to restore the company to health. The natural pride of a management in its own business can lead them to over-value it. Institutions who support such an operation with finance may be inclined to regret the persuasiveness management can bring to bear in such circumstances.

(c) Taxation

Acceptance of cash by the vendors can give rise to tax liabilities. They will be considered to have disposed of their shares and any capital gain will be realised at that point. This may simply be the penalty of having made a successful investment. However, there may be some advantage in offering vendors the alternative of taking shares or other paper. In this way, they may be able to 'roll-over' their investment so that no taxable gain will arise until they dispose of the securities they receive in exchange for their original holding.

(d) Cosmetic advantages of a paper alternative

The fact that cash is simple also means that there is no disguising that a sale is actually being made. It is not possible to suggest to vendors that they retain any kind of stake in the future of the business. If some alternative, even partial, can be offered in paper in addition to the cash, this not only gives the vendors another option but may also make them feel they are not being forced to part with their investment in the company altogether.

(ii) Deferred terms

As part of the negotiations between buyer and seller, it may be agreed that all or part of payment for an acquisition should be on a deferred basis instead of for immediate settlement. One reason may be because the acquiror cannot afford to put up 100% of the purchase price initially but there are a number of other circumstances in which deferred terms may be appropriate.

(a) As vendor finance

Deferred payment may be considered to be mainly to the advantage of the purchaser. It may be offered by the vendors if they realise that to demand cash is likely to restrict the chances of a sale. In some cases, the assets being purchased may not be acceptable as security for conventional bank borrowing. Vendor finance not only makes the transaction possible but gives the purchaser an indication of the vendors' confidence in the quality of the assets and the price being paid. For the vendors, provided security is retained over the asset, the worst outcome would be to take back the asset and retain the deposit.

Vendor finance is most suitable where a relatively straightforward asset such as a property is being sold. In the case of a business, the damage done by the changes of control can make this structure undesirable.

(b) As part of negotiation on price

Payment by instalments can be a useful negotiating device where a seller insists on the amount he must receive and the purchaser's best offer falls short. A compromise can be achieved through a series of deferred payments. These may add up to the nominal sum the vendor has in mind but have a discounted present value (allowing for interest) equal to the price the purchaser is prepared to pay. While this may seem purely cosmetic, it is surprising how frequently a vendor is concerned to claim he has achieved a particular figure, perhaps to avoid a book loss.

(c) To provide for a period of investigation

The purchaser will investigate an acquisition at the time of the transaction to find out what problems may exist. Without being in full control of the business, a purchaser cannot be entirely confident he has identified all the potential pitfalls. Difficulties may not become apparent for some period of time. If the whole purchase price is paid on completion, the purchaser may have to sue the vendor to recover any damages due. If, on the other hand, the purchaser retains some portion of the purchase price, he has the option to refuse to pay the balance if he feels the terms of the sale and purchase agreement have been broken. The vendor must then prove that the purchaser is withholding money unfairly. No question arises as to whether the vendor can actually repay the sum in dispute. If the vendor's business proves to have some financial weaknesses, it is likely that the purchase price, once paid over, will prove difficult to recover.

(d) To allow for variations in price

The price for an acquisition may vary depending on future performance. It is sometimes useful to have a performance-related element in the consideration so as to give management an incentive and to allow vendors to share in future growth. In such cases, payment has to be by instalments as the amounts due cannot be known at the outset.

Difficulties can arise with this structure. The new controlling shareholder may wish to change the accounting policies of the company. This will affect the reported profits in a way which may not reflect the performance of the business. In addition, disputes may arise over policies which are good for the business but may depress short-term profits. The new controlling shareholder may wish to establish a conservative base for growth for the future. The vendors will wish to maximise profits in the period during which the variable consideration is calculated.

(iii) Exchange of securities

An alternative to payment in cash immediately or on a deferred basis is to offer an exchange of securities. This is only likely to be a practical possibility where the securities being offered are, or will be, listed on a recognised stock exchange and so have a reasonable degree of marketability. The securities offered may be equity, debt or instruments combining both these elements.

An offer which includes an element other than cash can present problems of understanding for the shareholders to whom it is offered. The more elements there are in such an offer, the greater the likely problems become. It is a useful rule not to include more types of security than is really necessary and to ensure that the securities which are offered are as familiar as possible.

(a) Ordinary shares

The most obvious choice is ordinary shares of the acquiror which rank in all respects equally to shares which are already in issue. The acquiror must weigh up the percentage in the equity of the enlarged group which is being allocated to the shareholders of the company being acquired. The acquiror must expect that shareholders of a target company may not necessarily see the merits of the acquiror's paper as clearly as the acquiror itself.

The provision of a cash alternative by underwriting or some other method will establish the worth of the securities being offered. Firm arrangements are desirable to deal with a large number of shares being issued to investors who may not be long-term holders. In the absence of such proposals, the announcement of the bid may trigger a period of price weakness in the acquiror's shares. This can play havoc with calculations of the worth of the bid based on market prices before the announcement.

(b) Shares with different rights

Despite additional complications, it may be advantageous to offer shares with different rights from the existing ordinary shares. If the target company pays a high dividend, it may be necessary to offer shares carrying preferred dividend rights in order to be able to offer an attractive increase in income to the target's shareholders. An alternative might be for the acquiring company to raise its own dividends to match that of the target. However, this requires the higher dividend to be paid on all the issued shares of the acquiror, which may not be practicable.

As well as shares with improved rights, shares with restricted rights may be utilised in acquisitions.

Shares which do not, for the moment, carry any rights to dividends may be acceptable to vendors as consideration for an asset which does not currently generate income. An example is a property for development where the development period might typically be two to three years. In this case, shares could be issued which carry no rights to dividend during the development period, after which they would rank equally with the other shares. Until they do, they are unlikely to be freely tradable in the market.

Shares can also be issued with rights linked to the particular business being acquired. This is a useful device where the acquiring company is very large with a different major activity to that of the target company. The target company shareholders may feel little interest in being shareholders of a company so dissimilar to their original investment. To counter this, the dividend of the new shares may be linked to the performance of the business being acquired and not to the group as a whole. Accounting problems may arise but an acquiror may feel this is a fair price to pay where in any case it is intended that the acquisition should be run independently.

(c) Debt

Shareholders of the target company may also be offered debt obligations of the acquiring company. They may see an advantage in ranking ahead of shareholders in a company with which they are not familiar. The coupon on debt should provide a higher current income than dividends on an equivalent value of ordinary shares which should attract investors valuing high yields. The acquiror on the other hand can offer a higher nominal value without surrendering equity in the enlarged group. Where the company being acquired is asset rich, inclusion of some debt may seem appropriate to both sides. The vendors feel due consideration is being given to the assets contributed by their company, while the purchasers' equity is not diluted. The debt issued is prudently backed by assets and may be serviced by income from or disposals of such assets.

The inclusion of debt increases the debt/equity ratio of the enlarged group in the same way as a cash payment. However, depending on the repayment schedule of the debt, the impact on cash flow will be significantly reduced.

Debt may be issued on terms which enable it to be converted into ordinary shares. This allows the issuer and the holder to hedge their bets. If the underlying equity does not perform well, the debt will still hold its value to a considerable extent. If the company does well, holders of the convertible will benefit from conversion. The dilution effect to the issuing company's shareholders will be delayed until increased earnings can compensate for the larger number of shares in issue.

As an alternative to conversion rights, warrants to subscribe for the acquiror's company's securities (usually ordinary shares) may be included in the package. Warrants have proved rather difficult to value and may not be regarded as having much importance in the eyes of the target company's shareholders. They are viewed more as a general sweetener to the proposals.

In volatile and rising markets, warrants can have significant market worth. They may also prove useful to the issuing company. At the end of the warrant period, providing the underlying share price is above the warrant exercise price, new funds should be received by the issuing company through subscription of the warrants.

CHAPTER 16

Approach, negotiations and opening the attack

The time when analysis and planning stops and the initial approach to the potential vendors is made is a hurdle which many acquisition proposals fail to clear. An acquiror should try to tailor his method of approach to the particular circumstances of the case. The factors involved are discussed in 'I Initial approach' below. A general account of the art of negotiating is a subject in itself, but some basic points are covered in 'II Negotiations' below. 'III Opening the attack' below deals with tactics if no progress is made. Even the most delicate approach and skilful negotiating technique sometimes come up against a brick wall.

I INITIAL APPROACH

The right start to a transaction is likely to have an important bearing on its ultimate success. Where a company is owned and managed by different sets of people, a choice must be made as to which to contact first and what line to take. Sometimes the use of an intermediary can allow for more flexibility than a principal-to-principal approach. If the target company is listed, there will be constraints imposed by the need to keep negotiations confidential.

(i) Shareholders versus management

In companies with a wide spread of shareholdings and a professional management team, the executive control of the company is in the hands of management, divorced from the ownership of the company which lies with the shareholders. It is management's responsibility to run the business on behalf of the shareholders and in normal circumstances there is little reason to expect them to do otherwise. However, the interests of the two groups may diverge sharply in the case of an actual or threatened takeover bid.

Management may be concerned principally with retaining their power, prestige and livelihood, particularly if they are not well protected by service contracts. Shareholders, on the other hand, are understandably attracted by the chance of realising an immediate and substantial gain in the value of their investment. Particularly in the case of a cash offer, they may not feel greatly concerned about how the company is run afterwards or who is running it.

This divergence of interest may have two undesirable consequences. If an incumbent management is convinced that they have no future after an acquisition, they may well try to discourage proposals being put forward or disguise the fact that they have been. If they are forced to recognise the existence of an offer, their first reaction may be to criticise its terms whatever the financial advantages to shareholders. Emotive language may be used against the offeror who will be labelled a 'corporate raider' or 'asset stripper'. This may of course be true or partly true but misses the point. Shareholders wish to be told whether the long-term prospects of yet-to-be achieved profits justify rejecting the bird in the hand. Arguments put forward by managements as regards the need for stability to ensure the long run success of the company can sound very high minded but may be spiced with a dash of self-interest.

On occasions, managements have been prepared to pay 'greenmail' to an aggressive acquiror of shares who is bought out using the company's resources. This rewards the opportunistic buyer at the expense of the existing shareholders. It tends to leave the company with a weakened capital structure while denying the body of shareholders an equal offer for their shares. Once one raider has been bought off, another may pounce.

A similar danger for existing shareholders is a management which is wooed by an acquiror. Management may be flattered by comments on their abilities and the importance of their remaining in office after the acquisition. If they become convinced that a takeover would enhance their own position, they can make ideal advocates of the proposals to shareholders. It is not uncommon to find proposals from acquaintances or associates of existing management being recommended to shareholders as being in their interests only to be topped by a less welcome party whose appetite has been aroused by the prospects of a bargain. In this situation, the tactical advantage lies heavily with the less welcome party. The board of the target company has not only lost credibility by its premature recommendation of a low offer but has also deprived itself of a major defensive ploy, the argument that the price offered is too low.

(ii) Use of intermediaries

A mutual acquaintance, merger broker or other agent may be of assistance in making the first approach. A seller may indicate a willingness to deal to a third party without being thought to display weakness. In a direct contact, the potential seller might well be more cautious. The role of a 'marriage broker' to break the ice is as useful in this context as in a number of others.

A third party using 'shuttle diplomacy' between principals has more chance of narrowing the gap between two sets of proposals without being hung up on a particular structure or price. A skilful intermediary will seek to make both parties feel he is on their side. As someone who is committed to neither and paid only if a deal is consummated his interest lies in seeking ways to reconcile the objectives of buyer and seller.

If emotions run high, a direct meeting between acquiror and the target company's management or shareholders may be bad tempered. A clash of personalities can hinder the conclusion of a proposal which might otherwise have a good chance of success.

(iii) Publicly listed companies

If the target company is publicly listed, special considerations apply. A leak of the possibility of an offer being made or that negotiations are in progress may cause a rise in the share price. This works against the interest of the offeror by making his proposals look less attractive when compared with the market price ruling immediately before a public announcement. A sharp price rise may also embarrass a management which is seeking to be helpful.

Precautions aimed at keeping discussions confidential by restricting knowledge of them to the minimum number of people are essential. Holding talks on neutral ground is worthwhile if proposals reach an advanced stage. On the other hand, a management which wishes to frustrate an offer may resort to a deliberate leak.

The stock exchanges and other regulatory authorities are alert to unusual levels of trading of companies' shares and will monitor the position as a matter of course. Sometimes pressure will mount for an announcement which the parties regard as premature. Ritual denials can look very foolish in light of the unveiling of a detailed transaction, sometimes hours later.

If the proposals are not likely to be welcome to the target company, the acquiror may decide to maintain secrecy in order to achieve a surprise attack. If it is decided that negotiations in advance will be fruitless, the acquiror will wish to give the target the minimum time possible to marshall its defence and present its case. Announcements immediately prior to major holidays such as Christmas and New Year are not unknown. A public company offer usually has to be open for a minimum period (say three weeks) but holidays are not excluded.

II NEGOTIATIONS

Merger and acquisition negotiations tend to be particularly prone to breakdowns and other disruptions. It is hard to remain detached and objective while selling a business which has taken years to build up and which may be closely identified with one individual. Equally, the process of buying a company can be wrapped up with the ambition and prestige of the individuals involved. Takeover battles make good reading and, if one becomes public, the added glare of publicity can magnify the problems. The following paragraphs suggest some guidelines through this potential minefield.

(i) Knowledge of the other party

During investigation of a target, some information should have been obtained concerning its directors and shareholders. As the first approach would normally be to the chairman of the target company, a knowledge of this person's character and personality may be particularly valuable. The initial contact with the chairman is probably the moment of greatest danger as, if this goes badly, all subsequent negotiations may be irretrievably soured.

It may sometimes be possible to use a divide and rule tactic, splitting the directors into two camps. Experience suggests that an unsolicited approach to buy a company is one of the few things which will unite directors who may have been quarrelling bitterly over other matters.

If it seems likely that an appeal will be made to the general body of shareholders over the heads of directors, the personalities of the major shareholders (or, if institutions, their representatives) will be relevant. Do they regard themselves as 'loyalists' or will they treat a bid in an objective way? Has the company done anything in the recent past, such as missed a profit forecast, which would have unsettled them?

(ii) Assembling a team

A team approach to negotiations can be very productive. It is not easy for one person to grasp all aspects of a transaction and impossible for him to analyse thoroughly all the various alternatives which may be open. A properly briefed team of advisors is necessary to keep a negotiator effective 'in the front line'. The composition of such a team will depend on the business of the target company but will normally include a firm of accountants and lawyers as well as a merchant banking advisor and, if the company is listed, a stockbroker.

Presentation of the arguments and analysis carried out by the team may be put forward more effectively by a single person. Some effort may be expended by the negotiator to conceal the depth of analysis and planning which lie behind an approach. The negotiator may be significantly assisted by a go-between of some sort, perhaps a non-executive director of the target company known to both parties or a merger broker. The broker's objective will be to bring a deal to fruition. He will therefore seek to find solutions to the problems rather than to negotiate the toughest possible deal for one side or the other. Negotiations which result in a deal which is too tough on one side frequently collapse at a later stage.

(iii) Timing

The outcome of many negotiations is dependent upon timing. The state of mind of the vendor may critically affect his attitude to a sale. At times of difficulty, either for the economy as a whole or for a particular company, a realistic attitude towards doing a deal is likely to prevail on the part of the vendor. This however is precisely the time when a purchaser will need most courage to push forward.

Confidence born of a thorough analysis of the target is important. A well thought-through programme to assimilate the acquisition into the acquiror's group can pay great dividends at this stage. If the purchaser delays until the market recovers, he is likely to find that the seller has changed his mind or at least increased his expectations of price.

(iv) Win a recommendation

Recommendation of an offer by a target public company's board is probably the most single important factor in success. Recommended offers fail principally if they are topped by a third party, in which case the initial suitor can at least retire with a dealing profit if he has built up a share stake as a platform for a bid.

Obtaining a recommendation tends to deter third parties from entering the fray. Buyers who might have been interested may be reluctant to disturb an agreed deal. They fear rebuff and are conscious of the premium price they would have to offer. There may also be the risk of legal sanctions if they can be considered to have persuaded a seller to break a contract.

If a recommendation is not achieved and the bid vigorously opposed, it can often be repulsed. Even if it succeeds, a substantially increased offer may well be required, resulting in a pyrrhic victory which the purchaser lives to regret. On other occasions, the ultimately successful party enters later in the day and the bidder who has made the running finds that the prize is elusive.

A recommendation is so important that it can be regarded as a factor separate from the financial and business position of the target company. It has a value which may be estimated as equivalent to the cost of fees, expenses and management time of a contested bid, plus the intangible damage to business morale and image which may be caused by failure.

(v) Keeping something in reserve

Company chairmen spend a significant proportion of their working lives in negotiations of one sort or another. They like to believe that they are successful negotiators. Unless the target company is so vulnerable that it has to accept anything it can get, a purchaser should keep something in reserve in the initial approach which can be conceded at a later stage. The chairman or his advisers can feel that extracting this concession is their contribution to the deal.

Care must be taken that, in allowing some scope for improvement in an offer, the initial level is not pitched so low that it cannot be considered a serious offer. If it can be dismissed as a sighting shot, the purchaser may find he has to begin all over again from a higher base, without extracting any worthwhile response from the target. The alternative is to let the bid drop at a level which is far below what the offeror was in fact prepared to pay, which is even more unsatisfactory.

(vi) Setting limits

It is important for an offeror to consider his upper price limit before serious negotiations begin. Once personalities are engaged, it is all too easy to be carried away in 'hot pursuit' of an acquisition. Success becomes an end in itself, a matter of corporate and personal pride which can overwhelm other factors and lead to poor judgment.

It is legitimate to review prices set in advance if more information becomes available. This is in fact likely to happen during negotiations or as part of defence documents issued by a target company. However, strict control must be exercised to ensure that the information provided does indeed justify revision of the limits set in the cooler atmosphere before a bid began. Prices paid in contested bids tend to demand unrealistic rates of growth or very high increases in asset values to be justified.

III   OPENING THE ATTACK

It is necessary for the potential acquiror to monitor the progress of negotiations carefully. If negotiations lead to an agreement and a recommended offer, this virtually guarantees success. It is therefore worth expending a good deal of time and effort to obtain. On the other hand, it will be to the advantage of a board, even one which is determined to resist, to engage in negotiations if only to gain time to marshall their defences. An acquiror must be alert for a phase of negotiations which represent a target simply playing for time and which are highly unlikely to lead to any fruitful conclusion. At this stage, the acquiror will have to decide whether to let the transaction die or to make an offer without the blessing of the target company's board.

(i) Private companies

In the case of a private company, the room for manoeuvre is limited. The acquiror is normally faced with a vendor who controls the share capital and management of the company and is therefore not susceptible to pressures in this area. In addition, the standard articles of association for a private company contain a pre-emption clause, providing for shares being disposed of by one shareholder to be offered to other existing shareholders before they can be purchased by a third party. This presents a further hindrance to a forceful approach.

An acquiror may nevertheless be able to gain some advantage by establishing a timetable and pressing ahead with the events required before a deal can be completed. This assists in building up momentum and making a transaction seem more definite in the eyes of the principals. Setting of deadlines (as long as they are not unreasonable) for completion of various stages contributes to a sense of steady progress. The acquiror must be able to move decisively at each stage, including being prepared to incur professional expenses and line up the necessary finance even when it is by no means certain that it will be required.

(ii) Public companies

In the case of public companies, the option is open to appeal to the body of shareholders over the heads of the directors. The single most important factor in securing a successful outcome is probably a recommendation from the board of the offeree company. To achieve this, it may be advantageous to leave something in reserve when the initial offer is made so that the negotiators can claim credit for having extracted an increased price or other concessions in return for the recommendation.

(a) Price

If a recommendation cannot be secured, the offeror has relatively little room for manoeuvre and must rely on fairly blunt instruments. The major factor becomes simply the price he is prepared to pay. The opening price offered must be at a significant premium to the market price before the bid in order to grab the attention of shareholders. Although no hard and fast rules can be set, a premium of around 20% over market seems a common starting point.

In considering the premium, an analysis of the recent price history and levels of turnover must be taken into account. In many instances, the share price will tend to increase in the period prior to the announcement of a bid owing to market speculation and information leaks. The price is said in these circumstances to be 'frothy'. It would be reasonable for the acquiror to base his calculations on the price level which prevailed in the period before any rumours surfaced.

If a bid is timed after a steep decline in share price, many existing shareholders are likely to have acquired shares at prices significantly higher than the current market price. Although the acquiror may be able to make some mileage out of the premium at which the bid is pitched, he must nevertheless realise that shareholders may be reluctant to sell at prices which will result in a loss to themselves, in spite of the healthy premium over the prevailing market price. It may be found that there was particularly heavy turnover at certain prices, in which case these prices will be particularly sensitive to the shareholders who bought at that time.

If it can be said that the offer price is at a premium to the all-time high of the target company's share price, this is likely to be a powerful argument. All shareholders will make some profit. If the all-time high was reached some years ago, it will be relevant to look at the highs over the last two or three years to see if a more limited statement relating to those years only is possible.

(b) Timing

The timing of the bid may be partially determined by the progress and speed of the negotiations which precede it. Sometimes an acquiror will spring a surprise attack and time the announcement at a period of maximum difficulty for the target to mount an effective reply and organise its defence. A holiday season may be chosen or the attack launched just after an announcement of poor prospects or other problems by the target, particularly if this news comes at the time of the annual report. In these circumstances, it will be very difficult for the target to publish an optimistic forecast.

In the first place, as there will be a relatively long period before the next year end, prudence will demand a considerable safety margin should be built into any forecast. Second, if the chairman is already committed to some rather gloomy remarks about the future, he cannot turn round and forecast a sudden improvement without putting his own credibility in doubt.

Similar arguments apply if an acquiror can identify rivals for the target company. In that case, it will be advantageous to select a period when the potential competitor has other priorities or problems.

If the terms of the offer include an element of equity-linked paper, the acquiror should prepare the ground by choosing a time when it knows it can forecast good results and positive developments in its own business. This will be useful not only for supporting its own share price but in order to make favourable comparisons with the business and results of the target. The acquiror should pay attention to the rating of its shares in the period leading up to the offer. The higher the price of the shares and the greater the support of the shareholders, the more attractive the terms of the bid will appear to be for the acquiror. The share price is more likely to bounce back from the marking down which is often the initial market reaction to the announcement of a significant bid.

(c) Platform for the bid

A common procedure is to accumulate a block of shares in the target company to serve as a platform for the bid. There are a number of advantages to this. It may serve to lower the overall cost of the bid as shares are bought at market price rather than at the premium level at which the bid will be pitched. It also helps to give credibility and momentum to the offer if a significant number of shares are already 'in the bag'. In addition, it allows a dual strategy on the part of the acquiror as regards rival offers. The knowledge that the initial offeror has a significant stake may in itself deter possible rivals. However, if a rival does emerge and is ultimately successful at a higher price than the initial bid, the initiator has the consolation of a dealing profit to offset expenses and show some reward for his efforts.

If substantial blocks of shares can be identified beforehand, it may be possible to deliver a virtual knock-out blow by purchasing in the market or from selected major holders. Rapid purchase of an effective controlling stake is known as a 'dawn raid'. Some markets have introduced checks on the vigour with which dawn raids can be mounted. These restrictions are designed to allow a target company breathing space to put forward its defence and provide up-dated information to shareholders so that they can make an informed decision on whether to sell their shares. Such regulations may prevent an acquiror from carrying off the prize in one fell swoop via a dawn raid, but the arguments in favour of building up a stake in advance of an announcement remain powerful.

Purchases in the market or from major holders must be handled carefully if they are not to backfire. Market purchases may have the effect of supporting the share price of the target company or even of pushing it up. This may result in the acquisition actually becoming more expensive for the acquiror. If he is not able to buy many shares, the saving will be relatively small. It applies to only a few percent of the share capital whereas the offer for the remainder may have to be pitched higher in order to appear attractive as compared to the price before the announcement of the offer. The higher offer will apply to many more shares than have been acquired at the cheaper price in the market. Takeover codes (where they apply) commonly provide that all shareholders should be offered a price equivalent to the highest price paid for shares during the offer period. Consequently, purchases at a price higher than the offer value will require the entire offer to be revised, even for shareholders who have already accepted at the lower levels.

The ability to purchase substantial blocks of shares in the market after an offer has been announced may be a warning sign that some shareholders feel the offer may not be successful. If they also feel the share price will fall if the offer lapses, their best policy will be to sell in the market while the bid is still on the table. A purchaser buying such shares risks being caught with a substantial (and expensive) minority holding if his offer fails.

(d) Offer document

The wording of contested bids is fairly strong by the standards of professional documentation. This is one of the few occasions when the normally restrained language may go out of the window and the professionals involved have the opportunity to let their hair down.

The offer document sent out on behalf of the offeror will normally criticise the record of the incumbent management of the group under attack in terms of its financial record and business abilities. Published documents such as annual reports and circulars to shareholders will be carefully studied and any broken promises, over-optimistic comments or missed forecasts contained in them will be gleefully seized upon. The verbal warfare by circular may be backed by prominent advertisements in the press and sallies by supportive stockbrokers, journalists and public relations consultants.

A more staid part of the document will cover the financial arguments for accepting the offer. The aim in this section is to show that the shareholder enjoys a significant appreciation in the capital value of his investment under the terms of the offer. It will also try to show that his income (before and after tax) increases, or is at least maintained.

As an acquiror's shares will often be more highly rated than the target company's, it will not necessarily follow that, in a share exchange, an increase in capital value will be backed up by an increase in attributable assets and earnings. The acquiror should be aware of the likely defence in this area and do what it can to minimise the opportunity for a counter-attack. It may be limited by the wish not to dilute the attributable assets or earnings of its own shareholders, which would inevitably be the case if it was offering the target company increases in attributable assets and earnings.

The best that can probably be achieved in this area is that any dilution in the earnings and assets attributable to the selling shareholders will not be sufficient to outweigh the benefit to them of the increase in capital value. The target company's management cannot go too far on this point without leaving themselves open in turn to attack. Why are their shares apparently so lowly-rated despite the asset backing and earnings record?

Vigorous assaults may at the least persuade the target company to release more detailed and probably more favourable information about themselves. This will enable the acquiror to analyse the position in greater depth to satisfy itself that its own proposals are sound. To the extent that the information is favourable, the acquiror will have the ammunition to persuade its own shareholders and financiers that a higher offer is prudent and not just the blind pursuit of success.

Care should be taken that criticism of the target company and its management does not become a double-edged sword. If the criticism is of the company, the question may arise as to why the acquisition is so desirable in the first place. If the criticism is of the management, after the offer closes, assuming the acquiror does not intend to replace executives wholesale, the wounds of battle may make relations very bitter. A defensive and resentful management can cause a malaise in the period after an acquisition which jeopardises the value of the business being acquired. The South may rise again.

(e) Components of the offer

The offeror should attempt to tailor the components of its offer to suit the shareholders.

If shareholders are likely to have significant capital gains tax problems, they may prefer to receive securities in exchange for their existing holdings rather than cash. If they receive cash, there is no doubt that they have disposed of their shares and the gain would be crystallised. If they receive securities, it is normally possible to 'roll-over' the gain until the securities received in exchange are disposed of. Shareholders may prefer to feel that they still retain an interest in the business after they sell their shareholding. If they receive shares (or other equity-linked securities) in a group which includes the company in which they are currently shareholders, they will still participate in its future success. If they have no option but to receive cash, the deal may take on a rather more different complexion and possibly require a higher price for success.

On the other hand, shareholders may believe that if they are going to sell out they should receive cash, which gives them maximum flexibility for reinvestment. Why should they become shareholders in a group which they had not independently selected as a desirable investment? There may be a feeling that it is rather a cheek to offer paper instead of cash and that this is not a proper form of payment. The more complicated the securities involved in the offer become, the more likely this argument is to be heard, until the purchaser is accused of paying for the acquisition with 'funny money'.

The most versatile arrangement is to offer shareholders a choice between taking securities or an equivalent amount of cash. This can be achieved either by the company providing the cash alternative itself or by arranging for the securities which will be issued to be underwritten. In such circumstances, it is not unusual for the cash offer to be set somewhat below the nominal value of the paper offer. Care must be taken to ensure that the gap does not become too large as this gives the target company an opening to attack the credibility and value of the paper being offered.

If the company is providing the cash alternative itself, it may (subject to availability of funding) set the level of the cash alternative as it desires. However, if underwriting is being employed, the level of the cash alternative will be determined by the discount demanded by the underwriters. This discount will become an even more sensitive negotiating point than usual.

CONCLUSIONS

The scope for subtlety on the part of the acquiror lies mainly in the opening moves, in the way the target company is first approached and negotiations are conducted. The prime objective of the approach and negotiations is to secure an agreed or recommended deal. If this cannot be achieved, an aggressor must rely on decisiveness, determination and a sheer ability to pay. But in inter-corporate warfare, for most moves there exist a series of counter-moves and the emphasis shifts to the resourcefulness of the intended victim and the art of self-defence.

CHAPTER 17

The art of self-defence

It has been said that the price of liberty is eternal vigilance and nowhere is this more true than in the case of a public company whose shares are widely spread. Companies with no dominant shareholder group are always potentially vulnerable to an unwanted takeover bid. The announcement of a takeover bid can strike such a company's management rather like a heart attack. After it has occurred, there are only a limited number of steps which can be taken and time is running out. In addition, there may be legal or other regulatory or practical restraints on management's freedom of action once a formal offer has been announced. A management which wishes to prolong its life should adopt preventative measures in advance and review them on a regular basis.

The measures described in this chapter are divided into three categories. The first section deals with areas which can be considered good housekeeping, in other words, matters which a competent management would deal with as sound business practice rather than because it was nervous about a possible unwanted bid. The second section covers measures which while having a commercial basis, would be primarily undertaken to deter or repel an expected bid. The third section deals with the tactical steps which may be taken to defeat an unwanted bid after it has been announced.

I GOOD HOUSEKEEPING

Good housekeeping measures relate primarily to an awareness of and sensitivity to the market. This includes shareholders, potential aggressors and the investment community in general.

(i) Share price – keep it up

The surest defence against an unwanted takeover bid is not to receive one. The single most effective deterrent is a share price which fairly reflects the profit potential and asset-backing of the company. The most vulnerable companies are those with depressed share prices standing at a substantial discount to net asset value.

Some managements claim indifference to the ups and downs of the share price. In their eyes, their job is to concentrate on the company's fundamental commercial and financial health, ignoring the whims and fads of the stock market. This approach, although understandable, invites opportunist attacks from a more market-aware operator.

In the long run, a company's share price is likely to reflect the fundamental factors affecting itself and its industry. But there will be periods when this is not the case, and it is these periods an aggressor will watch for.

It is of course true that maintenance of a healthy share price is not wholly within management's control but neither is management helpless. Steps which are likely to assist the share price include:

(a) Repurchase of the company's own shares in the market in jurisdictions where this is permitted

Where such repurchase is not permitted, management may encourage major potential buyers sympathetic to them to enter the market in times of price weakness. Such a process tends to prevent a poor technical position developing in the market and helps to keep the price firm. It also serves to demonstrate management's views of the minimum value of the company.

(b) Cultivate a good market image

It is good sense for management to promote cordial relations with the major shareholders who can be identified. This may be done by telephone calls, by lunch meetings or other forms of entertaining and by off-the-record briefings on management's plans. In giving such contacts substance, care must be taken not to disclose to certain favoured shareholders specific price-sensitive information concerning the company which is not available to the market generally.

Management should also consider the merits of granting interviews and making background information available to research analysts employed by stockbrokers, fund managers and other professionals. A favourable broker's circular can assist the market rating of the shares and help in building up an institutional shareholder base.

Management should try to keep abreast of the preferences of the stock market which change from time to time. In differing phases, a market may emphasise low gearing, export sales, currency exposure or some other factor. Some markets show a distinct liking for bonus issues of shares or stock splits which keep a share price within a certain range.

A further step is to ensure that positive news or developments about the company receive favourable coverage in the media on a regular basis. There is a school of thought which favours this activity being handled by the company's own staff, particularly the chief executive or other senior director, if they have any talent for public relations. There is a natural tendency for the media to be flattered by being granted access of this kind, as there is to regard a public relations consultant as either a buffer or a channel for 'misinformation'. However, an individual may be a very capable executive but have little ability for communication outside the company, in which case the task is probably better handled by a professional firm.

Responsibility for shareholder, market and press relations should be recognised as a significant function. The responsibility should be one which is specifically allocated, whether it is carried out by company executives, external consultants or a combination of the two.

(c) Keep in mind the benefits of a steady profit and dividend record

Major transactions should be reviewed at the time they are undertaken to assess their immediate impact on the profit and loss account and balance sheet. While it is not suggested that short-term or cosmetic considerations should be given overwhelming weight when considering major corporate decisions, it is nevertheless naive to assume that shareholders will not be significantly affected by short-term results. As a highly successful investor remarked, in the long run, we are all dead. One of the skills shareholders demand from management is an ability to produce reasonable results in the short term while building for the future.

Financial years which are likely to show outstanding results offer a chance to review and provide against doubtful or uncertain items to establish a strong base for less good years. The market may not applaud a large dividend increase for one year if the increased dividend cannot be maintained for the next.

(d) Updating information

If fixed assets form a significant proportion of a company's balance sheet, consideration should be given to periodic revaluations of assets, say once every three years. The annual report may also disclose other types of information not necessarily required but useful for shareholders to base an analysis of the company's worth.

Some managements are reluctant to supply data on the basis that they may be giving ammunition to a bidder. However, a determined bidder may find out anyway; providing information to the market at large may well be the safer course if it results in the share price reflecting the underlying value more closely.

(ii) Shareholders – who are they?

If a takeover is announced for a widely-held company, the attitude of shareholders is likely to be decisive. It is therefore good sense for management to identify the company's shareholders and monitor changes.

Some managements seem ignorant or careless of the shareholder base of the company they manage and, equally important, how it is changing. Directors may be only familiar with a few long-standing shareholders, often friends and acquaintances, a smattering of institutions and the little old lady who asks a question each year at the annual general meeting. This probably presents a thoroughly misleading picture of shareholders in general and what their attitudes are likely to be in the circumstances of a takeover bid.

A sensible precaution is for the company secretary's department to compile on a regular basis (perhaps monthly or weekly in times of high stock market activity) a report on the numbers and composition of shareholders. Holders of, say, more than $\frac{1}{2}$% of the company's voting capital or of securities convertible into that amount of voting capital should be listed individually. Any changes in their shareholding and any new shareholders reaching this level should be highlighted.

Significant holders of preference share capital or debentures may also be relevant. Holders of such securities can normally block proposals which affect their rights. Preference shareholders may have considerable voting power on other matters if, for example, the payment of the preference dividend is in arrears.

Most public companies hire a specialist outside firm to maintain the register of their shareholders. Such a firm will normally computerise the register, in which case various analyses of the shareholders and the changes should be readily available.

Shares may not necessarily be under the control or ownership of the registered holder. The use of nominees to act as the registered owner of shares makes it more difficult to interpret shareholding lists. Nominee companies are not always sinister, often being used more as a convenience than as a cloak. Many nominees can be safely identified with a certain institution or group, either by a similar name (rather obvious acronyms are favoured), the same address or other clear connections, leaving a balance of potentially threatening holdings. In some countries, regulations permit a company to require nominees to reveal identity of the beneficial owner of the shares.

As a potential aggressor may not register shares promptly, the report on registered holdings should be supplemented by regular conversations with the company's brokers regarding concentrated buying from unusual sources. The level of turnover in the company's shares on the stock market and the price fluctuations should also be monitored to highlight any disturbing trends.

In some countries, the accumulation under the control of one party of a certain level of shareholding (however registered or held) requires public disclosure or notification to the company concerned. In the US and the UK, for example, an important check is at 5% of the voting capital, a level which may signal potential trouble but rarely confers control.

(iii) Public announcements

A watchful management will pay particular attention to content and presentation of all public announcements. Announcements of corporate results are often dictated by accounting or auditing timetables, with little opportunity allowed for an overall review of presentation and impact. Under the pressure of time to get an announcement out, implications which later seem quite obvious can be overlooked. Omissions can make management seem incompetent or insensitive to shareholder concerns.

In the case of an announcement of results, the market is likely to have formed expectations in advance which the company's brokers or other market contacts can be asked to relay to management. If the actual figures are significantly different from the market's expectations, an explanation should be prepared in advance. Explanations made later, perhaps under public pressure, rarely succeed in being wholly convincing.

Inconsistent comments, changes of policy, missed forecasts and other unpleasant surprises are useful sources of ammunition for potential bidders. All statements should be reviewed to identify what 'hostages to fortune' are being given. Comment or loose wording which runs the risk of coming back to haunt management in the future might be best omitted in the first place.

It is useful to bear in mind that the market tends to assume that delayed announcements of results mean bad news. If the news is bad, a delay in timing is not going to help.

(iv) Putting yourself in the aggressor's shoes

A useful exercise for management is periodically to view their own company in the way an aggressive bidder might. The exercise should include a valuation of all major group assets both on an existing use and on a best alternative use basis. Businesses with a below-average return on capital should be considered for management buy-out or other means of disposal at an acceptable price. Other possibilities include spinning off a part of the business whose worth may not be obvious to the market.

Incumbent management is in a position to know the company's potential better than any outside party and is able to apply the same analysis and techniques as a raider would. Inertia, sentiment or commitment to people or past decisions can make this a difficult or painful process. However, the options identified may strengthen the financial position of the company as well as anticipate and therefore neutralise a bidder's strategy.

A mechanism to identify such opportunities should be established so that they can be considered for implementation before management's hand is forced.

Such moves may be rejected as undesirable for the moment for many valid reasons but contingency plans should at least be prepared which can be activated at short notice.

Management may have fears that rationalisation along these lines will present the company to a bidder 'on a plate'. Experience suggests that taking the necessary steps to improve the performance of a business is much less likely to attract a hostile bid than neglecting them.

II   MEASURES TAKEN PRIMARILY TO REPEL AN EXPECTED BID

The measures discussed in this section are those for which some preparation is normally required (although some may, in emergency, be attempted after a bid has been announced) but which a management would probably not undertake except in anticipation of some hostile move. They therefore fall into a kind of twilight zone where the immediate benefit to shareholders may be questioned. On the other hand, a management may argue that it is part of their duty to protect the company in a wider sense and that they are therefore justified in taking measures which have the effect of safeguarding their position so that they may carry out their responsibilities without extreme short-term pressure.

The actions are divided into five categories:

(i)   Changing the rules.
(ii) Building obstacles into the financial or commercial structure.
(iii) Creating defensive shareholdings.
(iv) Making critical disposals or acquisitions.
(v)   Pre-empting the bidder.

The specific actions which fall into these five categories will change as laws, market sentiment or public opinion about their legitimacy change. However, the principles of how to repel a bid remain the same although they may appear in different guises at different times.

(i) Changing the rules

Procedures for managing a company's affairs are set out in the articles of association or bylaws. The rules of the game may be changed by management initiative (sometimes without reference to shareholders) in a number of ways:

(a) Place of incorporation of company

The directors may take steps to move the place of incorporation of the holding company to a jurisdiction which has more favourable rules from the point of view of incumbent directors. This process normally involves the merger of the existing holding company with a new company incorporated for the purpose. The State of Delaware is favoured in the US. Occasionally, the country of incorporation has been changed for reasons which may include factors relating to control. Examples are moves from the UK to Malaysia and from Hong Kong to Bermuda or the Cayman Islands.

(b) Directors

Rules concerning the nomination and election of directors not currently on the board may be tightened. For example, a lengthy period of notice and disclosure of candidates' personal, financial and business interests may be required. Election of directors may also be 'staggered' calling for, for example, one-third of the directors to be elected every three years, a move which would prevent a new controlling shareholder from obtaining a majority on the board for two years.

Existing directors may be given long-term service contracts. This does not prevent them being fired, but may make it a very expensive process to do so. Such arrangements are sometimes referred to as 'golden parachutes' but can backfire by making directors appear more concerned for their own welfare than the shareholders' interests. Amounts paid to retiring directors are often disclosed. They can receive wide publicity and prove deeply embarrassing to individuals.

(c) Proceedings at meetings

Rules may be introduced banning special meetings except with the consent of the board or requiring extended notice for resolutions to be put to meetings of the company without management's blessing. Higher majorities may be required for certain critical motions, such as those approving mergers or a repurchase of shares from a holder who has recently assembled a significant stake.

(d) Voting rights

Under the articles or bylaws of a company, classes of shares may be issued with different voting rights. A class of preferred shares for example, may carry a multiple of the votes applicable to ordinary shares. Ordinary shares may be issued with different par values and dividend rights but the same number of votes. Most stock exchanges are tending to refuse or cancel listings for shares in companies if different voting rights of this type are being introduced for the first time. Companies with such a voting structure already in place are normally permitted to maintain it.

(ii) Structural obstacles

Obstacles may be erected through the financial structure of the company or its commercial arrangements.

(a) Authorised share capital

Sufficient authorised but unissued share capital should be maintained to give management the ability, often without further reference to shareholders, to issue new shares. This gives scope for issues of new shares to supportive parties and to dilute a threatening shareholding.

New classes of shares with particular rights to be designated by management may be authorised, the basis for the 'poison pill' defence. In this manoeuvre, the defending company may declare a special dividend or bonus issue of a new class of share capital or of rights to subscribe for such capital. In some cases, the rights are only exercisable after a third party acquires more than a certain percentage of the outstanding share capital. The holders of the new shares may be entitled to receive payments or purchase shares in a new merged entity after a bid in such a way that the bid would be rendered prohibitively expensive for a bidder.

(b) Loans and loan stocks

The terms of listed convertible or unsecured loan stocks may include a provision that the stock becomes immediately convertible or repayable at par in the event of a change of control of the issuing company.

The origin of this type of provision was as a legitimate protection for the providers of long-term loan capital. It allows them to obtain repayment if the borrower's management changes in such a way that the loan stockholders' confidence is lost. However, the provision has sometimes been built in by the issuer itself in order to increase the cash requirements of the bidder. The terms of some syndicated bank loans also contain a provision that the loan may be callable in the event of a change of control of the borrower. In many instances, a default or early repayment of one loan may through cross-default clauses trigger wholesale repayments of a company's borrowings.

(c) Commercial arrangements

Companies may have valuable agency or licence agreements which are liable to be terminated in the event of a change of control. As in the case of bank loans, this practice has a legitimate commercial basis in that a licensor or other principal wants to know the party with whom he is dealing. However, it can also be used by a company entering into such agreements to erect further obstacles to a takeover.

(iii) Creating defensive shareholdings

As ultimately it is the votes that count, measures to form solid voting support are very effective.

(a) Voting pacts

Voting trusts or other voting agreements or arrangements between shareholders may be established. Sometimes family members, for example, or groups of associates, may agree that their shares should be held by a single company which votes for them as a block. This prevents an outsider from picking off individual members of the group or driving a wedge between groups who may not always see eye to eye.

(b) Allied shareholdings

An allied shareholding may be created by placing a block of shares in hands considered to support existing management. This might be done for cash or by the purchase of assets from a group or individual with long-standing connections with the company. The consideration would be satisfied by way of an issue of new shares. However, the asset or business acquired may not be ideal in commercial terms. There is also the danger of a change in attitude of the holder or an approach by an aggressor with an offer which cannot be refused.

(c) Cross-shareholdings

Cross-shareholdings, where two (or more) companies take substantial shareholdings in each other, have been commonly used to protect control. The position may be created originally by an exchange of shares, purchases in the market or other types of transaction. In a case where a third person has a substantial shareholding in one of the companies concerned, control of a large pool of assets may be secured for a relatively small investment.

Cracks in this structure may appear if any of the companies develop financial weaknesses. The interlocking nature of the shareholdings considerably hampers the making of issues of voting capital to third parties to raise further equity. The companies may therefore be locked into a vicious circle where new capital becomes increasingly difficult to obtain.

(iv) Disposals and acquisitions

(a) Disposals

It is part of sound management policy to review and, if appropriate, dispose of under-performing businesses. However, businesses or assets which cannot be sold easily or at an acceptable price but which may have great potential value to shareholders may require a different approach. They may, for example, be spun off through a distribution of shares to the existing shareholders of the company. In this way, shareholders have distinct shareholdings in two separate entities. This may serve to sharpen investor focus on both companies by unbundling a package of interests, in which case, the combined share prices of the two holdings should be higher than the share price of the group before the spin off.

The value of certain assets, such as oil or forestry reserves, may be made more directly accessible to shareholders by putting them in trusts and distributing units in the trust to shareholders. In this way, the shareholder can participate in the benefits of the income generated by the asset without the intervening layer of the corporate structure.

If there is one particular asset (sometimes referred to as a 'crown jewel') which is thought to be of particular interest to a potential bidder, it may be put outside the control of the company by one of the above methods or other arrangements whereby the management of that particular asset passes to other hands. In this way, the attractions of the company to a bidder are reduced.

(b) Acquisitions

A programme of acquisitions if properly planned will promote the growth of a company and improve the market rating of its shares. However, as sheer size is felt by many managements to be a barrier to a hostile bid, acquisitions may be made partly with a view to rendering the enlarged group too large for a predator to swallow. If such an acquisition is made for cash, it will also increase the level of gearing of the enlarged group which may be a further deterrent to an aggressor. Acquisition of a business in a specialised or sensitive area which involves government or other regulatory approvals can be an effective ploy of this type.

(v) Pre-empting the bidder

(a) Greenmail

Management may be inclined, where the law permits, to use the company's own resources to buy off a shareholder who has built up a potentially threatening stake. In cases where the price paid to such an aggressor is above the prevailing market price, this practice has been dubbed 'greenmail' and comes uncomfortably close to a management using shareholders' money to protect their own interests. It seems particularly blatant where a third party may have had as its principal objective to be bought off at a dealing profit rather than to seek control of the company or to take a long-term investment. A number of companies in the US have introduced measures preventing the payment of greenmail, on the assumption that this will dissuade an aggressor motivated by short-term profit. As a defence, it has had the drawback of displaying weakness, so that a management which pays greenmail once is likely to find itself faced with a similar demand soon afterwards.

(b) Defensive merger

On a 'better the devil you know' principle, some managements form understandings with a similarly-sized group to whom they can turn in the event a less agreeable suitor seems likely to press his case. This appears to be the driving force behind some mergers which lack any obvious commercial logic.

III   TACTICS AFTER THE ANNOUNCEMENT OF A HOSTILE BID

The third category of measures are those mainly applicable only after the announcement of a hostile bid, in other words, short-term tactical moves designed to combat a specific threat. After its announcement, an offer can be opposed in three broad ways:

(i) Releasing positive new information.
(ii) Attacking the terms of the bid and the bidder.
(iii) Taking actions designed to block or frustrate the bid.

(i) Releasing positive new information

A skilful bidder is likely to time his move at a time when it is difficult for the target to release encouraging news, for example just after an announcement of poor results has been made or following warning remarks on prospects by management. The main areas on which shareholders and investors generally will expect to hear the company's views are:

(a) Profit and dividend forecast

If increased profits and dividends can be forecast this serves not only to make the offer price look less attractive but also underlines the good performance of current management. In some countries, such forecasts must be reported on by the company's auditors and financial advisors. A past record of good growth and achieved targets assists in establishing the credibility of a forecast in circumstances where the directors would like to show an encouraging increase in profits.

(b) Revaluation of assets

If significant assets have been carried on the company's books at cost for a number of years, a revaluation may disclose a substantial surplus over book values which would tend to make the offer price appear less generous. Some allowance should be made for any tax which might be incurred on the disposal of assets at the valuation price.

(c) Other positive developments

A company may have projects on hand which can be announced at an important moment to bolster shareholder confidence in the future of the company. Such announcements might include promising new products and orders, contracts which are being signed or negotiated, hiring of new management and other similar items.

A target company must be aware that release of positive new information may be a double-edged sword in circumstances where the aggressor has considerable financial strength. The first offer may be a 'sighting shot' to force disclosure of information on the basis of which an increased offer can be justified. A management should therefore carefully consider how much new information it needs to release in order to repulse a particular offer. There may be arguments in favour of releasing information step by step saving the best until fairly late in the process so that it is difficult for a bidder to react with substantial changes to the terms of their offer.

(ii) Attacking the terms of the bid and the bidder

Attack is often the best form of defence. It is a rare bid and bidder that have no Achilles heel. Possible vulnerable points include:

(a) Value and type of consideration

An obvious tactic is to argue that the offer is not high enough, specifically that it does not adequately reflect the profits, dividends, assets and prospects of the company. Shareholders may be subject to taxation through a forced disposal of their shares, which will reduce the face value of the offer. An analysis of past share price performance may show that the offer price is below the market price at some period.

If the bid is not all in cash, the value of the securities being offered in exchange may be attacked. The bidder's shares may be vulnerable to the same type of criticisms as can be advanced against a target company.

If other more complicated types of security are being offered such as convertible or unsecured loan stock, the consideration may be attacked as 'funny money'. In a closely-matched contest, shareholders may through familiarity prefer to keep shares deliberately purchased rather than to accept shares in another company offered in exchange.

If a bid is in paper, the contribution of the two companies to the earnings and assets of the enlarged group may show that the shareholders of the target company are being 'short-changed' in some respect. Indeed, unless the bid is over-generous to the target, some disadvantage to the target company is inevitable and can be highlighted.

(b) Commercial and timing arguments

Often a bid can be attacked as being opportunist, taking advantage of some period of weakness in the target which may be temporary. Indeed, the bidder is unlikely to be motivated by pure altruism. The commercial and industrial logic of the transaction may be questioned, although strictly speaking this may be of little relevance to a shareholder offered cash or a considerable proportion of cash in exchange for his shares.

The argument may be put forward that if the company is as bad as the bidder makes out then why does he want it at all. Alternatively if a company is good, why should the bidder reap the benefits and not the existing shareholders? Sometimes the tables can be turned and pressure brought to bear on the shareholders of the bidding company to prevent that company making a high bid. If a bid is so attractive, in some sense it must penalise the bidder's existing shareholders.

An offer for the bidding company by the target has the potential to reduce the market to total confusion.

(c) Motives of bidder

Contested takeovers may rapidly become personalised, the more so the longer the bid continues. It tends to be seen as a duel between the two chairmen or other prominent executives of the companies. Public exchanges between the two sides can degenerate into mere abuse and personal attacks. A common tactic is to question the motives of the controlling shareholder or chief executive of a bidder, suggesting that the bid is made for reasons of ego or empire building and that such a person is unfit to manage the target company.

(iii) Throwing blocks

The third category involves not chiefly a debate on the pluses and minuses of the bid but spoiling tactics which can be applied almost equally well whether the bid is essentially good or bad.

(a) Legal/regulatory

In the US, a major part of the defence to a hostile bid is a resort to the courts for injunctions to delay or block the takeover, including attacks on both the bidder and his associates and financial advisors and backers for misleading or inadequate disclosure and violations of procedure. Takeovers may also be subject to government or other regulatory approvals particularly as regards anti-monopoly rules so that lobbying for such approval to be withheld is a possible tactic.

Whether a bid is vulnerable to such obstacles will depend primarily on size, sensitivity of the industry and the political clout of the bidder and the target. It may also depend on the political climate of the time. Most countries, for example, have restrictions on foreign control of local companies. How these restrictions are interpreted and enforced may vary with the attitude of the government of the day towards foreign investors. Equally, the strength of a domestic lobby at a particular time, for example the trade unions, may make the employment consequences of a particular bid a more sensitive factor than it otherwise would be.

(b) Market purchases

In the closing stages of a bid, perhaps the most critical factor will be whether the market price is at a premium to the value of the offer. A programme of share purchases in the market by associates of the target company will help to achieve this. In some countries, it is necessary to be able to demonstrate that the company has not provided any financial support for share purchases.

(c) Publicity and appeals to other factors

Management will send circulars and other material to shareholders containing information helpful to their case. Newspaper advertisements may also be taken out. The help of related parties such as stockbrokers may also be enlisted to prepare and send positive circulars to major clients who are shareholders or potential shareholders of the company.

Management can often appeal to a sense of loyalty in its shareholders particularly if the business has a long history and tradition. Companies with well-known products or brand names may be able to rouse the support of customers and suppliers. Employees who may be anxious about the effect of a change of control on their jobs can also be recruited.

(d) White knight

If management feels that the other moves open to it are unlikely to prevent the success of a hostile bid it may seek another suitor, commonly referred to as a 'white knight'. By gathering a consortium of institutional backers, management can become its own white knight through a management buy-out.

With the encouragement and support of existing management, a white knight knows that there is a high chance of success. In addition, an appropriate white knight will often have some interest in preventing the rival merger which may lead, for example, to a powerful competitive group being formed. These factors appear sufficient to guarantee no shortage of eager white knights, despite the fact that their late entry into the fray involves the payment of a price which they sometimes live to regret.

Blocking tactics may prove highly effective and are attractive in the heat of the battle. However, it may be questioned whether some moves, particularly legal and other technical steps which may be taken to block an otherwise attractive offer, are genuinely in the interests of the shareholders or whether their main effect is to preserve the power of an entrenched management.

CHAPTER 18

Formal procedures and techniques

The formal procedures and techniques used to implement mergers and acquisitions are a highly specialised area, requiring different skills and personalities from the cut and thrust of negotiations, attack and defence. The detailed steps involved are complex and vary with the provisions of the relevant company law, tax regulations and even fashions in professionals' views of how aspects of a transaction should be tackled. A step-by-step account of how a particular acquisition should be carried through is beyond the scope of this chapter. Participants in the market must be guided by specialist advisers on a case-by-case basis. Certain basic principles, however, remain constant and are capable of useful application in a wide range of circumstances. These principles are the subject of this chapter.

The first section deals with the acquisition of private companies and the second with public listed companies. In the case of private companies, it is likely that there will be restrictions on the sale and transfer of shares which will have to be taken into account. As it is only possible to proceed by negotiation, the formal sale and purchase agreement assumes a central position in the transaction.

In public company acquisitions, a wider range of procedures is possible. There is more flexibility in the level of control and the methods by which control is achieved. It will also be important to know how shareholders who do not agree to the proposals can be dealt with. The contents of circulars and any other communications to shareholders of public companies are subject to strict control.

I PRIVATE COMPANIES

There is in normal circumstances no alternative to carrying out the acquisition of a private company by negotiation with the directors or major shareholders, who are often the same people. Where the purchase is for less than the whole of the share capital, problems can arise with pre-emption rights. In order that the circumstances of the sale may be properly documented, the lawyers for the buyer and seller will prepare a comprehensive sale and purchase agreement. If a business has suffered serious financial problems, the seller may be a receiver or liquidator instead of the shareholders and directors. Additional steps will probably have to be taken to deliver the business or assets in a form acceptable to the purchasers. A management buy-out requires special financial arrangements to be made.

(i) Pre-emption rights and restrictions on share transfer

The articles of association for a private company may well contain a pre-emption clause laying down procedures which a shareholder wishing to sell shares must follow. For example, a typical clause might provide that a vendor of shares must notify the directors of his intention and his opinion of a 'fair value' for the shares and appoint them as his agents for the sale. The directors may accept the opinion of value or request independent professionals such as the auditors of the company or a merchant bank to establish a fair price. This exercise will be done on a willing buyer, willing seller basis, taking into account the limited marketability of the shares in a private company. The result could be a lower figure for fair value than a shareholder expects.

Once a fair price has been established, notice is given to all other shareholders in the company of the number of shares to be sold and the price asked. Each has the opportunity within a certain period to state what maximum number of shares he wishes to purchase. The directors will then allocate the shares available on a pro rata basis, allocating any surplus shares to shareholders who have indicated they wish to purchase more than their pro rata entitlement. If all the available shares are not sold in this manner, the directors may well have a right to sell to a third party within some specified period, say one month. Only after these procedures have been exhausted is the vendor free to sell the shares to a third party of his own choice.

Whether or not there is a pre-emption clause and whether or not the pre-emption procedure has been followed, the directors may still have the right to refuse to register the transfer of shares without giving any reason for their action. Without the purchaser being able to have his holding registered, it will be impossible to complete the transaction. Consequently the full co-operation of the board of directors of the company is in practice needed.

It will readily be seen that these provisions can create major problems for a purchaser who is seeking to acquire less than 100% of a private company. He can only carry the transaction forward to a certain stage and then has to await the pleasure of the existing shareholders. At the end of the day, the purchaser may feel that if the shares are worth buying they are almost certain to be bought by one of the parties who has the right of first refusal. The vendor too is at a severe disadvantage. Once he has indicated he wishes to sell he is at the mercy of an expert whose view he cannot challenge setting a price for the shares which he believes is too low. In addition, he is forced to impose on the purchaser a significant delay while the pre-emption procedures are exhausted.

(ii) Sale and purchase agreement

The transaction negotiated between the principals is embodied in a sale and purchase agreement set out in the form of a legally binding contract between buyer and seller. A typical sale and purchase agreement will include the following main sections.

(a)   The identities of the parties to the contract, recitals giving brief background information on the transactions and definitions to assist in the reading of the contract.

(b)   A description of the assets being sold and purchased and the price being paid.
(c)   Any conditions to which the contract is subject.
(d)   How, where and when completion of the contract will take place.
(e)   Any warranties and undertakings being given by the parties to the contract.
(f)   Other standard clauses dealing with such matters as governing law, notices, costs and announcements.

The details of what is being purchased, the price to be paid and how it is to be satisfied will have been the subject of intensive negotiations between the principals probably long before the involvement of lawyers. For this reason, these sections of the contract rarely cause difficulty at this stage. If they do, it is a sign that the negotiations have not really been concluded.

The conditions to which the transaction is subject will usually have been discussed, though they may not have been expressed in precise detail. Putting them down on paper may have the effect of making one or other of the parties believe that negotiations are being reopened. Some agreements have so many conditions that it is questionable whether it is worthwhile to proceed with a formal agreement at that stage. It may be better to try to satisfy the major conditions in advance, to establish that the transaction is a realistic one.

The area which frequently causes the most difficulty is the question of warranties to be given by the vendor. It may not be relevant for the purchaser to give any warranties, particularly if the purchase is for cash. Assurances may be obtained that the purchase has been properly authorised according to the purchaser's internal rules and any external regulations, if applicable. The vendor on the other hand is likely to be asked to warrant the condition of the business being sold in considerable detail. The areas which warranties will cover include the following:

(a)   That the balance sheets and other financial information provided about the company and its subsidiaries are correct and complete, and that there have been no material adverse changes since the date on which the information has been provided.
(b)   That there are no material capital commitments, unusual contracts, guarantees or any other contingent liabilities outstanding, including current or threatened litigation.
(c)   That the books and records of the company are correct and have been kept up-to-date and that all tax returns and other statutory returns have been made.
(d)   The group has good and marketable title to all its assets and that they are fully insured.
(e)   That the group has complied with all leases and other agreements.
(f)   That no shares of the company are under option and that there are no outstanding rights to subscribe for shares or securities convertible into shares.

A vendor will wish to limit the warranties as far as possible and put a time limit for any claims to be lodged. The purchaser will wish to make the warranties as broad and open-ended as he can. He may also seek to retain some of the purchase money to offset against possible claims under the warranties.

(iii) Sales by a receiver or liquidator

If a business encounters financial difficulties, it may come under the control of a receiver or liquidator whose main responsibility is to realise funds for lenders and other creditors within a reasonably short period. This may present an opportunity for an acquisition at an attractive price. The receiver may take the view that the value of the business will rapidly diminish unless a speedy sale can be concluded.

The sale of a business as a going concern is likely to generate more cash than selling assets piecemeal. It is also a more convenient and usually a quicker process. However, a purchaser may be reluctant to buy a business with its associated liabilities and commitments, some of which may be difficult to quantify.

To facilitate a sale, a new subsidiary of the failed group may be set up by the receiver and the relevant assets 'hived down' to the new company. The new company will have a low share capital and the consideration for the assets hived down will be left outstanding and perhaps undetermined for the time being. If a purchaser agrees to buy the business he will purchase the share capital of the new company for a nominal amount and provide funds to it to satisfy the debt to its former parent. The debt will at this stage be crystallised at the amount that the purchaser has agreed to pay for the business.

Through the hiving down procedure, the purchaser can buy a business which starts with a clean sheet and the liabilities and commitments of which can be precisely assessed. This method is perhaps most appropriate for manufacturing concerns where stocks form a considerable proportion of total assets. If operations cease, much raw material and practically all work-in-progress may be valueless. Customers may no longer be willing to take finished goods unless they are contractually bound to do so in case after-sales service and support are lacking. In these circumstances, the receiver, who may not have much practical experience in that particular industry, may well take a view of value which leaves some margin for a company engaged in a similar line of business to make an advantageous purchase. It is desirable that the purchaser should be able to assess the risks for himself. It is unlikely that the receiver or liquidator will be willing to give any warranties and to obtain a warranty from the vendor, the failed group, serves little purpose. In addition, it is unusual for a receiver or liquidator to accept any other terms of payment than cash.

(iv) Management buy-out

A buy-out by management (or any other group of investors) can be carried out in the context of a listed company as well as in a private group. However, if a public listed company is purchased the checks of the market-place will apply. If the price agreed is too low, a rival bidder will be attracted once the proposals are announced and it is clear that the company is 'in play'. In the case of a private company the price at which the sale is made may not be published and it is less easy to determine whether it is fair.

A diversified group may find it more practical to sell a subsidiary or division to an existing management team than to a third party. By taking this route they avoid potentially strengthening a rival group. Negotiations can be handled in-house and no information needs to be provided outside the group.

One of the main problems is likely to be finance. Management may not be able to put up more than a small proportion of the funds needed which may, however, be a very significant percentage of their own savings. It is likely therefore that they will need to attract further equity partners.

When management buy-outs first became popular the price of the buy-out tended to be reasonable and the backers specialists who were prepared to try to understand the business and play a continuing role in support of management. As the early transactions prospered, more deals were proposed and the weight of institutional funding which became available put pressure on prices.

A typical buy-out is likely to have a multi-tiered financing structure. High gearing is inevitable as the management group will want to retain voting control of the vehicle used. The financiers may also prefer management to have the deciding say in running the business. The pure equity base may therefore be very low. Next will come lenders with some rights to convert into equity or warrants to subscribe for shares. They will be prepared to sacrifice some immediate income for the prospect of capital gain. The top tier are outright lenders, commercial banks or institutions, who will expect above average interest rates to compensate them for the risks involved. Their attitude will be influenced by whether they can obtain direct security over the assets of the business being acquired which is not possible in all jurisdictions.

The former parent of the business being bought out may have to provide some assistance. Documentation may include a technical or services support contract with the former parent covering for example design rights or computer facilities until the newly independent organisation can develop all its own functions.

II   PUBLIC COMPANIES

In the case of a public company, a wider range of procedures is open to the would-be acquiror. It may be feasible to acquire a significant stake in the target company, either as a preliminary to a full bid or with the intention of achieving control without making a full offer. Where a full bid is made, there may be a choice between a public offer based largely on market practices for share purchases or a legal procedure called a scheme of arrangement. An important consideration will be how to deal with shareholders who do not accept the proposals.

Whatever procedure is chosen, shareholders have to be informed of the details of the offer and the up-to-date position of the target company. The contents of documents published in connection with proposals made to shareholders of a public company are subject to review and control by various bodies.

(i) Acquisitions of less than 100%

(a) Dawn raids

The technique of buying a significant stake in the market rapidly and from as few shareholders as possible is called a 'dawn raid'. Stockbrokers with major institutional connections will be key members of the war-party. The percentage of a company which may be purchased in a dawn raid is restricted in some countries and disclosure must be made when certain levels of shareholding are reached.

The effect of disclosures and enforced delays in the pace at which a significant stake can be built up have to some extent limited the effectiveness of the dawn raid as a tactic. However, despite changes in regulations, the acquisition of strategic holdings from major shareholders with whom negotiations are held privately can be a major blow to the target company's morale and a major boost to the offeror.

A dawn raid can have some drawbacks for the offeror. Depending on the percentage acquired, a raider may not be permitted to make a full bid without providing a cash alternative equivalent to the highest price paid for the shares during say the previous six months. If certain trigger points are reached, the purchaser may be required, whether he wishes it or not, to extend an offer to all other shareholders, in cash or with a cash alternative at the highest price paid.

(b) Partial offers

An offeror may have the option to make either a full or a partial offer. A partial offer may be made for any nominated percentage of a company's share capital, but usually for over 50%.

Market enthusiasm for partial offers varies widely. In the US, they are frequent. In the UK, and other countries which have adopted broadly the same system in the securities markets, the practice is to date relatively rare. It may not be permitted at all if substantial purchases have been made from the market in advance of the offer.

A partial offer is normally conducted on a tender basis. The offeror either fixes the number of shares he wishes to buy or he may indicate a range, with a maximum and minimum. He will also stipulate the price he is prepared to pay. Shareholders can tender any or all of their shares to the offeror.

If the offeror receives less than the stated minimum number of shares, the tender will lapse. If he receives a greater number, acceptances will be scaled down proportionately so that the offeror only purchases the number of shares he desires. A shareholder tendering all his shares may succeed in selling a larger percentage than the percentage for which the offer is made if other shareholders do not tender all their shares.

From the offeror's point of view, the procedure reduces the amount of funding required as compared to a full offer. As a minimum percentage of the shares will remain in public hands, the tender offer method ensures that the shares of the target company will continue to have a degree of marketability.

(ii) Choice of procedure for a full bid: offer or scheme

A full bid is an easier process for shareholders to understand than a partial offer and still leaves them with the option of assenting only a proportion of their holdings. The price of giving shareholders this choice may be uncertainty for the offeror about the final level of shareholding he will achieve. This uncertainty can be removed in some jurisdictions by the use of a legal procedure called a scheme of arrangement which, however, is inflexible in other ways.

(a) Need for recommendation in case of scheme

A scheme of arrangement is entered into between the company and its shareholders. The 'offeror' may have little or no involvement beyond providing the cash or other consideration called for under the scheme. Because of this, it is very difficult to employ a scheme of arrangement without the active co-operation of the board of directors of the target company. It may perhaps be argued that directors ought in any case to put advantageous proposals to shareholders for their decision. As a practical matter, it can be assumed that the option of using a scheme of arrangement is only available in a recommended offer.

(b) Expenses

Under the terms of a scheme of arrangement, existing shares of the company are cancelled and new shares issued. A cancellation and reissue of shares is not technically speaking the same as a transfer of existing shares. No payment of transfer duty therefore arises under a scheme, which can provide a significant cost saving. No capital duty is incurred when the new shares are issued under the terms of the scheme, so there is no offsetting cost in this regard.

As a scheme is a fairly complex legal procedure which includes court hearings, legal costs are higher than for a straightforward offer. These additional expenses should be outweighed by the saving in transfer duty. A scheme is particularly useful where a new top holding company is being created to merge two existing groups beneath it. If the groups involved are sizeable, the savings in transfer duty may be very substantial. However, capital duty will be payable on the entire share capital of the new holding company.

(c) Acceptance level required

There are important differences in the level of acceptances required. An offer is usually conditional on at least 50% of the total shares in issue being assented to it and must reach the high level of 90% acceptance before the remaining shares which have not been assented to the offer can be acquired compulsorily. A scheme, on the other hand, has an apparently higher percentage level of acceptance required (normally 75%), but this percentage relates to those present or represented at the meeting to consider the scheme, who may be quite a small number, and not to the total shareholding body. Consequently, it is possible for a scheme to be approved with a far lower total of votes than an offer.

On the other hand, it is also possible for a 25% minority to block a scheme completely. A minority of this size could not be certain of preventing a public offer succeeding at least to the level where voting and management control of the company passed to the offeror.

(d) Time needed to obtain majority control

A public offer will be open initially for a minimum period of, say, three weeks, after which it may be closed provided it has become unconditional. Voting control of the company can be immediately exercised if sufficient acceptances have been received. It takes appreciably longer to reach this stage under a scheme. The scheme proposals must be approved by meetings of shareholders, the notice period for which is approximately the same as the minimum period a public offer must remain open for acceptance. However, the need to comply with court requirements imposes delays both before and after the posting of the documents to shareholders, totalling about one additional month. Consequently, if taking control as quickly as possible is the main objective, a scheme will not be appropriate. Such instances are most likely to be unrecommended offers where, owing to the need for co-operation from the target company's board, a scheme is not a practical alternative in the first place.

(e) Time needed to obtain 100% control

If it is critical not simply to obtain majority control of the target but to acquire the entire issued share capital, a scheme is the quicker and more reliable route. A scheme is an 'all or nothing' procedure. If a scheme is approved at the meetings called to consider it, the scheme becomes binding on all shareholders, whether they attended or were represented at the meeting or not. If it is rejected, no shares are acquired at all. If a public offer is made, it is extremely unlikely that all shareholders will accept it in the first instance and there is no immediate way to compel them to do so.

(f) Degree of certainty

Because of the legal nature of the scheme and its use in agreed situations, from the first public announcement of the proposals, they are assumed to be virtually certain of success. The announcement of an offer does not carry a similar degree of certainty.

If a scheme is used, the offeror knows from the outset that he will acquire 100% of the company or none at all. No possibility exists for the level of acceptances to settle in a 'no-man's land', over 50% but short of 90%. This no-man's land is the most difficult outcome for an acquiror to finance. The amount to be paid out is considerably greater than the minimum required to obtain control, yet as minorities are still outstanding, no direct access to that company's assets is possible. This may not be a comfortable situation for the acquiror or his bankers.

(iii) Dealing with shareholders who do not accept

Special procedures exist for acquiring small minorities who may not accept the offer. It is unlikely that all shareholders will accept even an attractive and recommended offer as a percentage will be uncontactable or unable to give good title, for example, where probate has not yet been granted.

If a sufficient level of acceptances of a public offer is received (under British law 90% of the shares for which the offer is made held by at least 75% in number of the shareholders), the offeror may, in due course, acquire the balance of the shares compulsorily through legal procedures. However, this is a lengthy process which takes up to six months to complete from the date the offer was originally made. It is open to shareholders who wish to do so to raise objections before the court. During this period, there will be minority shareholders outstanding in the offeree company, some of whom may be actively opposed to full absorption of their company in the new group. Revisions of the group structure and redeployment of group assets may not be possible until the minorities have been acquired.

Under a scheme, control of 100% of the shares of a company is obtained at completion of the required procedures. No question of outstanding minorities can arise. This is likely to be some four months after the inception of the scheme. However, this is some two months before compulsory acquisition of outstanding minorities would be completed if a public offer had been employed.

(iv) Contents of takeover documents

Whether a partial offer, a full offer or a scheme of arrangement is employed, a document will be required to be circulated to shareholders on behalf of the acquiror. In most jurisdictions the person sending out such a document is required to be licensed as a dealer or securities adviser in order to assist the authorities in controlling the contents of the offer documentation. The contents of such a document are determined by law, stock exchange rules and other regulations including those contained in a takeover code if one applies in a particular market. The main components of this type of document are as follows:

(a) Chairman's letter

This letter sets out the broad principles and terms of the acquisition and explains why it is being put forward and what benefits are expected from it. The tone of the letter will vary greatly depending on whether the proposals are agreed or not, or whether it is hoped that they will be agreed in due course.

If the offer is agreed from the outset, the letter is more effective coming from the chairman of the target company. His views about the attractions of the offer may be felt by the shareholders of that company to be more relevant than those of the party making the offer.

(b) Offer letter

The offer letter will be written by the acquiror's financial advisers who make the offer on behalf of the acquiror. The letter will state the terms of the offer and describe the different elements in it. It will include the terms and conditions attached to the offer and explain the timing for acceptances and the level of acceptances required. The financial effects of acceptance will be spelt out with examples of the effect on capital value, income and possibly attributable net assets and earnings. More technical matters relating to the validity of acceptances, how to tender share certificates and when the consideration will be received will also be explained.

(c) Financial information

Financial information about the offeree company will be set out. The information given will normally be a summary of the past five years' results together with the latest audited balance sheets. If a forecast of results is being made, details of the basis and main assumptions will be supplied. Any material changes since the date of the audited figures will also be given, particularly an up-dated statement of the indebtedness and commitments of the group.

If the offer is in cash, little financial information about the offeror need be shown. A confirmation will be given by a financial institution that the maximum amount of cash required under the terms of the offer will in fact be available to the offeror.

Where the acquiring company offers its own shares or other securities in exchange for those of the target company, the offer document also serves as a prospectus. Financial information about the offeror similar to that required for a listing must be given, including a working capital statement and if possible a profit and dividend forecast for the current financial year.

Where a profit forecast is made by either the offeror or offeree it must be verified and reported on by the auditors and the financial advisors of the company making the forecast.

(d) Legal requirements

Differing levels of disclosures are required by the stock exchange and other official bodies in various markets. The disclosures emphasise dealings in shares, areas relating to any conflicts of interest which might arise and significant contractual arrangements which have been entered into.

(e) Notice of meetings

A scheme requires at least two meetings of shareholders. Other offer arrangements may require meetings to approve certain steps being taken, for example to issue substantial numbers of new shares or dispose of major assets. The notices convening the meetings will be attached to the offer document. The information included in the offer document forms the basis for shareholders' decisions on how to vote at the meetings.

CONCLUSIONS

The procedures for completing acquisitions are specialised and in their detailed application may depend on quite obscure tax or other legislation in particular countries. The principles underlying the techniques change much less than the techniques themselves. Negotiations for control of a private company may prove frustrating because it is only possible to follow a limited number of paths. It is the greater range of routes available in a public company acquisition which make the procedures more complex. A number of difficult choices face the acquiror. His task is to match the methods selected with his objectives and complete the transaction with a minimum of disruption, delay and expense.

CHAPTER 19

Role of professionals and technical aspects

Mergers and acquisitions require a range of expertise to bring about a successful conclusion. Individuals who generate ideas are not always the most successful negotiators. Negotiating and dealing with people in turn demand different skills from the specialist task of devising the most efficient method of implementation from a tax, accounting or legal standpoint.

Merchant banks are often the prime movers in an acquisition. They put up ideas, offer advice and provide support with financing. Accountants will be involved from the evaluation stage and particularly in assessing such aspects as the impact on published results. Lawyers play a central role in the documentation and completion phases of the acquisition. Tax advice is often critical. It may be provided by accountants or lawyers working on the acquisition or by tax specialists. If the companies are listed, the help of a firm of stockbrokers will be highly desirable. Other professionals may be consulted depending on the specific type of acquisition under consideration.

(i) Role of merchant banks

Merchant banks have made a speciality of merger and acquisition work although it has little connection with classical banking business. In some cases, there is no significant outside funding required and the company's lawyers or accountants may have a closer relationship with the principals. However, it is the investment and merchant banks who have taken the lead in building large departments of full-time professionals and such departments now dominate the field. They are closely involved in all facets of merger and acquisition work from the initial identification of targets to the completion procedures.

(a) Preliminary stages

Merchant banks actively go out seeking mandates to act for a buyer or a seller of a company. A mandate for a committed seller is preferred. All managements worth their salt wish to hear about opportunities. Few will say they are not interested in acquisitions. This is a far cry from actually concluding the deal.

It is a simpler matter to determine whether a potential seller is serious about a sale. Once the parameters (price, terms, timing) have been established, one side of the transaction is firm. It should then not be too difficult a task to identify a buyer in the marketplace.

Acting for a seller also has advantages when it comes to fees. A firm mandate to act exclusively can be obtained from a seller whereas few buyers will wish to commit themselves in this way. In addition, a seller who has received a satisfactory price is normally quite willing to pay a reasonable fee out of the proceeds. A buyer who is already facing large payments for the acquisition may be unwilling to shoulder heavy professional fees as well.

Merchant banks will try to keep lists of current buyers and sellers in their files. However, the chances of arranging a transaction 'off the shelf' in this manner are remote. Good deals tend to be done quickly. Deals which have been in the market for some time go stale. It is likely that a specific search will be needed to identify a target which is not being actively offered for sale. In a large market such as the US, an initial screening may be made by computer to identify a range of suitable propositions.

Merchant banks will assist, if desired, in assessing the price which may have to be offered to bring an acquisition to a successful conclusion. A merchant bank's approach will tend to be market-orientated, concentrating on the price needed for success which is not necessarily the same as a valuation.

The merchant bank will often be involved in the negotiating process. Questions of price and negotiations tend to merge. If a buyer is willing to pay a high price, the negotiator need not be very skilful. A merchant bank will seek some room for manoeuvre in negotiations to improve the chances of bringing the discussions to a successful conclusion. As merchant banks are often paid substantially on a 'no foal, no fee' basis, they have a strong interest in getting the deal done. This is not to say that they will not fight hard for their corner but they may also be inclined to feel that it is in their client's interest to show some flexibility.

(b) Takover code

Takeover codes operate in a number of markets where practice is traditionally based on the UK system. In the UK, takeover activity has primarily been self-regulated through a voluntary code of practice. Such a code and its administrators rely heavily on the cooperation of the participants in the market and can be made to seem toothless when confronted by an operator determined to go his own way. On the other hand, since legal procedures are avoided action within the scope of the code can be taken swiftly and informally. Not all concepts need to be precisely defined, as considerable reliance is placed on the 'spirit' of the code. This discourages participants from exploiting loopholes in the rules which may be considered legitimate where regulation is by law alone. It can, however, lead to considerable argument about whether an action, particularly when a new tactic first emerges, is within the spirit of the code or not. Voluntary codes are based on a core of general principles designed, among other things, to ensure equal treatment for all shareholders, proper provision of information and advice and adequate time for response to an offer. The principle that all shareholders should be treated equally has gained particular prominence, although in some markets it is freely acknowledged that a block of shares which confers control should be valued more highly than a small holding.

Detailed rules are drawn up or amended in response to specific problems which arise. This approach can resound to the clang of stable doors being locked after the horse has bolted. Rules are designed to prevent perceived abuses. By the time new rules are introduced, the market conditions which generated those particular abuses may no longer exist.

A number of important provisions have proved relevant despite changes in the market and include the following:

(i) if a certain percentage holding (ranging from 20% to 35% in different markets) is acquired by one person or a group of persons acting together to obtain control, an offer must be made to all shareholders, essentially on the same terms on which control has been acquired;

(ii) up-to-date financial and other material information must be disclosed in time for shareholders to make an informed judgment of an offer. A detailed list of what is required is incorporated in the code, corresponding largely to the stock exchange's regulations for disclosure about significant acquisitions and disposals;

(iii) the target company may not without shareholder approval at an extraordinary general meeting take any action which would effectively frustrate an offer or prevent shareholders deciding on an offer on its merits;

(iv) the contents of all documents and publications addressed to shareholders during the period of an offer must be prepared with the same standards of care which would apply if the document was a prospectus;

(v) dealings for a period before and during the offer are subject to disclosure to the authorities and publication. If the offeror buys shares of the target company at above the offer price, it must raise its offer correspondingly;

(vi) guidelines are laid down for the initial and subsequent public announcements. Arrangements may be made for suspending market dealings in the shares briefly when critical new information is released. Any conditions to which the offer is subject must be announced from the outset; and

(vii) directors of an offeror or offeree company have a responsibility to act solely in their capacity as directors, without regard to their own position.

As there is an element of vagueness in voluntary codes which rely on compliance with the spirit as well as the letter of the regulations, it is essential to have an informed and responsive body to administer the code. This body is constantly available for consultation and to give rulings on points of doubt. It is normally staffed by a combination of civil servants and practitioners. There may be a full-time secretariat plus a committee which can be convened at short notice to consider urgent questions. There will be provision for appeal against the committee's decision. Practice notes supplementing the rules will be published regularly to provide up-to-date information about significant decisions made by the committee or the secretariat.

(c) Other procedural aspects

When negotiations have been concluded, the merchant bank will usually take the lead in co-ordinating documentation. Offer documents contain much legal and accounting information which the merchant bank will not have prepared. The merchant bank's role is to draw the various parts together into a consistent whole. This document will then be submitted to various regulatory authorities for their comments.

Once the document has been put together and cleared by the relevant regulatory agencies, the merchant bank will oversee the process of distributing it to shareholders. The merchant bank will also monitor response, often drafting in numbers of people to assist in contacting shareholders or soliciting proxies.

If a company meeting is involved and difficult questions are anticipated, a rehearsal may be held to prepare the executives involved for what may be ahead. A list of expected questions and model answers will be drawn up.

Throughout this period, the merchant bank will be monitoring the reaction in the market and watching for an opportunity to pick up shares in the target company at advantageous prices. In addition, it may organise some support for the shares of the offeror.

(d) Financing

When necessary, the merchant bank may organise and provide finance for acquisitions. Although merchant banks rarely do much straightforward lending, they may be involved in identifying suitable lenders and negotiating terms with them. If the takeover is being financed by the issue of securities, the merchant bank, in conjunction with the company's stockbrokers, may assemble a syndicate to buy or underwrite the securities being issued.

(ii) Role of accountants

(a) Accountant's report

It is prudent for a purchaser to seek a full accountant's report on the business he is buying. A seller is likely to oppose an accountant's investigation, at least until a late stage in the negotiations. Not only does the report represent a further substantial hurdle at which the deal may fall, it involves disruption to day-to-day business and can be damaging to the morale of existing staff.

The basic methodology of the accountant's report is to take each significant item in the financial statements and examine it to ensure that any unusual or doubtful aspects are brought to the attention of those deciding the offer price. Any items of potential under- or over-valuation will be highlighted, together with items which may not be directly reflected in the balance sheet but could have an impact on value such as guarantees, litigation and lease obligations. Comments may be made on the adequacy of systems and the general competency of management.

The quality of earnings should be scrutinised by the accountants. It is normally possible for a company to produce better than average results for one year by including items which may previously have been held in reserve. Particularly in a private company there is no incentive for the owners to increase their tax bill by showing a high level of profitability.

Companies may follow different policies in accounting for profits. Certain sales of assets may be included in profits before taxation by some companies and treated as extraordinary items by others. In general terms it is only to be expected that the sellers will groom their company for sale and present the figures in the best possible light.

An accountant's report is a very useful reference point in the analysis. Often the seller refuses to allow it to be carried out. Where permission is given the buyer should regard the report as a thorough check but not a substitute for thought and analysis of their own. In the final reckoning, the acquirors must form their own view of value.

(b) Impact on acquiror's accounts

An acquisition can have a significant impact on the balance sheet, profit and loss account and dividend paying ability of the enlarged group. The acquiror's accountants are in the best position to assess this impact. The factors they will consider will include the following:

1   Cost of acquisition.   The cost of acquisition is based on the consideration provided by the vendor. In the case of cash or loan stock, it is the amount paid or issued. In the case of shares, it is the market value at completion of the number of shares issued, unless some unusual factor makes the market price misleading, in which case some other measure such as net asset backing could be substituted. The expenses of the acquisition may also be added.

2   Goodwill.   The cost of acquisition is compared with the 'fair value' (based on open market value) of the assets acquired.

There has been considerable debate about the correct method of accounting for takeovers, particularly where it may be argued that a merger has occurred. It is difficult to define a merger precisely but it would seem that to qualify the two companies of approximately equal size must come together in such a way that one does not dominate the other and that both sets of shareholders continue to have substantial equity interest in the new group. In such circumstances a 'pooling of interests' method may be used to account for the new group. The individual financial statements are aggregated with only the minimum adjustments. No goodwill arises.

The 'purchase' method of accounting for acquisitions is more frequently applied. Any excess of the cost of acquisition over the fair value of the net assets acquired will appear in the consolidated balance sheet of the acquiror as goodwill.

If goodwill is assumed to represent a payment made in anticipation of future income, it is appropriate to treat it as an asset to be written off against the income generated on a systematic basis over its useful life. The useful life will vary depending on the type of industry, the competitive environment and other factors affecting the particular company purchased. Periods of up to 40 years are used.

More extreme views of goodwill are possible. One view is that any goodwill should be written off as soon as an acquisition is made. Goodwill may be too nebulous a concept to account for on a long-term systematic basis. Others would argue that goodwill is not an asset which necessarily depreciates at all. As long as the company acquired thrives, and profits are maintained or increased, no write-offs are appropriate. For example, a company holding a licence to operate in a growth industry is likely to become more valuable rather than less, although presumably this should be reflected in the price paid.

The directors of predatory companies dislike goodwill appearing in their balance sheet. Banks and other analysts tend to regard it as an intangible asset to be deducted from the capital base of the group, increasing the gearing ratios. If the auditors insist on regular amortisation, the contribution the acquisition makes to the profits of the combined group can be severely reduced. This makes it all the more important to establish at the outset the auditors' view of the effect of the acquisition on reported earnings of the group.

(c) Pre-acquisition profits

When a company is acquired, the retained earnings of that company are designated as 'pre-acquisition'. They cannot be treated by the acquiror as distributable to its own shareholders. However, the new management may wish to write-down the value of the assets of the company acquired which can be done against pre-acquisition profits. The bulk of the profits in the year of acquisition may in this way be judged to have occurred post-acquisition and so can be distributed. 'Clearing the decks' allows the acquiror to report better profits from the acquisition in justification of its decision.

Where a new company is formed to control a group, the problem of pre-acquisition reserves is particularly acute, since the new company will initially have no distributable reserves.

If this structure is put into place by a scheme of arrangement, the opportunity can be taken as part of the scheme to reduce the capital and reserves of the new holding company from the aggregate cost of acquisition to the level of the share capital and share premium accounts of the subsidiaries. By this means, distributable reserves are created in the new holding company equal to the combined existing level of distributable reserves of the subsidiaries.

(iii) Role of lawyers

In an acquisition of any complexity, legal advice will be required at an early stage. Specific legal problems may arise as regards the powers of a target company's directors, actions which can be taken by its shareholders and the rights of holders of, for example, preference shares or loan stock. The procedure for the conduct of a meeting or arrangements for voting may be of great tactical significance in an attempt to take control of a company. Many lawyers are skilled negotiators and act as spokesmen rather than simply behind the scenes advisers. Their formal role will include:

(a) Heads of agreement

As the framework of an agreement emerges the lawyers may be involved in drawing up a preliminary summary of the transaction called a 'heads of agreement'. Opinions vary as to whether it is helpful to reduce the main terms of an agreement in principle to a written form, which is signed or initialled even though it is not legally binding. A heads of agreement can serve to clarify and record the intentions of the parties and to bring into focus any major areas of dispute. Some vendors regard a heads of agreement as a necessary stage before they are prepared to release sensitive information about their business.

Another view is that to sign an agreement that is not legally binding is to interpose an unnecessary step in the negotiations. Because the parties know the agreement is not binding there may be a tendency to fudge difficult issues so that the meeting of minds is more apparent than real. The parties may feel that there is a substantial measure of understanding between them when in fact there is not. Frustration may set in later because negotiations appear to be going backwards. The transition from a heads of agreement to a legally binding contract can be as difficult as arriving at the heads of agreement in the first place.

(b) Formal sales and purchase agreement

If the principals intend to sign a formal sale and purchase agreement, the lawyers for both sides will play a prominent part in drawing it up. Successive drafts of the agreement may be used as a vehicle for advancing the negotiations so the role of draughtsman and negotiator become mingled. At this stage, the person drafting can insert ideas of his own as well as reflecting the results of discussions which can give rise to antagonism and accusations of bad faith. A lawyer may gain the trust of his opposite number as well as his own clients if he can fairly reflect in the documentation what has been agreed between the two principals. This approach is often ultimately more effective than a more adversarial style.

(c) Public offer

The lawyer's role in the formal stages of a public offer is pervasive. He will be closely involved in reviewing all aspects of the documentation with particular attention to the matters required to be disclosed by law and other regulations. The detailed terms of the consideration under the offer, its conditions and the rights of the securities which form part of it will be carefully examined and precisely worded. If the takeover is by way of a scheme of arrangement, the legal procedures will set the framework and timetable for the entire transaction.

(d) Tactics

A number of tactics, particularly in defence, are the province of the lawyer. Various provisions may be built into the company's articles of association, designed to repel an unwelcome bidder or make his bid prohibitively expensive. To be effective, such measures need to be introduced and worded with extreme care. The company's lawyer will be called upon to shepherd the directors through each step. Other defensive manoeuvres may include appeals to anti-monopoly legislation and contact with the bodies which administer it. The company will look to its lawyers to take the lead in organising the necessary presentations and meetings.

(e) Approvals

Offers and defences require a plethora of approvals by boards and individual directors. In a situation where their handling of affairs may come under close scrutiny, directors will seek such comfort as they can obtain that all the documents are accurate and complete. The lawyer will be responsible for organising the necessary verification procedures and documentation. They will also prepare detailed board minutes for use as an agenda for directors' meetings to ensure that all necessary areas have been covered. After documents have been approved, the lawyer will ensure that they have been cleared or filed with all the relevant authorities.

(iv) Tax aspects

Advice on tax may be provided either by accountants or lawyers involved in the transaction or by specialist tax advisers.

The taxation aspects of an acquisition are often the most technically complex part of it, particularly in countries such as the US and the UK. General guidelines can be misleading in particular circumstances but points which an acquiror should be alert to include:

(a) Transfer duty

When shares are bought and sold, a duty is normally payable on the registration of the transfer. In a stock market transaction, the practice is for buyer and seller to pay their own duty. This practice may be followed in the acquisition of a private company. In the case of a public company, the terms of the offer generally include a provision for the buyer to pay both buyer's and seller's transfer duty.

Various methods are available to eliminate or reduce the transfer duty payable. A scheme of arrangement, which works by cancellation and reissue of shares, does not technically involve a transfer and therefore no duty is payable. If a scheme of arrangement cannot be used, it is sometimes possible to reduce the value of the shares being transferred for example by the issue of new shares. Existing shares are converted to deferred shares carrying inferior rights and therefore having a low value. Transfer duty, which is charged by reference to value, is reduced. However, tax regulations are subject to change to counter this type of reorganisation.

(b) Capital duty

Where shares are issued as part of the consideration, it is likely that capital duty will be payable. The duty is based on the value at which the shares are considered to have been issued. Loan capital does not normally attract such duty.

(c) Tax on income stream

When calculating the return from an acquisition, it is important for a purchaser to determine what return he requires in cash and where it is to be received. In the case of acquisitions outside the acquiror's own tax domicile, the dividends, interest, management fees and the other components of the return may be subject to withholding and other taxes. The appropriate domicile of the ultimate holding company will be influenced by political stability, ease of communications and access, taxes on capital and income and other expenses of operation.

In countries which permit grouping for tax purposes, it is likely to be advantageous if the immediate holding company for the investment is domiciled in the same jurisdiction as the investment. This may permit interest payable on loans used to finance the investment to be offset against the taxable profits of the acquisition. It is unlikely that the investment holding company will make profits on an unconsolidated basis if there is even a moderate amount of gearing in its capital structure.

Countries which levy a withholding tax on dividends normally tax payments which may be made in place of dividends, such as interest on shareholders' loans, management fees and royalties.

(d) On sale of investment

The individual tax position of shareholders who receive an offer, particularly in cash, will be relevant. Shareholders may be subject to tax on a disposal which will reduce the apparent attractiveness. A share-for-share exchange on the other hand is not normally treated as a disposal until the shares received in exchange are themselves disposed of.

Where an investment is likely to be sold again, it may be useful to place it in an intermediate holding company. The tax implications of the disposal require prior planning to enable the most suitable holding structure to be established. It may well be advantageous to sell an offshore company holding or controlling an investment rather than to sell the investment itself.

(e) Tax liabilities of company being acquired

In countries where the depreciation bases for tax purposes and for accounting purposes vary, it will be necessary to ensure that any discrepancy between the tax written down value and book cost of assets has been taken into account.

On occasions, a major item of value, or even the prime purpose of an acquisition, is a tax loss available to offset future profits earned by the company being acquired. There may be limitations on whether such tax losses can be fully utilised after a change of control of the business which require careful examination. If the nature of the business also changes, the continued availability of the tax losses will be further jeopardised.

In the case of private companies, tax liabilities may arise through the tax position of their previous controlling shareholders. An indemnity from the vendor in the sale and purchase agreement is usually considered sufficient to cover this point.

(v) Role of other professionals

Depending on the nature of the transaction various other professionals may be involved in one or more stages.

(a) Stockbrokers

In a public company takeover, firms of stockbrokers will have a particularly key role. They will normally handle the necessary liaison with the stock exchange authorities as regards public announcements, trading arrangements and clearance of the offer documents.

The stockbroker is in a position to offer informed advice on what price may be acceptable to major stockholders and will liaise with stockholders who are their customers to obtain their views on the situation. Both the offeror and offeree companies may organise market operations to provide support for their respective share prices and sometimes to destabilise their opponent's. This cut-and-thrust role in the market is very much the province of the stockbroker.

If the offer requires financial support through underwriting, the stockbroker will play a leading role in lining up a syndicate of underwriting institutions.

If a substantial volume of commissions is generated through dealings in the market, the stockbroker may be prepared to handle other functions for a fairly low fee. On other occasions where a stockbroker has provided a corporate finance advisory service without handling a large volume of market transactions, a higher level of fee will be charged.

(b) Valuers

If the companies concerned in a takeover have a substantial amount of fixed assets it may be desirable (or required) to commission a revaluation. The valuer chosen should be independent of the board and of sufficient reputation that his opinion will stand up under any cross-fire which may arise. He should be alive to the possibility of different valuations for different uses of the property and should present a 'best alternative use' value so that this can be considered in negotiations and communications with shareholders.

(c) Others

In the closing stages of an offer, the registrars or receiving bankers may be heavily involved in counting acceptances. There have been occasions where two parties have claimed to have received over 50% acceptances.

A measure of double-counting and other mistakes are likely to occur under pressure. Last minute circulars and other documents may be required so that the less glamorous functions of proofing, printing and getting documents despatched can become highly critical.

Merger and acquisition work requires a decisive hand. Behind the high profile announcements and decisions, a great deal of teamwork and specialist support is required. Constant co-ordination is essential to ensure that the various professionals involved are not either treading on each other's toes or missing an important area on the assumption that someone else must be covering it.

CHAPTER 20

Disposals

The criteria and procedures for disposals should be the mirror image of procedures for acquisitions. For every buyer there must be a seller. It would seem logical for a management to spend as much energy and enterprise on identifying and preparing for disposals as it does on acquisitions. This rarely proves to be the case. Attitudes to disposals tend to be ambivalent at best, if not downright negative. An approach to this problem and other factors relevant to taking the decision to make a disposal are discussed in 'I Deciding to make a disposal' below. If it is decided that a business should be considered for sale, it should be groomed in advance to look its best on the day. 'II Preparing for and promoting a sale' below covers how to prepare a business for sale and other practical steps which may be taken to achieve a successful outcome. 'III Disposals made in special circumstances' below deals with such matters as defence against an unwanted takeover bid, a management buy-out or a sale in connection with a flotation.

I DECIDING TO MAKE A DISPOSAL

The first element in taking the decision to make a disposal is subjective, an attitude of mind. The second is analytical, what specific criteria should be used to decide that an asset or business should be sold.

(i) Attitude

Acquisitions are associated with growth and achievement. Disposals tend to carry a connotation of decline and failure. The initial reaction to even an over-priced acquisition may be more positive than to a well-judged and lucrative disposal. At the opposite extreme is the equivalent of zero budgets, that everything is potentially for sale and that it is retention which must be justified.

It is important for senior executives to encourage the attitude that consideration of a business or an asset for disposal need not be any reflection on the executives responsible for it. The best use of an asset may change for reasons entirely unconnected with the performance of the business in which that asset is employed. For example, a plantation which gradually becomes part of the suburbs of an expanding city will inevitably be more valuable if redeveloped for residential purposes. It would be impossible for an industry whose profits are largely determined by world commodity prices to earn a return equal to that from redevelopment.

Apprehension about disposals among staff is partly rooted in a very practical concern about remaining employed. Particularly in the case of horizontal mergers, there is likely to be some duplication of functions, resulting in loss of jobs as the corporate structure is rationalised after the acquisition. This is likely to take a higher toll of the staff of the target than of the acquiror.

It is unrealistic to expect that executives employed in a company targeted for disposal will show any real enthusiasm in this respect. Potential damage to morale may make it difficult to involve such executives as fully in the planning and execution of a disposal as is desirable. A reputation for protecting the rights of employees in negotiations and attempting to offer displaced staff some alternative will assist in these circumstances.

At the corporate level, planners and analysts should be encouraged to consider identifying group companies for disposal to be as much part of their job as sifting through acquisition candidates. Regular reporting requirements from group companies should be partly drawn up with an eye to keeping the necessary information readily available. If a special request has to be made, it is likely to cause delay and trigger the negative reactions noted above.

(ii) Measures of performance

In order to compile a reasonable basis for assessing a disposal, accurate measurement of the company's performance over time is required. If a business is to be retained, it ought to meet or be capable of meeting the same financial and other objectives which would be expected when an acquisition is made.

Most control systems are based on setting budgets and monitoring performance against them. Budgets tend largely to be expressed in numerical terms and on the financial side, some of the most important numbers will relate to capital employed and profits. The way these figures are calculated and presented becomes very important.

(a) Capital employed

Capital employed in a business must be properly assessed. Book values may not properly reflect the worth of the assets being employed. Property may have increased in value due to inflation or may have a higher value to an alternative user. The best alternative use value should be adopted as the basis for analysis, taking into account costs which would have to be incurred to realise this value. Plant and equipment may have been written-off over a period of time but should not for this reason be ignored. A company may appear to be making a reasonable return but may, in fact, be running down by not earning sufficient for reinvestment in up-to-date equipment. Working capital requirements and whether they are managed tightly are also relevant. If cash can be released by improved control of current assets, this benefit can be obtained without a sale.

(b) Profitability

The method of computing profits must also be monitored to see that the information it produces is a fair basis for measuring performance. In a group of companies, the allocation of overheads, for example, may be done in a rather arbitrary way. Transfer prices between one related company and another may not reflect the reality of the market in which case profits will be distorted. Standard costs may be used which are out of line with actual costs. Tax planning and other strategic corporate considerations may also affect the results.

Apparently inferior performance can be caused by accounting policies. The weak points occur in the same areas where a purchaser needs to be wary in assessing the quality of an acquisition's earnings. Capitalisation or writing-off of research and development and some types of interest expenses can make a significant difference to the costs charged against earnings. The treatment of disposals of assets can greatly affect the level of reported profits. Lower reported earnings may also paradoxically reflect a period of growth for the company, especially if costs are being incurred which are not capitalised but which may contribute to performance over a prolonged period. For example, an increased marketing effort may not bear fruit immediately. A management which feels it is under the gun to produce good results may be tempted to sacrifice projects which they realise are to the long term advantage of the business but which will penalise profits in the short term.

(c) Incremental costs/benefits

In monitoring a business for disposal, the analysis should reflect accurately what the incremental costs and benefits of selling the business are. If a business is sold, what income would actually be lost? It may be possible for other parts of the group to assume some of the business of the unit which is being sold. Equally important, would all the costs being charged against the business be saved on a disposal? Would head office costs allocated to it actually be reduced? Would material sold to it or services provided by related companies generate income in its absence? Have the full costs of disposal such as those associated with any redundancies been fully taken into account? Could stocks be realised at book value if production ceases?

(d) Strategic considerations

It is important that decisions on disposals are not taken on a purely short-term view. If financial criteria are applied too rigidly, it may appear that a particular line of business can no longer be carried on profitably. This indeed may be the case, but the poor results may also be attributable to a low point in a normal business cycle. A loss-making business should not immediately be put up for sale. Its future potential should be assessed as would be done in the case of an acquisition. Indeed, on the theory of 'better the devil you know', it may be reasonable to set somewhat lower financial targets for a business familiar to management. The risk of a business of which management has significant experience can be more fully evaluated than for a new acquisition, so that a lower level of return may be acceptable.

The apparent attractions of alternative investments may also be illusory. During a property boom, it may appear profitable to close a factory and redevelop the site. However, conditions may change during the course of the redevelopment to make the expected earnings unrealisable. There is a risk of having the worst of both worlds, no longer having the cash flow from operations but being unable to carry through the alternative project.

Management has to consider the strategic implications of ceasing to carry out a certain type of activity. It may have a broad impact on the morale of employees and the reputation of the group in general. Such a decision should not be taken 'by default' by allowing return on investment criteria to dictate policy.

II PREPARING FOR AND PROMOTING A SALE

Once the monitoring system has alerted management that a business should be considered for sale, it is beneficial to spend some time preparing the ground so that the business can appear in as favourable a light as possible. This will assist in the task of attracting potential buyers. Buyers may need a certain amount of persuasion or assistance from the vendor to reach the stage where a formal offer is made.

(i) Preparations

It is a useful exercise for the seller to try to put himself in the buyer's shoes. What strong and weak points would he be looking for particularly? The seller can then examine these points to see if any improvements to the existing position can be made. The points to be considered might include the following:

(a) Profitability

If the business is likely to be valued on an earnings basis and there are certain loss-making activities, it is preferable to close down or transfer them to another group company before the business is offered for sale. The presentation of financial information should be adjusted to exclude the results of the business which is to be discontinued or transferred. If there are unfavourable internal pricing policies or particularly conservative accounting treatments consideration should be given to making appropriate changes.

It may also be advisable to curtail major items of capital expenditure. Increased depreciation charges will reduce the earnings of the company in the period before the benefits of the project come through. In any case, a potential purchaser is unlikely to have precisely the same technical requirements or assessment of the market needs.

(b) Balance sheet

The main items on the balance sheet should be examined to see if there is anything which might deter a potential purchaser. It is inevitable that the purchaser will scrutinise major balance sheet items in great detail so it is worthwhile anticipating any criticisms he might make. Independent valuations of the larger assets serve to defuse arguments.

(c) Commercial

If a lease on key premises is due to expire soon a renewal may be negotiated in advance. It may be easier for someone familiar with the landlord to obtain fair terms than for a newcomer. There is always a tendency for an outside party to allow some discount for real or imagined difficulties in this regard.

If there are valuable agreements or licences which a change of control could jeopardise it may be advisable for the seller to sound out the relevant parties in advance so that he can provide reassurance to the purchaser on these points at the outset.

(d) Inter-company accounts

If there are any inter-company dealings preparations should be made to put them on an arm's length basis. Any accounts outstanding should be settled. If the funding of the business has been on non-commercial terms negotiations should be commenced with outside banking sources to replace the internal facilities. Temporary agreements may be required to cover transitional arrangements on such matters as provision of technical assistance or computer services.

(ii) Timing

Successful sales of businesses depend critically on timing. Most markets are subject to cyclical forces. Towards the end of the upward phase of the market, the profits generated by a business should be near their peak allowing an attractive price to be set. At the same time, a purchaser can still look forward to some further improvement in performance. The confidence of potential purchasers will be high, a very important factor in a bridging the gap between simply talking about a transaction and making a final commitment.

It is at this point of the cycle that finance for acquisitions is also likely to be most readily available. The availability of finance can significantly influence a purchaser's judgment. Apart from making a purchase possible at all, the backing of a banker may provide some comfort to a purchaser that the transaction is financially sound. While no bank loses money on purpose, the record of banks in evaluating their customers' decisions near market peaks is not without blemishes.

A major obstacle is often indecision by a seller who is loathe to part with a company that is apparently doing well. There is a tendency to assume good times will last forever. Some of the most successful managers of major groups of companies are people whose strengths include the ability, without emotion and at the correct time, to dispose of businesses they have built up. If a vendor delays until the business turns down, the attitude of potential purchasers will be substantially different.

(iii) Supplying information

The initiative at the opening of negotiations lies with the offeror. However, the seller need not simply be a passive recipient of proposals from the buyer. He may have prepared a presentation on the company and have his own ideas about the structure of the deal. It will be of advantage to appear the 'reluctant' bride no matter how desirable a sale may be in actuality. This will mean not showing too much eagerness in negotiations. Supplying information will appear like drawing teeth. Many regrets will be expressed at the passing of independence.

The provision of information can backfire. In acquisition negotiations, it is almost impossible to provide all the data a purchaser could want to consider. At some stage, it may be counter-productive to provide further details. The receipt of such information spawns delays, pending its analysis by the purchaser. The moment of decision is postponed while the purchaser begins to flounder under mountains of paper. In these circumstances, he may become incapable of making up his mind. Moreover, it is likely that the analysis will itself suggest additional questions which may never have arisen at all unless prompted by the further information disclosed. While it can be thought unhelpful to refuse to provide all the information requested, it may prove that retaining some of the mystery is a better strategy than removing all the 'seven veils'.

(iv) 'Sotheby's' atmosphere

A useful tactic for a seller is creating what may be called the 'Sotheby's atmosphere'. In obtaining a good price for a business, it is helpful to generate an aura of excitement as sometimes happens in an auction room. A spirit of rivalry, often involving companies well-known to each other, fosters an atmosphere where a higher price may be paid than can be justified objectively. Deadlines may be imposed which are not strictly required, but are designed to force a purchaser to overcome final doubts and create suspense, as when bidding reaches a climax before the hammer falls.

Buyers like to believe they are not the only party interested or they begin to wonder why. A little competition can do wonders for the enthusiasm of a purchaser. A seller should if necessary try to create the sense of a competing offer in the wings even if one does not exist. Skilful sellers have resorted to mysterious meetings and sudden business trips, accompanied by profuse apologies. If the seller can succeed in building up this kind of atmosphere, not only may the price paid be increased but the chances of the deal being concluded will be substantially improved. A sense of occasion is created where the buyer must say yes or no.

(v) Use of intermediaries

In negotiating with potential purchasers, it is often advantageous to use a third party such as a merger broker or investment banker. This allows even a keen seller to maintain a distance and avoid seeming too eager to sell. It also may provide a purchaser with confidence if an investment banker has prepared a presentation on the company and reviewed the financial information provided.

A seller has probably more to gain than the purchaser from the use of an intermediary. While few people mind being known in the market as a buyer, for a seller to indicate a willingness to deal is often thought to display weakness. If the approach is made through an intermediary, the seller can always claim if the news leaks out that he was misinterpreted and that the intermediary was exceeding his instructions.

An intermediary may be in a position to achieve an increased price for a seller. A third party using 'shuttle diplomacy' between principals has more chance of narrowing the gap between two sets of proposals. At times, he can be more shameless in insisting on price as the major factor than a seller, who will tend to emphasise other factors, even if price is the main thing.

A skilful intermediary will seek to make both parties feel he is on their side. As someone who is committed to neither and paid only if a deal is consummated, his interest lies in seeking ways to reconcile the objectives of buyer and seller.

If emotions run high, a direct meeting between the seller and the acquiror may be bad tempered. A clash of personalities can hinder the conclusion of a proposal which might otherwise have a good chance of success. An experienced intermediary can see the warning signs and intervene to avoid unnecessary antagonism.

(vi) Assistance with finance

A seller may have to consider assistance to a purchaser in financing an acquisition. Insistence that the purchaser arranges funding for the entire purchase at arm's length may make the transaction impracticable, especially if the business being purchased makes poor collateral for bank borrowing.

A willingness to take some shares in the purchasing company not only helps in raising the total amount required, but may promote a feeling of partnership. By accepting paper, the seller is expressing a degree of confidence in the management and business of the purchaser. Alternatively, a seller may agree to become a shareholder in a new vehicle formed to acquire a business or assets from himself. In this way, he retains an interest and avoids being thought anxious to sell out entirely.

A vendor may agree that a portion of the consideration should be paid on a deferred basis. This is equivalent to the vendor being paid out in part from the cash flow of the business being sold, which some vendors find objectionable. The purchaser would, however, still have the obligation to pay if the cash flow falls short of expectations.

A loan may be made to the purchaser by the vendor, secured on the business or assets purchased. This may be done so that an acquiror can complete a transaction for which sufficient third party financing is unavailable or as part of a package which the seller provides to attract a buyer, even though he could raise finance independently. In such circumstances, the seller cannot really regard the sale as being completed until the money is fully repaid. It may happen that the seller needs to continue with some management role in the business or even take it back if the purchaser fails to meet his commitments. For this reason, this structure is most suitable for a relatively simple asset such as an investment property or a hotel.

III   DISPOSALS MADE IN SPECIAL CIRCUMSTANCES

Occasions arise where a disposal is made not primarily because performance is below standard but for other tactical reasons. Some examples are given below.

(i) To raise money

A group may be forced by financial pressures to make a disposal in order to raise money. In this situation the normal logic is reversed. Instead of singling out a business with a disappointing return, one of the more promising assets of the group may have to be selected to ensure that the sum required is realised within a reasonable time.

The bargaining position of the vendor will be weakened if he waits until the market is aware of his financial difficulties. A skilful operator has sometimes managed to take the initiative by proposing to merge with or even buy a rival company thus succeeding in setting in motion a process which eventually leads to an offer for his own company. This type of manoeuvre takes time and planning as well as skill to accomplish.

A group which has encountered financial difficulties often finds itself under a number of restraints. A sale of an asset which is heavily borrowed against may reduce gearing significantly but will not generate the free cash which may be necessary for survival. A disposal at a book loss may be sensible commercially but may draw the market's attention to problems. The accounting effects of a disposal may also be critical if the company has little leeway on borrowing restrictions and other covenants contained in loan stock or bank loan agreements.

(ii) Defence against an unwanted takeover

A takeover may be launched principally because of a particular business or asset a group controls (sometimes referred to as a 'crown jewel'). In normal circumstances, this would probably be the last item the directors would consider selling. However, to deter a raider, approaches may be made to potential purchasers in order to put the prize beyond the raider's reach. Sometimes this may be done in such a way that existing shareholders of the group retain an interest in the asset for example by spinning it off into a separate company or by putting it in a partnership in which shareholders participate. This tactic has the merit of protecting the position of existing shareholders whereas to sell the asset outright simply to prevent a takeover seems in some sense self-defeating.

If the whole group is threatened with takeover, the directors may seek a defensive merger to make the enlarged group too big for a predator to swallow. Alternatively they may seek a more acceptable suitor called a 'white knight'.

(iii) Management buy-out

In a diversified group, certain businesses may become neglected because of operating problems or a strategic decision to emphasise development in other areas. Administrative controls may deprive management of the flexibility to make key decisions and funds for expansion may be difficult to obtain. This may lead to a demoralisation of management and a decline in performance. It may even endanger the survival of the business if allowed to continue indefinitely.

It may therefore suit both the parent company and the management in question to arrange for a disposal of the business to the management. The business will become independent and managed by a motivated board with a significant personal stake in the business. Finance for the purchase may be provided partly by the vendor, by offering deferred terms or vendor finance, partly by management from their own resources and partly by outside investors. Merchant banks have become very active in organising funds, partnerships and syndicates of institutions willing to finance this type of transaction.

For management, a buy-out may represent a chance to realise an ambition of owning their own business. Freed of the shackles of an unsympathetic parent, the business may indeed recover and management make a success of its declaration of independence. In the early stages of this type of operation the price at which groups were prepared to dispose of businesses to management were fairly low. As availability of financing has increased, prices have risen. A buy-out which partly replaces equity by debt inevitably increases the financial gearing of the company and consequently cuts into safety margins should the business encounter any unexpected set-back.

(iv) Flotations

When a group is being groomed for flotation it may be preferable to sell or even give away a loss-making subsidiary. If the price of the flotation is being set by reference to a multiple of earnings, a loss incurred by one member of the group will reduce the overall valuation by a factor equal to the multiple being applied. On occasions a company has been disposed of to a private associate of the group going public, with an option to reacquire the business subsequently once the flotation is complete or the company restored to financial health.

A listed company may be sold primarily for the sake of its listing. Most of the assets will be sold out of the company leaving it effectively as a 'shell'. A purchaser wishing to obtain a listing for some of his interests can then buy control of the company and inject assets into it either for cash or new shares. The listing which is being sold may be considered to have a value independently of the other assets of the company. This value will correspond roughly to the costs involved in going public via the full flotation process plus an intangible element for the added certainty and control which the shell route offers. The premium which the shell can command will also depend on the attitude of the Stock Exchange and other regulatory authorities towards obtaining listings via this route.

CONCLUSION

Disposals ought logically to occupy as much of management's time and attention as acquisitions do but this is rarely the case. The principal reason is that whereas acquisitions are associated with progress and growth, disposals carry a negative connotation. Nevertheless, a well-judged disposal can be critical in the development of the group. The technique of making a successful disposal is a subtle one and the personality which makes an executive an effective acquiror of companies will not necessarily mean he is a good salesman. Sometimes a disposal is forced on a group by financial circumstances and there are other particular circumstances which may dictate policy in this regard. While the philosophy that everything for sale is anathema to many corporations it seems that greater attention to the merits of an organised disposal programme and policy could pay great dividends.

Conclusion

SOME REMARKS ON CURRENT CONCERNS AND FUTURE DEVELOPMENTS

(i) Scope of corporate finance work

Corporate finance activities, as defined in this book, are primarily concentrated on the two major fields of activities which are described in Parts 2 and 3, namely going public and making further issues of equity capital, and takeovers, mergers and disposals. From time to time, corporate finance specialists become involved in a wide range of advisory activities in response to market conditions. In periods of financial difficulty, teams of corporate finance specialists have been put in to manage companies instead of a receiver where it is thought that by making disposals and rationalising the corporate and financial structure the company may have a chance of survival. Changes in capital structure are also required in major loan restructuring exercises. It has often been a corporate finance function to assist companies with reconstructions and negotiations with creditors. Fields such as leasing and some forms of project finance have been pioneered by corporate finance staff in the early stage of their development before they become specialities in their own right. However, the core of corporate finance work has remained equity issues and takeovers.

Although these two areas of concentration may seem rather dissimilar, there are in fact many similarities between them. The motivation in both cases owes much to the forces of ambition and the desire for growth. The ways of using and valuing securities are central to both and are essentially the same, although they must be interpreted differently in line with the objectives of the particular exercise. The components of the documentation, the accounting investigations and disclosure requirements form a familiar pattern. They may be assembled in a different order and with a different emphasis as a marketing exercise or in response to changes in tax laws, but the fundamentals remain, rather as a manufacturer may create product lines by a new design and packaging of essentially the same components. The markets, the regulatory authorities and the people who run them are generally the same.

Close links exist between the activities of floating companies, raising capital and engaging in takeovers. A life cycle of development can be observed, in which flotation forms an important part of the first phase of growth. In the second phase of growth, further issues and takeovers are common and the company may become the victim as well as the aggressor, followed by a slower phase where regeneration may be needed to avoid eventual decline. During the final phase, the company may itself be taken over or be subject to various types of reconstruction. These successive phases of corporate development feed on each other and provide further grist for the corporate finance mill. A satisfaction can be observed among the participants in a flotation. The total market is expanded; a takeover leads to one less independent company.

The phases of the market tend to reinforce this inter-relationship. Bull markets are largely a time for flotations and issues. Merger and takeover activity may also be strong, buoyed up by premium ratings for aggressor companies and availability of finance, even though prices are high. Bear markets create opportunities for companies who have preserved their resources to negotiate bargain prices. Rescue packages are required for financially troubled companies. An atmosphere prevails in which normally reluctant sellers may feel it wise to complete disposals. Corporate finance transactions fail more from a lack of commitment on the part of sellers than any lack of eager, if not always capable, buyers.

(ii) Some potential conflicts

The role of a corporate finance adviser has in it some inherent conflicts. The most obvious conflict arises during the setting of a price for underwriting an issue. Pricing must be left until the last minute at which time it is primarily a market-related exercise. When taking soundings in the market, the underwriters will seek to provide a contingency for uncertainty. They will need to be able to convince sub-underwriters that an adequate discount on the expected market price has been secured. There is an obvious incentive therefore for the lead underwriter to suggest an issue price at the low end of the range which may have been discussed. It will advance such arguments as the possibility of a 'flop' if the issue is priced too finely, the need to encourage active trading and the value of the remaining shareholdings which are not being sold. All these points have a certain merit but they all are in the underwriters' interest. The company may be forgiven for wondering whether the underwriter is being unduly influenced by its own risk and its desire to keep major investment clients happy.

This same underwriter has for a considerable period, possibly up to six months, been advising the company closely on the best course of action. It is very difficult, if not impossible, for the company now to consult someone else on whether the underwriting terms are fair. The problem is made more complicated if there are two groups of sellers. Existing shareholders may be forgiven for wanting simply to secure the maximum price for their shares. If the company is issuing new shares to raise money, it may be an easier matter to take the broader considerations into account.

In takeover activity, the major area of potential conflict is when a merchant bank should advise a bidder to drop out or advise a board resisting an offer to recommend its acceptance. A merchant bank making an offer on behalf of a bidder is very much identified and bound up with the success of that offer. Advice is being given to individuals whose personal prestige and future career prospects may also be riding on the outcome. Shareholders of the offeror are rarely consulted at all unless the bid requires a large number of new shares to be issued. Yet there must come a point when it is simply not worth paying any more for a company or continuing a struggle which is distracting senior management from running its own business. How and when this advice should be given is a very delicate matter. It is helpful if some limits have been agreed in advance which can be used as reference points. It would also ease the blow if the aggressor has at least acquired some shares in the target company which it can sell to meet its costs.

It is an equally difficult task to advise a board which has been determined to resist a bid that it is time to surrender. There is a fair price for every company and once that price has been reached the board of directors has an obligation to make its views known to shareholders, particularly if they are aware that a sharp drop in share price is likely after the offer is defeated. Again, career prospects may be at stake, as the management of a company which has resisted bitterly and possibly engaged in bad-tempered exchanges of circulars and other communications can expect little sympathy from an eventually victorious but bloodied bidder. Service contracts may provide a cushion. Even an aggressive bidder may prefer a substantial degree of management continuity and may be willing to give assurances about the integrity of the business being taken over.

The potential conflicts are likely to intensify in a world where financial institutions engage in many different roles. If commercial banks, merchant banks, stockbrokers and dealers are all rolled into one, the difficulty of keeping confidential information segregated becomes more acute. Even the Great Wall of China has numerous gaps in it. New types of potential conflict are created. A group with a major lending exposure to a client can hardly ignore its position if called upon to advise on a takeover by a financially stronger group. A vigorous defence will inevitably result in substantial expenses and a heavy cost in management time and it may be in the bank's wider interest for the bid to succeed in any case. A bank may be more prepared to underwrite an issue of securities if it knows that one of the main effects of the issue is to make its own loans more secure. Of course it can be argued that the ability to provide an overall package of services is the most important factor. Certainly, many client companies can be heard to support this line. On the bank side, the arguments seem to bear a remarkably close correlation with whether the proponents are working for an independent house or a financial supermarket.

(iii) Markets are becoming more international

An interesting trend is the growing internationalisation of corporate finance markets. International takeovers and mergers are scarcely a new phenomenon but the number of transactions and the willingness of companies to look outside their own domestic market is on the increase.

Practical experience suggests that an international transaction of any size is much more difficult, costly and time-consuming to bring to a successful conclusion than a comparable domestic transaction. The reasons for this seem to include the added regulatory and tax complications which may be encountered, under-estimating of practical difficulties of assessing a company in another market and general unfamiliarity with the negotiating style of a foreign management. Nevertheless, the greater range of opportunities and the glamour of international deals are powerful enough factors to ensure considerable persistence.

Some techniques which have worked well in one market seem slow to take root in another. For example, leveraged buy-outs have developed into an enormous business in North America without sparking off much of a reaction in other major markets. There does seem to be a tendency among companies going public to try and pick a market which suits them best. Small manufacturing and distribution companies may find they are accorded a higher rating in the American market than in their home base and are beginning to take seriously the possibility of going public in an overseas market. Companies are also increasingly tapping the international markets for subsequent issues. These markets may follow different practices from their home markets on such matters as issues of further shares by way of rights. Some disputes are likely to arise until a method of issue is established which is internationally acknowledged as fair.

Companies which are listed in one major market are also examining the merits of having their shares listed on overseas exchanges as well. Experience varies as to how much extra documentation and expense is required and whether it is worthwhile. There is a tendency for shares to drift back to the market where most trading is carried out. Even if a placing on the local market has been made in conjunction with the listing, local trading tends to dry up subsequently.

(iv) Securitisation

Another major development is securitisation. Part 2 of this book is mainly concerned with the issue of shares or equity-linked debt instruments. The bond market is a separate subject in itself. However, as more commercial paper issues, mortgage loans and other commercial loans become tradable on the stock market or between market-makers, the field of corporate finance is likely to be increasingly affected by these activities. Either it must expand to encompass them or find its traditional role as prime mover in the securities markets under increasing pressure. Certainly the advantages of adding marketability to such instruments makes the trend irreversible.

(v) Effect of takeover activity

There remains the vexed question of whether takeover and merger activity generates any real economic benefit (other than the fees for the various professional advisers involved) or whether it is basically just a numbers game. The inherent conflict between shareholders and their supposed servants, management, is central to this question. In circumstances where the shareholding body and senior management are separate, the receipt of a takeover bid crystallises the differences between the two. One side is principally concerned about a gain which may be short-term but is nevertheless tempting. Management has to struggle against its outrage and sense of being attacked. It must balance its own desire to remain in control with the benefits that a bid confers on shareholders. Management is likely to have a (no doubt) sincere belief that their knowledge of the company makes them better placed to realise long-term benefits for the shareholders than an opportunist bidder. The bidder can hardly argue that he is not in some sense opportunist. Otherwise, why would he have launched the bid in the first place?

The use of highly leveraged bid packages have made corporate minnows potentially capable of swallowing whales. This has brought the conflict between shareholders and management to an unprecedented level. It has coincided with a trend for the handling of takeover bids to become more 'show biz'. The extensive involvement of major advertising agencies has prompted the use of publicity techniques previously more associated with the selling of cigarettes or presidents.

Index

Opening attack—*continued*
 public companies—*continued*
  offer,
    components of, 176
    document, 175
   platform for bid, 174
   price, 172–173
   timing, 173–174
Options
 grant of, 113
Ordinary shares. *See* SHARES

Paper
 alternative to cash, cosmetic advantages of, 163
 highly rated, opportunity to increase, 134
Performance
 measures of. *See* DISPOSALS
Philosophy
 going public, change caused by, 48–49
Placement
 private, as method of gaining listing, 98
Placings
 cash, for,
   costs, 111
   debt securities, placings of, 111–112
   market reaction, 111
   pricing, 111
   procedures, 109–110
   timing, 110
 generally, 39–40, 109
 pricing of, 29
 shell company, marketing of, 95
Pre-emption rights
 formal procedure, 191
Preference shares. *See* SHARES
Preferred shares. *See* SHARES
Price earnings ratio. *See* VALUATION
Pricing
 flotation, 28–29
 fundamental analysis,
   generally, 69
   multiple of earnings, 69–70
   net asset basis, 70
 generally, 37–38, 69, 73
 market, realities of,
   comparable companies, 71
   generally, 70–71
   market soundings, 71–72
 opening attack, 172–173
 placing, 29
 placings for cash, 111
 practical skill, as, 28
 rights issue, 29, 102–104
 takeover, 29–30
 tender method of,
   advantages, 72
   disadvantages, 72–73
   procedures, 72
   stagging, effect on, 72–73

Pricing—*continued*
 valuation distinguished from, 19
 See also VALUATION
Printers
 flotation,
   expenses, 64
   forming team, 62
Private company. *See* COMPANY
Procedures to implement mergers. *See* TAKEOVERS AND MERGERS
Professionals
 accountants. *See* ACCOUNTANTS
 lawyers. *See* LAWYERS
 merchant bank. *See* MERCHANT BANK
 role in mergers and acquisitions, 126–127, 200
 stockbrokers. *See* STOCKBROKERS
 valuers. *See* VALUERS
Profitability
 measure of performance, as, 211–212
 preparation for sale, 213
Profits
 flotation, criteria for, 51
 forecast,
   release after announcement of hostile bid, 186
   report in prospectus, 78
 pre-acquisition, 205
 prospectus, information in, 76
 steady record, benefits of, 179
Promoter
 meaning, 33
Property
 interest in, inclusion in prospectus, 76–77
 net assets, 24–25
Prospectus
 main components of,
  appendices,
    accountant's report on group, 77
    general information, 78–79
    professional valuations, summary of, 78
    profit forecast, reports on, 78
    statutory information, 78–79
  background industry information, 75
  balance sheet, 76
  business of group, 75
  commitments, 74
  contingent liabilities, 74
  directors, 75
  dividends, 76
  generally, 38, 74
  guarantees, 74
  history of group, 75
  indebtedness, statement of, 74
  interest in properties, 76–77
  management, 75
  parties involved in issue, 75
  past results, 76
  procedures for application, 79
  proceeds, use of, 77